Getting Used to Being Shot At

Getting Used to Being Shot At

The Spence Family Civil War Letters

Edited by Mark K. Christ

The University of Arkansas Press
Fayetteville
2002

06 05 04 03 02   5 4 3 2 1

Designer: John Coghlan

⊚ The paper used in this publication meets the minimum requirements of the
American National Standard for Permanence of Paper for Printed Library
Materials Z39.48–1984.

Library of Congress Cataloging-in-Publication Data

Spence, Alexander E., d. 1864.
  Getting used to being shot at : the Spence family Civil War letters /edited by
Mark K. Christ.
    p. cm.
Includes bibliographical references and index.
  ISBN 1-55728-726-0 (cloth : alk. paper)
  1. Spence, Alexander E., d. 1864—Correspondence. 2. Spence, Thomas
F., d. 1864—Correspondence. 3. Confederate States of America. Army.
Arkansas Infantry Regiment, 1st. 4. Confederate States of America. Army.
Arkansas Mounted Rifles, 2nd. 5. Arkansas—History—Civil War, 1861–1865—
Personal narratives. 6. United States—History—Civil War, 1861–1865—
Personal narratives, Confederate. 7. Soldiers—Confederate States of
America—Correspondence. 8. Arkadelphia (Ark.)—Biography. 9. Spence
family—Correspondence. I. Spence, Thomas F., d. 1864. II. Christ, Mark K.
III. Title.
  E553.5 1st .S84 2002
  973.7'82—dc21

                                                              2002000241

To my parents, Karl and Betty Christ, with love and respect.

Contents

List of Illustrations

Acknowledgments

This book would not have been possible without the kind assistance of many people. I would first and foremost like to thank Bill Gatewood, director of the Old State House Museum, for giving me the opportunity to work with this collection. Joellen Maack, the Old State House Museum curator, was a constant source of support during the project and provided valuable leads and information on the Spence family. Adam Bergfeld, Larry Ahart, and Georganne Sisco of the Old State House staff also have helped in the course of this project. Gail Moore, exhibit designer *par excellence*, created a beautiful setting for the Spence letters exhibit and also gave much-needed moral support.

My boss, Ken Grunewald, director of the Arkansas Historic Preservation Program, has been extremely supportive and understanding of the demands of this project. Frank Arey, deputy director of the Department of Arkansas Heritage, gave yeoman aid from editing chapters to guiding me to sources for understanding obscure references in the Spence letters. Department of Arkansas Heritage director Cathie Matthews and Bobbie Heffington, deputy director for museums, also have been supportive of this effort.

Others who gave great assistance include Wendy Richter of Ouachita Baptist University, who I cannot thank enough for her generosity in locating Clark County information; Bryan Howerton and Ken Byrd, who shared their knowledge of Rueben Reed's obscure cavalry unit, among other things; John Lawrence Smith, for his extensive research into the life of Amanda Willson; Daniel Sutherland, whose suggestions for improving the initial manuscript proved both accurate and helpful; Margaret Curley, Bob Ewing, and Mark Gillin, who provided genealogical information that clarified the family ties of the Spence, Cook, and Ewing families; Howard Norton, both for bringing the Spence collection to the attention of the Old State House Museum and for helping to decipher hard-to-read words and cryptic references; Judi King of the Arkansas State Library for interlibrary loan aid above and beyond the call of duty; Willard Gatewood; Bobby Roberts; Amy Bennett and Frank Latimer of the Arkansas Historic Preservation Program; Andy Zawacki, Dana Simmons, and Tammie Dillon of the Historic Arkansas Museum; the staffs of the Butler Center for Arkansas Studies at the Central Arkansas Library System's Main Library and the Arkansas History Commission; Tom Wing of Fort Smith National

Historic Site; Connie Langum of Wilson's Creek National Battlefield; Leslie Anne Rawlings of Stones River National Battlefield; the Southwest Arkansas Regional Archives, and old friends Don R. Simons and Bill Frazier. Thanks also to Larry Malley, Brian King, Archie Schaffer IV, Amy Ramsden, and John Coghlan of the University of Arkansas Press. I apologize to anyone I may have failed to mention as helping in this project, and please do not take my memory lapse as an indication that your assistance was not appreciated.

As always, my love and thanks to my wife, Kim, and daughters, Emily and Cassie, for their patience with my frequent absences over the past year in the course of researching this book.

Mark K. Christ
September 2001

Introduction

The Spence Family Collection

The Spence Family Collection at the Old State House Museum in Little Rock features more than fifty letters from and to members of the Solomon Spence Sr. family of Arkadelphia, Arkansas. It contains thirty-eight letters from Alex Spence, ten from Tom Spence, two from family friend Isaac W. "Babe" Cook, one from Mary Ann Hood of Caldwell, Texas, a sister of the Spence brothers, and one from Amanda Willson of Madison, Georgia, Alex Spence's fiancée. In addition, the collection contains a letter from T. B. Yancey, a comrade of Alex Spence in the First Arkansas Infantry Regiment; two from James Candler, who served with Tom Spence in the Second Arkansas Mounted Rifles; and two from Robert E. Hearn, Sallie Spence Hearn's brother-in-law and a trooper in a Tennessee cavalry regiment. A letter that probably was written by Sallie's husband, A. G. Hearn, appears in Appendix 1 and discusses details of the 1864 battle of Poison Spring, Arkansas. Among other materials in the collection are images of Tom and Alex Spence, a newspaper clipping listing Clark County casualties at the battle of Murfreesboro, Tennessee, and a handwritten obituary of Solomon Spence Sr.

Through this collection, we can learn much about the experiences of the common soldiers and junior officers of the Army of Tennessee, especially those who served in the First Arkansas Infantry and the Second Arkansas Mounted Rifles in battles in Missouri, Arkansas, Kentucky, Tennessee, Virginia, Georgia, and Alabama, marching literally thousands of miles during their four years of service. The letters contain not only accounts of the many battles in which the Spence brothers served, but also reflections on the hardships of campaigning, the pride of serving in battle-proven units, and the pain of losing comrades to combat and disease.

The Spence Family Collection was the basis for the 2001–2 exhibit: "Brothers in Arms: The Spence Family and the Civil War." That exhibit placed the Old State House Museum's extensive collection of Civil War battle flags in context through the words of the Spence brothers; this book is intended to share the letters of Tom and Alex Spence with a broader audience. In preparing the letters for publication, I have endeavored to place the letters in the context of their times by following the regiments and campaigns in which Alex and Tom Spence fought. Each chapter begins with explanatory narrative describing the period in which they were written. The letters from that period follow, sometimes accompanied by brief notations if they were written by someone other than Tom or Alex Spence or if they are fragments of letters. References to names, places and events are explained in endnotes wherever possible. For the most part I have not corrected spelling or capitalization errors, though punctuation is added to make the letters more readable.

The Spences of Arkadelphia

Arkadelphia, Arkansas, was a prosperous little town in 1860, located on the bluffs on the west side of the Ouachita River. One of the earliest places settled in southwest Arkansas, it was Arkansas's seventh-largest city and boasted a two-story brick courthouse, four churches, a thriving commercial district, and the Arkansas Institute for the Blind. One of the leading centers of commerce in south central Arkansas, the town was home to 817 residents in the year before the Civil War began, of whom 600 were white and 217 were slaves.[1]

Among the best-known residents of the town were the members of the Solomon Spence family. Patriarch Solomon Spence Sr., a native of Virginia and veteran of the War of 1812, and his wife, Frances Caruthers Spence of North Carolina, settled in Clark County in 1849, after living for some years in Alabama, where several of their ten children were born. Spence owned a popular hotel on Main Street in Arkadelphia, a two-story brick Greek Revival–style building erected in the mid-1850s to replace Jonathan O. Callaway's two-story log structure, the town's first hotel. Solomon Spence Sr. had a comfortable fortune in 1860, owning real estate valued at $8,000 and personal property valued at $2,500, which included three slaves.[2]

Also living in their parents' household were Alexander E. Spence, age twenty-two, who worked as a clerk, and Thomas F. Spence, twenty-five, the popular young sheriff of Clark County.[3] Tom Spence enjoyed a measure of personal wealth, listing $1,500 in real and $250 in personal property in 1860. Son-in-law Alfred G. Hearn, age thirty-four, an Arkadelphia lawyer, and his wife, twenty-eight-year-old Sallie Spence, owned $10,000 in real property and $6,000 in personal property including five slaves. In addition to their two daughters, the Hearns shared their home with an eighteen-year-old nephew, Rufus D. Hearn of Wilson County, Tennessee. Another son-in-law, Arkadelphia merchant Joshua Elder, and his wife, the former Martha Spence, owned a comfortable $2,500 in real and $50 in personal property. Over in Clark County's Greenville Township, son Dudley

Joshua Elder was married to Martha Spence, daughter of Solomon Spence Sr. and sister of Tom and Alex Spence. Martha would not survive the war; Elder remarried in 1865 and had several more children. (Courtesy of Margaret Curley)

Solomon Spence Sr. owned the Spence Hotel in Arkadelphia, and both Tom and Alex
Spence lived there before enlisting in Confederate service. The hotel, shown here in a
postwar image, burned down in the 1870s. (Courtesy of the Clark County Historical
Society)

Spence, a thirty-nine-year-old farmer, recorded $3,000 in real and $12,000
in personal property, including eleven slaves.[4] Frequent visitors at the
Spence home included Isaac W. "Babe" Cook, a close friend of Alex Spence,
and his sister, Mary, the widow of Solomon Spence Jr.

With their successful and public careers and extensive holdings in
property, both real and personal, the extended Spence family could be considered among Clark County's best known and most prominent when the
shadow of secession fell across Arkansas. Four years later, Arkadelphia
would be ravaged by war, Martha Spence Elder would have passed away,
and Tom and Alex Spence would lie in soldiers' graves, far from their Clark
County home.

Tom and Alex Spence

Tom and Alex Spence died young, but their letters reveal something of the personalities of the popular young brothers from Arkadelphia. Tom Spence, who had assumed the duties of Clark County sheriff at age twenty-three following the death of his older brother, wrote short letters, straightforward and to the point. The affection with which he was viewed by his comrades in the Second Arkansas Mounted Rifles is evident in their electing him captain of Company E in 1862, in references to him in contemporary letters and postwar reminiscences, and in the official citations of his valor in Civil War battle reports. Before and during the war, Tom Spence was a man of action.

Alex Spence, a clerk in 1860, was both younger and more verbose than his brother. Through his letters the modern reader can meet a dedicated, somewhat idealistic young man who was tempered in service to become a hardened soldier and devoted leader of the men of Company B, First Arkansas Infantry, a man proud to be serving with Patrick Cleburne's vaunted Trans-Mississippi troops. In one of his earliest letters, Alex Spence is outraged by the cavalier treatment of the young recruits of the Clark County Volunteers on their voyage across the Mississippi River. Three years later, he is matter-of-factly reporting the deaths of men he has known for years, and callously recounting in one of his letters how he "had the pleasure the other day of making two Yankees 'bite the dust' & got me a fine hat." Perhaps the saddest aspect of Alex's story is his courtship and affiance to Amanda Willson of Georgia, a betrothal cut short by a Union bullet in the carnage at Franklin, Tennessee. Amanda's letter to Sallie Spence Hearn, written two years to the day after Alex's death, provides both an ending point for the Spence Family Collection and a reminder of the high cost and tragedy of the American Civil War.

The Secession Crisis

Arkansians were divided about whether to follow South Carolina in announcing secession from the Union following the 1860 election of Abraham Lincoln.[5] As was the case in many Southern states, residents of areas in Arkansas that depended heavily on slave-based agriculture for their livelihood leaned more toward secession than those of upland regions with fewer concentrations of slaves. Nevertheless, the Arkansas General Assembly called for an election to be held on February 18, 1861, for Arkansas voters to decide whether or not to hold a secession convention.[6]

Thomas F. Spence, the popular young sheriff of Clark County, enlisted in the Second Arkansas Mounted Rifles in 1861 and saw action in Missouri, Arkansas, Mississippi, Kentucky, and Tennessee before dying in a charge at the battle of Murfreesboro, Tennessee. (Courtesy of the Old State House Museum)

Before the election could even take place, Arkansas nearly became the flash point to plunge the nation into civil war as rumors spread through the state that reinforcements were being sent to bolster the Federal garrison at the U.S. arsenal in Little Rock. Nearly one thousand militiamen from

Alexander E. Spence rose through the ranks to become captain of Company B, First Arkansas Infantry Regiment. Wounded at Shiloh, he fought in most of the major engagements of the Army of Tennessee before suffering a mortal wound in the doomed Confederate attack at Franklin, Tennessee, in 1864.
(Courtesy of the Old State House Museum)

central, western, and eastern Arkansas descended on the capital to prevent this from happening. On February 6, Gov. Henry M. Rector called on Capt. James Totten to surrender the arsenal to state forces. Totten complied the next day and was presented by the ladies of Little Rock with a sword engraved with a poem: "When women suffer, chivalry forbears / The soldier dreads all dangers but his own." Such niceties would become increasingly rare in the years of warfare to follow.[7]

In the February 18 election, 27,412 Arkansians voted in favor of holding a secession convention, while only 15,826 cast ballots against it. Significantly, however, 23,626 votes went to Unionist candidates as opposed to 17,927 for secessionist delegates. The convention met at the state capitol in Little Rock on March 4, 1861, the same day Abraham Lincoln was inaugurated as president of the United States. After some two weeks of debate, a vote for immediate secession was defeated, thirty-nine to thirty-five, and the delegates adjourned until August 19.[8]

The tenuous Unionist victory at the secession convention came to naught the following month, when Confederate artillery opened fire on U.S.–held Fort Sumter in South Carolina's Charleston Harbor. A day later, on April 13, Fort Sumter surrendered and on April 15 Lincoln called for seventy-five thousand troops from the states.[9] In response, Governor Rector ordered state militia to seize the federal post at Fort Smith, which U.S. troops abandoned by April 23. David Walker of Fayetteville, president of the secession convention, called for that body to reassemble at the state capitol on May 6. In marked contrast to the March meeting, only five delegates voted against secession on the first vote. Four of them changed their votes as a token of solidarity, with only Isaac Murphy of Madison County refusing to vote in favor of leaving the Union. Arkansas had cast her lot with the South.[10]

The Spence brothers, too, went with the South. Alex Spence was among the first to enroll in a volunteer outfit that later became Company B of the First Arkansas Infantry Regiment, a regiment that would see action at Manassas, Shiloh, the Kentucky campaign, Murfreesboro, the Tullahoma campaign, Chickamauga, Ringgold Gap, the Atlanta campaign, and the cataclysmic battle of Franklin, Tennessee. Tom Spence followed his younger brother a few months later, enlisting in the Second Arkansas Mounted Rifles, with which he would fight in Missouri, Arkansas, Mississippi, Kentucky, and Tennessee.

Chapter 1

"The ball I expect will open before long . . .":
The First Arkansas in Virginia

With secession came a call for troops, and Arkansians, particularly those from the agricultural counties, rushed to serve beneath the banner of a local company, many of which were sewn and presented in tearful ceremonies by the ladies of the communities from which the recruits hailed.[1] Among the companies formed in April 1861 was the Clark County Volunteers, an enthusiastic group of ninety-four men under Capt. Charles S. Stark that included Alexander Spence and Isaac W. "Babe" Cook. In early May, the volunteers were ordered to Little Rock, where they were consolidated with nine other companies to form the First Arkansas Infantry Regiment, C.S.A., which was enrolled for one year of Confederate service on May 8, 1861.[2] Stark's command was designated Company B. At Little Rock, Capt. James F. Fagan of the Saline County Volunteers was elected colonel of the regiment, and it was ordered east to aid in the defense of Virginia.[3]

Spence's company left Little Rock on May 11, 1861. From Memphis, the First Arkansas rode the Memphis and Charleston Railroad through northeast Mississippi and northern Alabama, switching to the Nashville and Chattanooga Railroad at Stevenson, Alabama, to head north to Chattanooga, Tennessee. They then changed to the East Tennessee and Georgia Railroad to ride to Knoxville, finally switching to the Tennessee and Virginia Railroad for the last leg of the trip to Lynchburg, Virginia, where the regiment arrived on May 18.[4] At Lynchburg, the First Arkansas Infantry was formally mustered into twelve-month Confederate service on May 19, 1861.

The First Arkansas Infantry Regiment was part of Brig. Gen. Theophilus Holmes's brigade on July 21, 1861, when Union general Irvin McDowell advanced an untried Federal army against Rebel troops under his old West Point classmate Gen. P. G. T. Beauregard at Manassas Junction, Virginia. The raw troops bludgeoned each other throughout the day, but a flank attack by fresh Confederate troops arriving by train set the Yankee

Capt. Charles S. Stark of Arkadelphia raised the Clark County Volunteers in May 1861. The outfit later became Company B of the First Arkansas Infantry Regiment and served under Stark until his resignation following the battle of Shiloh in 1862. (Courtesy of the Old State House Museum)

This card captures the fever of early 1861 with its declaration that "Arkansas Men With Elephantine Power, Will Make The Yankees Quake and Cower." (Courtesy of the Old State House Museum)

army into a retreat that soon became a rout, with U.S. congressmen who had come to watch the battle mingling with blue-clad privates in a head-long race to the capital. Though present on the field, Alex Spence and the First Arkansas did not go into action at First Manassas. Two days after the battle, the First Arkansas marched to a campsite near Evansport, Virginia.[5] During the next few months, many of the foot soldiers volunteered for detached duty building and manning Confederate siege guns that sought to deny passage on the Potomac River to Federal traffic.[6] The soldiers built shelters to protect them from the elements during extended stays in such places as Camp Holmes, typically constructing rough log buildings for the four to ten men who formed a mess. With typical ingenuity, these cabins were made as homey as possible using such locally available materials as supply boxes, ammunition chests, and kegs.[7] The cold, damp weather of a Virginia winter, as well as the close living conditions of thousands of soldiers, caused the men of the First Arkansas to suffer from camp diseases and epidemics such as diarrhea, measles, and pneumonia.

On December 26, after spending their first Christmas away from home, the First Arkansas moved into winter quarters on Aquia Creek, where proximity to Fredericksburg allowed the men access to amenities not normally available to soldiers.[8] The relative comfort of the camp was tempered by cold duty guarding the Potomac at night in freezing temperatures without fires that would attract Union artillery. As their twelve-month enlistment drew to a close, much of the talk in the camp centered on who would remain in the army and the incentives to do so: a furlough to visit home and a fifty-dollar bonus.[9] An overwhelming majority of the men of the First Arkansas reenlisted, and the regiment left Virginia for the Western theater, in part to facilitate visits to Arkansas but also to stand against Union movements in west Tennessee.[10] Alex Spence cast his lot with the regiment, reenlisting for two years and receiving his furlough to Arkansas.[11] On February 28, 1862, the Third Arkansas Infantry replaced the First Arkansas in the camps on Aquia Creek; the Third Arkansas Infantry would be the only Arkansas regiment to serve the duration of the war in the Army of Northern Virginia.[12]

• • •

Fourteen of the letters from Alex Spence contained in the Spence Family Collection were written in Arkansas and Virginia in 1861 and early 1862. The letters, all of which are included in this chapter, begin with his departure from Little Rock in May 1861 and include his reflections on the First Manassas campaign, the winter of 1861–62 in Virginia, reenlistment, and the possibility of transfer to the Western Theater.

Little Rock Ark,
May 10th, 1861

Sallie,

Agreeable to promise I have seated myself to write you a few lines as it will be the last opportunity I will have for some time. We leave here to morrow morning for Va. 5 Companies have already left. 4 besides ours leave in the morning. The Camden Company and ours go on the same boat.[13] The Camden Co. are all nice men, but the worst of it is we all have to take "deck passage." Our company now numbers 110 men. We have the name of being the most civil, moral and gentlemanly C'mnd that compose the regiment. I believe ours is the "favorite Company" with the Citizens of the place. The Ladies here have been very kind to us, have done a great deal of work when they would not for other Companies. We have been encamped here in the arsenal for four days. I have a special permit from the Captain to let me pass when I chose. A soldiers life is a hard one, but I can't say that is worse than I expected. The "Convention or State" has appropriated $10,000 for paying the expenses of this regiment to Va. Each one of Company is to receive $10 when the boat leaves in the morning. I shall not receive *anything yet a while* as I shall most assuredly quit the Company at Memphis unless there is a change in some things. Mr. Monroe was elected Lieut Col. of the regiment & Mr. Starke is Captain.[14] I don't think he is enough. From the late telegraphic dispatches I think we will have big fighting *and plenty too.*[15] The Northern States are every where preparing for battle. Lincoln says the United States Flag shall *float* over every seceding state, a *glorious* time he will have in placing it over them. There was a large steamboat brot up this evening that was captured at Pine Bluff by Capt. Jno M. Bradley.[16] She was loaded with provisions for the west. Mr. Ashby is here just from Gin. He says northern people all swear vengeance against every Arkansian.[17]

I will try and write to you again from Memphis. Please write to me and direct your letter to Lynchburg, Va. If I do not go there I will write and have my letters forwarded to the place I go to. You need not look for me home as long as I have an arm to strike for the "Southern Confederacy" should she need my Services. I expect the most of us have seen Arkadelphia and its inhabitants perhaps for the last time.

So far I have enjoyed fine health, and I think Camp life will agree with me. All of the Company are standing it fine. You would be amused to see me seated at our "provision chest" writing this. I find camp life is attended with great inconveniences.

Sallie I must close this, as it is getting late and our drum has beat for retiring. Tell all the folks to write and do so yourself.
My love to all
Yours,
Alex E. Spence
I will write to Marcha soon[18]

• • •

Stmr Kentucky
Monday 11th/1861

Dear Tommy,

We left LRock on Saturday morning and are now aboard the Stmr Kentucky.[19] We will reach Memphis about 3 oclock this evening.[20] The Camden & Eldorado Companies are with us.[21] The two other Companies that were at the arsenal left on the same day we did. We are ahead of them some I reckon. There is a great deal of dissatisfaction among all three of the companies in regard to the treatment we have recd on board this Steam Boat. We have got up a card which is to be published in Memphis. We are all kept down on deck, have no place to sleep and nothing to eat. The officers of our Company do not seem to study the wants of their men, without the men are treated like *free and white men* ought to be. I fear the Arkansas Regiment to Va. will be a failure so far as these three companies are concerned, for without they have guarantees that they will be treated better, some of the men will refuse to leave Memphis.

We have met but one or two Boats coming down the river. The Blockade at Cairo is said to be completed, and no Boats from above that point can come down.[22] There was a fight in St. Louis so we heard yesterday in which there was about thirty Killed.[23] I reckon the war has ere this actually commenced—no telling where it will end. I fear many of us have seen Arkadelphia for its last time but I hope not. A good many of our company are sick. Babe and myself are standing the trip very well, John Callaway & Stamp Jones quit us at LRock, could not part from "Jimmy" I reckon.[24] I telegraphed to Tom Ewing before leaving L Rock.[25] If the officers are willing I shall pay my passage from Memphis to Va, so that I can fare like *white men* ought to. I sent my trunk key by Mr. Kingsbury.[26] Take care of all of my things so that I can get them if I should be lucky enough to reach back home in safety. We shall reach Memphis in a short time and if we stay there any while I will write again. If this regiment should be broken up—you must not look for me back. Write to me at Lynchburg Va—and give all the news. My respects R. C. Davis and all other friends.[27]

My love to all the folks.
Yours,
Alex E. Spence

Excuse bad writing etc, I have no pen handy and am sitting on a box writing this. I do not think you ought to leave Arkansaw, yet awhile, plenty of others that can leave easier than you can.
A.E. S.
• • •

Richmond Va
Thursday Night, May 30th 1861

Dear Tom,

On yesterday morning I received your very kind letter directed to me at Lynchburg. The Company left Lynchburg on yesterday morning and reached this place last night. Pitner and myself staid and brought up the baggage to day.[28] We are encamped about 1 1/2 miles from the city. Have not got near as good a place to camp as we had at Lynchburg.[29] There are a great many troops encamped near this place, several thousand must be. They are leaving here every day for the "Seat of War." Our Regiments are expecting orders to leave now every day. It was reported this evening that we were ordered to leave for Manassas Gap on to morrow, but as we are not preparing for travelling to night, I am pretty confident that we will not leave here to morrow.[30] President Davis came out to review the "Arks Regiment" this evening on Dress Parade. He and Gov. Letcher made us speeches, tho the President seemed to think *we would have work to do.*[31] The people crowd after him everywhere. They say the old woman just hang after him, Kissing him all the time. He is a fine looking old man and looks like he is "the right man in the right place."

I presume ere long we will have work and that plenty to do. We drew our guns/muskets at Lynchburg.[32] They are very good ones. The Captain shot mine 310 yds this evening and made a good Shot. If we get into an engagement, we are only to have two Shots and will then have to charge bayonets, a thing to be dreaded sure, but there is no use in flinching—the issue has to be met and I reckon it is as well now as any time. I fear some of Our Boys boast too much about what they will do and when it comes to acting they will not be found there. God forbid that this Regiment should do as the Arks Regiment did in Mexico.[33] If it does, if it does I never want to go back to Clark County.

I was sorry to hear that you had a notion of joining a Company and going out on the frontier. I think you had better stay with Pa and Mother.

Old Jno Callaway had to turn back at Lynchburg. The old fellow was willing but was not able to go. We made him up enough money to carry him back and left him to take the cars yesterday evening.

I understand Col Bozeman and some others did not show their liberality *very much* when you all were making up a purse to buy ammunitions.[34] Tis the way I have always thot such men would act . . .

The letter ends here.

• • •

Camp McGregor Va[35]
Friday Night, Aug 16/61

Dear Pa,

This will be handed to you by Mr. Ewing who leaves in the morning for Arkansas, he will give you all the news. I wrote you some time ago about sending me some money. I have got the money from Mr. Ewing and give him an order on Barkman Kingsbury & Co.[36] I want you if you please to see that the money is paid to him. The money I get from Tom is money Dave Meadour has won and is sending back to his wife.[37] If it happens that you have sent the money, assist BK & Co or Ewing in raising the money and I will pay Ewing back when he comes here. The money I get this time I think will do me through the war.

I wrote to Tommy to pay Davis, Ewings overseer, Five Dollars for Randle.[38] If he has never done it please pay him yourself. I have written in this to Sallie about sending me some clothes. By Liza's letter I recd today I expect you have already sent them by Dr. Ward.[39] Send me the Winter Clothes, I enclose in the within list any way, as most of the other clothes I wrote for was for summer, the Cotton Under Shirts & cot Drawers. I will not need the pants I reckon you have sent in addition to the list of clothes I have given. Please tell Mother to have one Fatigue Jacket made & sent, have it made out of grey or blk cass.[40] You all can guess at the size. There has been so many soldiers in Arkadelphia I reckon you all know how they are made. If you do not, Mr. Ewing will tell you all how it is made. I could buy these things here but would have to pay too much for them. I am glad to hear you are having made for me a knife from the [portion torn] . . . making him I think we will have wo [portion torn] . . . ere long. Cannons were firing all day [portion torn] . . . the Creek. The ball I expect will open before long with us. I am not particularly anxious to be in a fight but I think I shall do my part when we do get in an engagement.

Pa I want you if you please to be sure & not let Mr. Ewing be disappointed in that money & please have the clothes sent. The money I get this time I think will last me the balance of the war. We have to have something to eat and that is about the way the most of our money has gone. I shant be quite as extravagant hereafter as I have been. Tell Mother I did not get to see Lincolns Carriage at Manassas.[41] Have you ever got your fine carriage or not?[42]

What in the world is the reason you all don't write me oftener. Liza's letter to day is the only one I have recd. for about two weeks. It does seem you might write oftener. I wrote you not long since. Tell Mr. Kingsbury we all would be very glad to have him come on to see us.

I will close this. Mr. Ewing will give you all the news. I expect he will be asked a thousand & one questions. Do you all ever hear from Tom, I would write him if I knew where to direct my letters.

I will write you all every few days. Did Dr. Ward get any recruits in Arkadelphia for our Regiment? Be sure & write and give all the news by Mr. Ewing, & please attend to the things I have written about in this (the money & clothes.)

I hope I will hear from you all very soon
My love to all, Yours,
Alex E. Spence

• • •

Friday Evg, August 11/61

Sallie, I commenced this yesterday but did not finish. Today the mail was brought in but one letter for me from Liza Aug 6th/61. She writes you all get no letters from me. I write at least 3 times a week to some of you. She writes about the clothes. I would be glad now if you all have not sent them as you can now send the winter clothes. Send the things I need anyway. I fear Pa has sent the money. I will get the money from Ewing anyway & give him in the order on B.K. & Co. Dr. Ward the recruiting officer is a great friend of mine. Tell Pa I heard he was having a knife made to send me. Tell I will be much obliged to him for it. Knifes are the things in close quarters with the Yankees. The Tiger Rifles from La tried theirs at Manassas on "Ellsworths Pet Lambs."[43] Liza writes that I write too much about the Cos and citizens of Arkadelphia. I dont expect there has been one of our Com that ever wrote a letter home before the artillery life but what said something disparaging of the artillery. Well Ill stop it now as they have gone.

I want you all to be sure & write & give all the news. Mr. Ewing will give you all the news.

My Love to all, yours, etc.

Alex E. Spence

You can burn this when you get through reading.

• • •

This fragmentary letter was written after the battle of Manassas and before the First Arkansas went into winter quarters on Aquia Creek near Fredericksburg, Virginia.

. . . have to pay the man exorbitant prices here for everything. The rations we draw is nothing but "Sugar, Coffee, Beef & Flour" & you know one can not live on this always. I shall not be quite as extravagant hereafter & think the money I get this time will last me over twelve months out. Do not send me any common or white shirts in the clothes you send. I have plenty of them. The undershirts and socks I think I have in my trunk you may also send. Genl Holmes is talking of fixing up our winter quarters at this place if we do not get in an engagement before the 1st November.[44] I do not think our Regiment will ever get in a fight. There has been a good many writing here inquiring about our officers, how we are treated, etc. Ewing will now give you all "a true state of affairs," what we think of our officers & particularly our 1st Lt who is looked upon more with pity and contempt than anything else.[45] Fred Greene is one of the very best men I ever saw.[46] Lindsey does very well, is a good friend of mine.[47] So does Capt. Stark seem to be. Mc pretends to be also. I understand Tom was elected "Orderly" of Flanagan's Co. Well he will find it a hard birth, has more work to do & gets less credit than any other officer.[48]

How does Rufus stand the "artillery" business?[49] Poor fellow, he will have a hard time of it. We have a good many advantages over the frontier Soldiers in case we get wounded or get sick. We have the best of hospitals to go to & if prefered we can go to private residences. I am in first rate spirits. Think I will get through this war & back home all safe.

Bill Alexander has a trunk at Cassarts & wants it here.[50] You all can get it & put mine and Babe's clothes in it and send as I have no use of a trunk here. If it is a large trunk, fill it with something to eat if nothing else. Any things you all think of that I will need you can send. Ewing will tell all the things necessary for a Soldier. You need not hint to mother about her "cakes." I am afraid she might send some of them, but they would not Keep I reckon.

Sallie I have written this to you to attend to these things not that I think but what the others Marcha, etc. would attend just as well and with as much pleasure, but because I have written to all the others since you. In the trunk you all will have a good opportunity of sending me letters. Tell all my friends to write & send. I wish to Gracious you all would write. I have never heard a word from Tom since he left Arkadelphia.

• • •

Two letters from Isaac "Babe" Cook, Alex Spence's friend whose sister was the widow of Spence's older brother, are included in the Spence Family Collection. The first of these includes an account of the death of a comrade.

Camp McGregor Virginia
Wednesday Sept. 4th 1861

Dear Sister
Your very kind letter of the 20th August came direct to hand. That afforded much pleasure to have from with the rest of the family and to hear that you was all well. This leaves me in very good health. I written you by Mrs. Marbury.[51] I also intend writing by Maj. Bourland. I was at Fredericksburg when Pen and Maj Bourland left for Arka.[52] Went down expressly to see them leave. I should of written by them if I had of had time. They left Fredericksburg early in the morning. Pen appeared quite anctious to get off. His health was improving very much when he left, but we have had the painful misfortune of loosing one of our Brother Soldiers that is long to be Remembered by all of our Company. Poor Calhoun bid fun not more than three weeks ago to live as long as any man in our company, but Sunday last it was the will of God to take him from our midst. A noble young man, he was two. Every one in the com-

pany was his friend. Has was not thought to be dangers when sent to Fredericksburg. Nor even until the Evening before he died. I learn Since his departure that he Said when first taken that he did not believe that he would get well. None of the company thought of his being dangerous until the word came to us that he was dead. It will be almost heart breaking to his old Masster to hear of it. His things were sent back by Mr. Bourland.[53]

We have but few cases of sickness in the company at this time, none considered dangerous. Jan had herd I was sick. My health is very good now. If I should get sick, I will certainly leave camp and go to a private home. Sister, I have almost saw a full account of the fight at Springfield, Mo.[54] An account of the Killed and wounded. All things came through right by Dr. Ward. They came through in good time. I was beginning to Kneed [sic] some of the tricks. We are still at the Same place & I would not be Surprised If we were to remain here all winter. Give my love to the Old Man & Lady Spence and tell Mrs. Elder it is out of the question for me to send her the flag she spoke about. My respect to Mr. Elder & Joshua, Mr. Hearn & family, Parson Beatties & family & say to him I rec'd his letter and will answer it in a Short time.[55] I must close. Write often. I remain your loving Brother,

Babe Cooke

• • •

The Spence Family Collection includes one letter from Sarah Ann Hood, a daughter of Solomon and Frances Spence who lived with her husband and family in Caldwell, Texas. Her letter to her sister Martha Elder provides insights into the domestic situation in rural Texas in the early months of the war.

Caldwell Texas Novbr. 7, 1861[56]

Dear Sister Martha,

As usual, I am found writing to my relations. You all in Arkansas have entirely forgoten me, and perhaps my writing may refresh your memory. Sometimes you will write. It has been a *long long time* since I received a letter from any of you. Sallies writen July 15 was the last. In it she informed me of Thomas departure to the scene of war. Immediately wrote to him at Fayettville Ark, have received no answer yet. I would be glad to know where he was that I could write. Alex writes occasionally. On the 5 of Sept his last was wrote. When did you hear from him and Thomas? I hope they are well. Every mail for the last four weeks I have expected a letter but Alas none have come. Still I shall hope for one. To night I am more anxious if possible now than ever to hear from you all.

Thomy and Alex I am uneasy about all the time, wish I could hear from them all the time.

Novbr. 10—Sister, as company come in to spend the day, I was prevented from finishing this to get in that evening mail. To night I shall finish. This holy sabbath evening we are all alone, and all in good health. This part of the county is ver healthy this fall. I do hope you all are in good health and your dear little baby, what is her name? Who does she favor? I wish I could see you all once more that we could talk over our matters but, alas, dear sister, I fear that is too much pleasure for me ever to realize. You have heard that Mr. Hood had gone to the War with a company. He is stationed in Galveston.[57] All this I wrote to Mother. It is now going on three months since he left. We have indeed a lonely time of it. Miss Johnston stays with me all the time. You all would naturally want to know how we are geting along. I can say we do as well as any one could expect under the circumstances. We have a good many hogs, plenty to make our own meat; ten head of cows, chickens, and Buddy has a fine pony so that I can send him to the country after any thing I want, and a pleanty of the whear with to buy any thing I want has been deposited where I can get it in three day notice. I have met with very many kind friends who have voluntarily offered to protect the War Widows during the absence of there husbands. Corn sells at 50. Pork at $500. Beef 3 1/2 cts. Sweet potatoes 50 cts, Molasses 75 cts per gallon. Sugar a shilling a pound. Coffee 50 a pound. Tea one dollar per pound. Butter 12 1/2 cents per pound, egg 12 1/2, dozen. Chickens 12 1/2 piece. I buy butter hear and send to Mr. Hood and a great many other things, a mattress and beding. Tell me, sister, has mother and Pa sent Thomy and Alec a mattress and bed clothing, and do they send them an[y] clothes? I know if they have, they will not suffer. I have socks comforts and blankets for the soldiers and would cheerfully send them to my brothers if I knew how to get them there, one package to Alec in Virginia and one to Thomas in Missouri. Would in all probability never reach them unless there were other things sent to each of there companies. I am determined for one to do my part for the soldiers. I have already done much sewing and kniting and will continue to do. It is heart rending to think our relation that are out on the battle ground and on the tented field should want for warm clothing and a comfortable place to rest there wearied limbs. Sister, if our dear brothers have not been furnished, get ready and send on thoes things as quick as possible. They will know how to appreciate it. When did you hear from them? Where are they now? I wish they would write. Well, how are Pa and Mother & Eliza? Lonely enough, I dare say. Are they well? Do they visit you and Sallie often? You should both visit them very often and make there time as pleasant as possible. Oh, what would I give to see Mother and Pa. Tell them I will live in hope of seeing them if I dye in despair. How is Sallie, Mr. Hearn and the children? Tell her if she could but know what a pleasure it was to read letters from loved ones, she would write. You all are there to see and talk with each other while I am hear one alone. How is brother and Sarah Ann? Are both well? Ask brother to write to me. Martha, will you ask Mother and Pa, Brother, Sallie and you with the rest send me your likenesses. They are frequently brought hear in the male from the states. The postage is but little an Eliza, tell her. She promised to send me brother Sallies. I have long looked for it, all in vain. Ask her for me to send it and she, too, must write. I would be glad if Mr. Elder would write. I cant see why we don't correspond with our brother in laws. We ought to feel that we are all one family. Marcha, I had a letter from Sister the other day. They were well except colds. Mr. Stinnett has not joined the army as he expected. Lucie says he will go when needed as an independent volunteer. I wrote to her to come down and hope to see here this week. We still hear of battles being fought in V[irginia,] K[entucky,] an[d] Missouri. What an anxiety of mind. We are daily expecting an attack at Galveston. The women and children have all left the city. Troops are going in by every train of cars and if they get the large guns there before the enemy, they can hold the Island. Those guns have been looked for there for the last four weeks. There is a mystery about them some way. They hung four men that were following after thoes guns. They are 4 and the mud is so deep and stiff, it takes 40 yoke of oxen to move one gun.[58] Negroes so far have done much better than was anticipated. It may be to get us off our guard. Dear Sister, when you read this, goe to Mothers and let her hear from us. Fannie, Buday, Namie, all join in sending their love to Mother, Pa, you, Sallie, Brother, Sarah Ann, Eliza, Mr. Elder, Mr. Hearn and Bettie, Fannie and Lizzie. Tell all to write. I regret we have no school and no prospect for one soon. Dear Sister, I must close and write to Alec. As soon as you get this, do sit down and write to me. If you please, my dear sister, write soon and often. So, good night to you all. I remain your affectionate sister, Mary Ann Hood.

My own dear sisters, dont forget to write. I will write some of you soon.

Good bye, Marcha Elder

• • •

Camp Holmes Banks of the Potomac Va
Sunday, Dec. 8th, 1861

Dear Sallie,

I received your kind & welcome letter of 23rd ulto a few days ago.[59] This being Sunday, have concluded to answer as I could not pass it more pleasantly than writing home. Sunday is a long day in Camps. It is a day for general inspection of arms, etc., hardly ever drill and seldom have preaching. Our Chaplain is of the Episcopal Denomination and as he never preaches, I suppose he dont care much for the spiritual welfare of the Regiment.[60] Guess he is something of the "Parson Kerr order." By the by, Sallie what has become of this distinguished Reverend, he paid our Regiment a flying visit but forgot I reckon there was a company from Clark in it.

Rumors are as thick as leaves with us in regard to the advancing of the Northern forces. The last one we heard is that there would be a large fleet of vessels at this place to day to commence the attack on our Batteries at this place.[61] Last night we were cooking up provisions so as to be prepared for them to day. As the fleet has not yet made its appearance I suppose the report like most others we hear is false. We never know when to believe anything in Camps. The Yankees still continue to increase in numbers on the Maryland Shore, keep a balloon up nearly all the time. Yesterday our Batteries fired at the balloons and I tell you they brought it down double quick.[62] We may have a fight here but I dont think we will unless we attack the Yankees. Col. Fagan tells us we will be moved to Brooks Station in a few days and take up quarters for the winter as soon as the excitement dies away about this "big fight" expected. I suppose we will go.[63]

By this time I reckon you have heard of the death of Capt. Swink who died in the hospital at Dunfries a few days ago. His son is getting well and will be at home as soon as he gets able to travel.[64] There is not many sick in the Co. at present. It seems what little sickness we have is more fatal than it has ever been before. Mr. Jas. Coffman that used to clerk for Capt Cook died in Fredericksburg a few days ago. He belonged to a company from Camden.[65]

We have had some very cold weather, plenty of Snow. I have felt as cold weather in Arkansas as we have had yet. In regards to the clothes it will not make much difference about them as I reckon I will have plenty to do without them. The blankets have not yet arrived.

Well when did you, from Tommy, the report of the fight in Mo was all false [sic]. Tom Ewing got a letter from Tommy of the 17th ulto a few days ago, he says he has never received a letter from me yet. I have written him several letters. What has become of Marcha, she seldom writes me. I received a letter from Liza yesterday and will answer in a few days & tell Marcha I will write her as she won't write me. I am sorry you have had so much sickness amongst your folks. I am in hopes this will find you all well. I am glad to hear Pa & Mothers health is good. Tell Mr. Hearn I will write him before long.

As I have nothing more to write I will close. Write often and give all the news, and tell all to write.

My love to all. Your Bro etc,

Alex E. Spence

Tuesday morn, Dec. 10th, 1861

Dear Sallie I have an opportunity of mailing this this morning. All of our baggage is being sent away to Fredericksburg & everything being prepared for our march. None of us have any idea which way we will move. Some think we will go towards Manassas, & others that we are only going to Brooks Station. None of us have the least idea there is any chance for a fight.

I will write again in a few days.

Yours,

Alex

• • •

Fredericksburg Va.
Dec 25th 1861

Dear Pa,

I wrote you a few days and promised to write again soon. Am sorry though I can not say I am well. I thought by this time my fever would be broke but tis not. I have had a slight fever every day for the last ten days. Comes on about 7 in the morning and lasts until two in the evening. I am very weak. After the fever cools off I am able to walk about the house. The Doctor says its nothing but cold and I will be well in a few days. Hope he speaks aright. A young man by the name of Cowan belonging to our Co died in the hospital at this place with Typhoid Fever last night.[66] I don't know when I will be able to go to Camp. I wish if you have it you would send me about 20 Dollars. You can send it in one bill. Tom Ewing has never been able to pay me all you sent by him. If I have to stay here much longer I will need the money. I will write you again in a few days. I hope you are all well. My love to all

Your son,

Alex E. Spence

Tell Mother not to be uneasy about me.

• • •

Camp Price Near Aquia Creek Va
Saturday Janry 11th 1862

Dear Pa,

I wrote you not long since by Mr. Ewing but being at leisure to day thought I would write you a few lines again. Have no news. Yesterday I recd two letters from home, the first in some time. We are all having a pretty easy time of it, too cold to drill and in first rate quarters. Bhoys get to go to town about whenever they want to. Officers getting very easy on us.

Yesterday Genl Holmes & Walker made us a speech on the absolute necessity of the "1st Arkansas" reenlisting for two years.[67] The greatest efforts will be made to get the whole Regiment into it and I expect they will come very near doing it. Capt Starke is raising a company, has very near the Number required by law. I suppose they will get enough and in a day or so organized. Alexander, Bourland, Yancey & Jno Lindsey are the only Boys from Arkadelphia that have yet gone into it.[68] The others from our Company live in the country. As for my part I shall not reenlist and will be at home when my time is up. The Bhoys that have reenlisted will get furloughs and leave for home in a few days.

The Health of the Company is very good, but few sick. I am as "hearty as ever." We are all living fine, plenty of "fresh oysters." Should we remain here, Our time will soon pass away. There is no prospect of a fight anywhere near here. The roads are so bad it would be impossible for the Yankees to make an "advance." The expected fleet up the Potomac has not made its appearance nor do I think it ever will. I am truly glad to hear you have enough groceries to do you. Sometimes it looks like there is but little hope of the Blockade being raised.

I suppose by this time Tommy is at house. I would like very much to have met him there but no chance for a furlough here now.

When we were fixing to leave Arkadelphia Capt Cook proffered to give me a letter or so of introduction to some of his friends in this State. I wish you would see him and if he has any acquaintances in Richmond and is willing to do so he would write me a letter of Recommendation to them. And you can send me. All that I want for him to speak of business Capacities & character, which I presume he will be willing to do. Tell him I will be very much obliged to him for it.

I was sorry to hear of Mr. Millers death. Reckon though he deserved it.

By the time this reaches you Tom Ewing will have reached Arkadelphia I reckon and will give the news from our Camps. I hope your & Mothers continues good.

I wish you all would write me oftener, it has been some time since you wrote me. I will write again in a few days.

My love to all. Your Son, etc

Alex E. Spence

• • •

Camp Price Va.
Febry. 4th 1862

Dear Sallie:

Your kind letter of 25th ulto was received yesterday and it is the first one I have got from you of a later date than 25th Dec. I am truly sorry to hear you are all sick. It does seem "your folks" have their share of sickness. I hope by this time you have all got well of the "chills." I have so far been very fortunate in having good health. A good many of our Company are sick, none seriously though. All of our sick are allowed the privilege of going to town either to the Hospitals or private Houses if they prefer.

We are having some pretty bad weather now. Yesterday the snow fell to a depth of 6 or 8 inches. To day it is warm and pleasant and the ground melting off very fast, but it is *awful* muddy, I assure you. I have felt no such cold weather here yet as I expected from what people said, think I have suffered more with cold in Arks. than I have here. The "old Residenters" here think now we will not have much cold weather this winter- which I hope will be so.

By this time I suppose the Bhoys of our Co will have reached Arkadelphia. I expect they will have lively times for a while. I did write Mr. Elder. I had no notion of enlisting did not have at that time. The Virginia Legislature are about passing a law Keeping all of her 12 mo Vol in the field for two years after this present term is up. Probaly the other states will pass the same law. I wrote you last week asking your advice. I suppose as Tommy is at home he can tell something about the Cavalry service and what he thinks about New Companies being made up from Clark. I would prefer going in the Cavalry service on the frontier if there is a good Company made up to go. One in the service here is cramped most too much in his movements. Write me what kind of a company Mr. Love is making up.[69] The gentleman I wrote you about wanting me to remain with him was speaking to me yesterday, he is very anxious for me to stay with him. Says I need not enlist though until the Regiment is reorganized and he gets his appointment. If I agree to stay, probaly I may not be able to go home until next fall. I shall not enlist until I hear from you all again. There is no use in talking about staying at home after my time is up.

I learn there is a great deal of dissatisfaction in the Artillery Company.

I never thought much the Captain would do. Re-enlisting dont take with them, so they write us.[70] How does Rufus get along—you all never mention him.

Tell Tommy I shall expect that long letter from him. I reckon Mr. Ewing will get there in time to see him.

If you have not written before you get this, be sure and write and let me know what you all think about my staying.

I will write to Pa in a few days. Has Marcha forgotten me? Tell the folks all to write me.

My love to all

Your Brother,

Alex E. Spence

• • •

Camp Price Banks of the Potomoc Va
Thursday Night, Feby 6th 1862

Dear Pa,

Yesterday I received your kind letter enclosing those of Capt. Cooks for which I am very thankful to you for sending me. I have written to the Capt. thanking him for his kindness to me. I do not know that I shall make application for a situation, but I reckon there is no harm in having the letters in case I should see an "opening." Re-enlisting still goes on in the Regiments. The balance of our Company that have enlisted will leave next week for home. We will then be very lonesome. Several of our Company are going to work in the "Navy Yard" that is to be established on the Rhappahannock River near Fredericksburg until their time is up. The Bhoys are all in very good health. We have had some "awful weather" here lately. I think we have more sudden changes here than in Arkansas. We have nothing but "mud."

I have not enlisted and don't know yet that I will. Shall wait and hear what you all say about it. I wrote Sallie last week and expect to get an answer in the course of ten days. I think though the "frontier service" will suit me best. As Tommy has had some experience, I am in hopes he will advise me. Two years is rather a long time for one to sell himself for & I think troops will be accepted for a shorter time out west. I would have liked very much to have met Tommy at home. It seems they are particularly fortunate in getting furloughs to go home most any time they chose.

I reckon Tom Ewing has reached home by this time and will meet with Tommy.

To day I received a letter from Texas from Lucie of 18 ulto. All well so she writes. As it is getting late, I shall close. I am in hopes this will reach you all well. Tell Mother I shall take care of myself, for I want to see home about as bad as you all want to see me.

Tell all the Folks to write and please do so yourself. My love to all, Your affectionate son, etc.

Alex E. Spence

• • •

Camp Price Va,
Tuesday, Febry. 18th 1862

Liza

Your kind letter was received a few days ago, it being the first one I have had from home in some time. I was right glad to get it I assure you. I thought I had better write you to night for there is no telling what a day may bring forth. The Yankees seem to be making gigantic strides towards cutting us off from the other Southern States.[71] Whether they will succeed or not remains yet to be seen, but here of late it looks like they have been successful in all their undertakings. We "are all excitement" here now. This evening a telegram was received stating Fort Donelson was taken yesterday by the Federals. We know there has been fighting going on there for several days and fear the report is true.[72] There has certainly been a great battle fought there within the last few days, and many a poor soul sent to his long home.[73] To morrow evening we will get the correct news. The Artillery Company are pretty near the Yankees as I see our Forces have evacuated Bowling Green and the Federals have burned the place.[74] I fear we have been inactive too long. It will be a long time before we recover what we have lost in the late defeats our forces have met with. Re enlisting still goes on. Lt. McIntosh is trying to raise an artillery co., will leave for Arkadelphia in a few days for recruits. He may get up his company. I have not yet enlisted. Will return home and go either to the Indian Country, Mo, or Ky. Am getting tired of this country. Babe I suppose will do the same. I have no doubt but what we have an easier time here than we would have most anywhere else, but still I prefer a change. There will be a considerable difference in the next Company that represents Clark Co. in this Regiment and the present Co. You know very near all that have enlisted. Look and see how many intimate associates there is in it of Babes & mine, but few of the Bhoys immediately from Arkadelphia will be in the next Company. Tommy writes he dont Know what he will do. From his letter I don't think he is very well pleased with soldiering. Ask Pa if he can buy a good horse for me by the time I come back. I don't want to foot it the next time. I think when the time of Capts. Flanagan & Witherspoon Companies are up that there will be more companies made up from Clark. Tell Mother she need have no doubts about my remaining in the Service, for as long as there is a Yankee foot on Southern soil, I expect to try and serve "Our Country" in some way. By this time I suppose all of our Bhoys have reached home. Guess they will give a glorious account of how we are getting along, etc. "Well for a wonder" our boxes of Blankets etc, all reached here in safety a few days ago. Come in a very good time as it is pretty cold weather. Ground covered with snow again. Tell Marcha I am in hopes she will write me one more time before I go home. Has Sallies folks got well, I hope they have. Tell Mr. Elder I shall write to him in a few days. Write and give all the news. I am in hopes this will find all well. My love to all,

Yours etc.

Alex E. Spence

• • •

Thursday Eveg. Feby 20th 1862

Dear Pa,

I did not have an opportunity of mailing this letter on yesterday to Liza. All excitement around here now on account of the news of the fall of Fort Donelson and the probable surrender of Nashville into the hands of the Federals.[75] Col. Fagan leaves here this evening for Richmond to try and get leave to remove the remnant of the Regiment to Helena Ark. and have an order issued from the Department for all those belonging to the Regt. off on furloughs to rendezvous at Helena immediately. He thinks if he can get "the order," he will be able to have the Regiment in "full trim" for fighting within 20 days from this time. If he succeeds, I shall try and come home from Helena, but if I do not get a furlough, don't know when I shall be able to see you all, for if we are ordered either to Tenn or Ky, I believe I shall stay with the Regiment. I will write some of you again on Sunday, for by that time we will know whether we go or not.

I hope this will find all, well,

Your Son,

Alex E. Spence

• • •

Camp Price Va. Feby 23rd/62

Mr. Elder,

I recd. your welcome letter of a recent date a few days ago and have delayed writing until to day Sunday thinking I would be able to write whether we would be removed from this place as I wrote Pa about a few days ago. No news has been recd from Col. Fagan, so I fear he was not able to get permission to move us. If the Regiment is sent to any other state, I believe I shall remain with it, that is, if they will agree to give me a furlough after the reorganization of the Regiment. If the Regiment is to remain in this state, I don't think I shall stay. You all are very partial to the service in Va. I don't see why you should be. Tommy dont think I can stand the campaign in Mo. I beg to disagree with him, for I think I can stand any hardships that are to be borne by "Confederate Soldiers."

Yesterday we received the news of Genl. Prices victory over the Federalists in Benton Co Ark.[76] As the Yankees have at last set foot on Arkansas soil, I reckon every one will now "shoulder his musket," so then there will be no necessity for Gov. Rectors intended draft.[77] The Virginians are reenlisting very slowly. I expect they will have to make a draft to get her to furnish her quota of 68,000 men.

A Telegraphic Dispatch was received this morning stating that Nashville had been evacuated by our forces and they were falling back to Memphis. I don't know whether it is true or not, but fear it is. You will have heard before the receipt of this. The Federalists seem to be making "good headway" towards cutting us off from the balance of the Southern States.

Our Bhoys that are back I presume are having a lively time. 60 Days will seem a pretty short time with them I guess.

Tell Marcha I recd her letter a few days ago and will answer this week. Am very thankful for her advice. As it is getting "dinner time," I shall close. Lt Greene and myself are attending to the Commissariat Dept. of the Regiment, have a very easy time.

Please write on receipt of this and give all the news, general & special. I trust all are well. My love to all.

Yours truly, etc

Alex E. Spence

I will write again soon.

Chapter 2

"We had a very hard Fight . . .": The Second Arkansas Mounted Rifles in the Trans-Mississippi

Alex Spence's brother Thomas followed him into Confederate service, leaving his duties as Clark County sheriff to join the newly forming Second Arkansas Mounted Rifles. The regiment, containing 662 men in ten companies, was mustered into service on July 29, 1861, at Osage Prairie near Bentonville in Northwest Arkansas, and Tom Spence was made the regiment's ordnance sergeant.[1] In addition to the Clark Countians who comprised Company E of the regiment, the Second Arkansas Mounted Rifles included companies raised at Bentonville, Galla Rock, Paraclifta, and Washington, as well as the "Texas Fencibles," a company of horsemen from Daingerfield, Texas.[2] Col. James M. McIntosh, a West Point graduate who resigned his U.S. Army commission to fight for the South, was named colonel of the new regiment.[3]

On August 4, only a few days after their formation, the Second Arkansas Mounted Rifles joined Brig. Gen. Ben McCulloch on a march into Missouri to aid the Missouri State Troops under Maj. Gen. Sterling Price, who had been driven into southwest Missouri by Union troops under the aggressive Brig. Gen. Nathaniel Lyon in the battle to control that key border state. McCulloch's Arkansans and Texans linked with Price's Missourians near Carthage, and on August 7 more than fifteen thousand Rebel troops arrived at Wilson's Creek, about twelve miles west of Springfield. Many of Price's men were unarmed, however, and proved to be more of a hindrance than help in the battle that followed. Those of McCulloch's men who were armed had a wide variety of weapons; Thomas Spence went into battle bearing his late brother Solomon's old shotgun.[4] McCulloch's spies gathered information on Lyon's command, bringing it to the Rebel commander on August 9, but the Texan delayed a planned advance on Lyon at Springfield that night because of heavy rain. The U.S. commander, however, did not sit idly by and wait to be attacked.[5]

Lyon was heavily outnumbered at Wilson's Creek, where he commanded some 5,600 Union soldiers. McCulloch led 10,175 men, while

James McIntosh was the first colonel of the Second Arkansas Mounted Rifles, leading the regiment at Wilson's Creek, Missouri, and Chustenenlah, Indian Territory, in 1861. He was promoted to brigadier general and was shot dead minutes after assuming command of Ben McCulloch's troops at Pea Ridge. (Courtesy of the University of Arkansas at Little Rock Archives)

Ben McCulloch, a former Texas Ranger, commanded Confederate forces at Wilson's Creek and part of the Rebel army at Pea Ridge. He was shot and killed at Pea Ridge while reconnoitering the Union lines. (Courtesy of the Old State House Museum)

Price commanded 5,221 troops. [6] Lyon gambled and split his forces, attacking the Confederate front with part of his army on the morning of August 10, while Brig. Gen. Franz Sigel circled around McCulloch to hit the Rebel camp in its rear. The Confederates, who had withdrawn their pickets the night before in expectation of a morning march, were caught by surprise. [7] Lyon's command hit the Confederate lines as McCulloch and McIntosh sat down to breakfast with Price, leading the former two commanders to ride at the gallop to rejoin their commands. [8] The Federal general's initial thrust from Capt. Joseph B. Plummer's battalion of U.S. Regulars on the Rebel right was stopped by a slashing counterattack by the Second Arkansas Mounted Rifles and Third Louisiana Infantry Regiment. The two forces fired on each other at close range along an overgrown fence row, then McIntosh ordered a charge in which his nine hundred men swept away Plummer's three hundred Northern troops. McIntosh personally led this charge "upon a division of the regular Federal troops stationed up our north. In the charge many of the enemy were slain and the rest repulsed." Tom Spence was in the thick of this fighting, and Lt. Jonathan Callaway reported his actions in a letter home: "The first platoon shot about four rounds doing good execution—as its enemy had advanced within fifty paces Tom Spence gave them 8 Doz[en] buck shot at that distance & he urged them up to charge. . . ."[9] The enthusiastic Confederates followed Plummer's command until they came under Union artillery fire, which drove them back to shelter behind a small hill, where McCulloch found them and urged them back into battle.[10] Sigel attacked the Confederate rear, enjoying initial success but then fleeing the field after mistaking gray-garbed Rebel troops for a similarly clad Iowa unit, allowing the Southerners to get fatally close before opening fire. McCulloch then turned his full attention to Lyon's troops atop Oak Hill.

The Yankee attacks on Price's command on Oak Hill had come close to breaking the Missourians when McCulloch arrived to stiffen their line. The Second Arkansas Mounted Rifles joined this "close and bloody contest" on the Confederate right; the regiment's Lt. Col. Ben Embry reported: "[I]n a short time after reaching the scene of action the regiment became engaged with the enemy. We remained here for an hour and a half, at different times skirmishing with the enemy." The Arkansians later were removed from the fighting at Bloody Hill to guard the Wilson Creek ford against a Union cavalry attack that never transpired.[11] Lyon committed his reserves but was mortally wounded leading a counterattack against the doughty Rebels. Realizing that Sigel would not come to their aid, the Union army retreated toward Springfield. McCulloch and Price were too exhausted to follow.[12]

This first great clash of arms in the Trans-Mississippi was a bloody one. The five hours of combat left 279 Rebels dead and 951 wounded. Lyon's troops suffered 258 fatal casualties, 873 wounded, and 186 missing or captured. The Second Arkansas Mounted Rifles suffered 10 killed, and 44 wounded, the first of hundreds of casualties the hard-fighting regiment would suffer over the next four years.[13]

Perhaps as a result of these losses, Sgt. Tom Spence was sent to Arkansas on a recruiting mission and to gather supplies. Lt. Jonathan Callaway of Company E noted on October 5, 1861, that "we expect Tom Spence back soon with recruits and Clothing. we now muster 26 men rank and file about enough to roll logs." On October 11, Callaway reported that Company E's Capt. Harris Flanagin received a letter "written at Paraclifta in which he says Sgt. Spence has in listed about the required No. of recruits + will be along in a few days—we are anxiously awaiting his arrival [and] hope he has forty men with 'Sand in their Craw.'"[14]

Because Missouri had not seceded from the Union, McCulloch pulled his troops back into northwest Arkansas, leaving Price and his troops to campaign in their home state alone.[15] In December, McIntosh led a force of 1,600 that included some 130 men from Companies A, B, C, and E of the Second Arkansas Mounted Rifles into Indian Territory, where members of the Creek tribe who remained loyal to the United States were attempting to retreat into Kansas.[16] The aged chief Opothleyahola's Creeks, joined by Unionist Cherokees and Seminoles, had defeated a force of Texans, Creeks, Choctaws, and Chickasaws at Caving Banks on December 9 and remained a disruptive influence on Confederate efforts to gain control of the tribes in Indian Territory.[17] McIntosh left Fort Gibson on December 22 with a force of 1,380 Texans and Arkansians in pursuit of the Creek chief, catching up to his party on December 26. The Unionist Indians occupied a "high and rugged hill, with its sides covered in oak trees. . . . Each tree on the hill-side screened a stalwart warrior." At noon, McIntosh ordered his forces to charge, and the desperate assault crashed through a skirmish line of Seminoles, bringing the Confederate soldiers into Opothleyahola's main lines. The Unionists broke and scattered, pursued by McIntosh's troops and forces under Col. Stand Watie, who arrived late on the field. Opothleyahola's forces lost around 250 men killed; 160 women and children were captured, along with 20 blacks, 30 wagons, 70 yokes of oxen, 500 horses, hundreds of cattle, 100 sheep, and other property. Confederate losses totaled 8 killed and 32 wounded (including 7 from the Second Arkansas) in the one-sided victory at Chustenenlah.[18]

After returning to Arkansas, Thomas Spence and the Second Arkansas Mounted Rifles received a new commander. Confederate president Jefferson Davis, in an effort to alleviate long-standing tension between McCulloch and Price, created the Military District of the Trans-Mississippi on January 10, 1862, placing it under the control of a dashing, romantic, and incompetent Mississippian, the West Point-educated Earl Van Dorn. Despite a military career that dated to 1842, Van Dorn had little strategic vision, summing up his goals for his Trans-Mississippi command in a letter to his wife: "I must have St. Louis—then Huzza!"[19]

Opposing Van Dorn was the Federal Army of the Southwest under Brig. Gen. Samuel R. Curtis, a West Point graduate, former congressman, and one of the founders of the Republican Party. While lacking his gray-clad foe's dash, Curtis would exhibit steadiness, initiative, and innovation in the upcoming campaign. The Army of the Southwest advanced against

Price, who abandoned Springfield on February 12, 1862, and retreated into Arkansas. Curtis and his army followed, and on February 17 the cheering Yankees invaded Arkansas.[20]

The rapid advance of the Union army compelled McCulloch, now joined by Price's Missourians, to abandon his comfortable winter quarters at Cross Hollows in Northwest Arkansas and fall back on the Confederate supply depot at Fayetteville. The Rebel general ordered his men to destroy those supplies that they could not carry away as they fell back into the Boston Mountains, resulting in widespread looting and the burning of several city blocks in the Washington County town. The Southern army established miserable camps in the Boston Mountains, with the Second Arkansas Mounted Rifles settling in near Hogeye. Curtis maintained aggressive mounted patrols, including one that occupied Fayetteville from February 22 through 26, to shield his exposed position hundreds of miles from his base of supplies in Missouri.[21]

Van Dorn left his headquarters at Pocahontas to assume personal command of his Army of the West and reached the Boston Mountains on March 2, 1862. The impulsive general, often feverish following a dunking in the frigid Little Red River during his race to join his army, ordered the Rebel troops to advance against Curtis on March 4. He set a killing pace that hobbled the Confederates, who had grown soft after months in winter quarters. Warned of Van Dorn's advance, Curtis placed his troops along the high ground bordering Little Sugar Creek and awaited the Confederate advance in the bitter cold. Confederate horsemen under McIntosh nearly cut off a small Union force under Franz Sigel, who had tarried over breakfast at a Bentonville hotel, but the German-born general managed to cut his way through and join the main body of Yankee troops.[22]

Finding his foe entrenched in a commanding position across Little Sugar Creek, Van Dorn ordered his exhausted, freezing troops to march around Curtis's army on the night of March 6 and 7, intending to place his Rebels between the Army of the Southwest and its Missouri supply line. The Confederate advance was slow and disjointed, and Van Dorn, confident his enemy remained in his works at Little Sugar Creek, made a momentous decision: He would send half of his army on a shortcut, reuniting at Elkhorn Tavern around noon.[23]

On March 7, McCulloch led his troops, bolstered now by Indian and Texas troops under Brig. Gen. Albert Pike, along the shortcut on the Ford Road north of the small hamlet of Leetown. Around noon he encountered

Yankee troops under Col. Peter J. Osterhaus, who Curtis had dispatched to hinder the Rebels as he prepared to turn his army to face the new threat to his rear. Placing his troops in line of battle, the former Texas Ranger rode ahead to reconnoiter the situation. Skirmishers of the 36th Illinois Infantry loosed a volley, and McCulloch toppled dead from his horse, shot in the chest.[24] McIntosh was with his old comrades in the Second Arkansas Mounted Rifles, who were footsore from marching in their high-heeled riding boots, when McCulloch died and he assumed command of the Southern forces at Leetown. The regiment, near the center of the Rebel lines, was marching through a thin belt of trees toward the Yankee troops when the impulsive McIntosh raced around their right flank and was himself shot through the heart and killed. He was carried to the rear by the men he had commanded for so long and through so many hard fights.[25] Command of the Leetown battle then passed to Col. Louis Hébert, who was leading an attack from the Confederate left himself and was captured after becoming disoriented in the thick woods and smoke and wandering into the Union lines. Pike attempted to take command but was ignored by many of the officers on the scene. The Southern troops milled around, essentially leaderless. By late afternoon, the action at Leetown was over. Having lost four killed, fifteen wounded, and eight missing, the Second Arkansas Mounted Rifles were out of the Battle of Pea Ridge.[26]

The remainder of Van Dorn's command, meanwhile, was overcoming a stiff Federal defense around Elkhorn Tavern to the east of Leetown. Price's Missourians drove the Yankees back from their positions, finally being stopped at twilight by massed Union artillery firing canister. The Federal spoiling attacks had allowed Curtis time to wheel his army 180 degrees from their works on Little Sugar Creek, and he consolidated his scattered commands during the night of March 7 and 8. The next morning, his twenty-seven cannons bludgeoned the Confederate lines for two hours before the Union general ordered some 10,000 troops forward in a general advance that swept the Rebels from the field. Curtis lost 203 men killed, 980 wounded, and 201 missing from his 13,000-man command. Confederate losses are uncertain but probably numbered in the neighborhood of 2,000 soldiers killed, wounded, and captured. The key border state of Missouri was saved for the Union.[27] Van Dorn's defeated host now wandered footsore and hungry back through the Boston Mountains, most gathering at Van Buren, though many decided they had had enough of war and left for home.

Following the retreat from Pea Ridge, Gen. P. G. T. Beauregard ordered

Van Dorn to move his army east of the Mississippi to join in an attack on Union general U. S. Grant's army at Pittsburg Landing in west Tennessee. Van Dorn obeyed the order with characteristic enthusiasm, stripping Arkansas not only of troops but also of weapons, livestock, equipment, machinery, and supplies, leaving the state virtually defenseless.[28] Appalling road conditions and flooded streams slowed the Southerners' eastward movement, though, and by the time Tom Spence and the Second Arkansas Mounted Rifles crossed the Mississippi, the western armies already had met near a small, tranquil church called Shiloh.[29]

• • •

Tom Spence's first letters in the Spence Family Collection include accounts of his regiment's actions at the battle of Wilson's Creek, Missouri; conditions in northwest Arkansas in February 1862; and the aftermath of the fighting at Pea Ridge, Arkansas.

At Camp near Springfield
August 12th, 1861

Dear Pa & Mother,
    I now write to you to let you know that I am still on foot. We had a very hard Fight with the Federal Troops on last Saturday morning. The Enemy attacked us about sun up. We was all taken on supprise. Our Pickett Gard was called in the night before the attack. We expected to attack Springfield the night before they made the attack upon us. The weather would not do to travel with firearms.
    The Enemys forces is estimated at about 10,000 commanded by Lyons and Sickills. Our Force was supposed to be about 20,000 under McCulloch. I was in Springfield to day. The Citizens think the Federal loss to be between two or three thousand. Our loss was I guess six or seven hundred. I never saw the like of dead men in life. Our Company does tolerable well. Their was eight or ten that Fought well. The ballance Run. I led the Regiment, that is McIntoshes, into the field and was the last one that left it. Cap. Flanagan is a Brave man.[30] Calloway, it is said, gave his commands . . . [portion blacked out] . . . scared I could see but very little.[31] One Minney Ball glanced my fore finger on my left hand which you will see in my likeness if you examine close.[32] The barrell of my Shot Gun was shot through which you will see. I send my Gun by Mr. Kingsbury. Take care of it. If I ever get home, I will want it as Brother Solomon give to me. I took a miney muskett from a dead Dutchman. We had to fight the Kansas Rangers—the Best Drilled troops in Missouria.[33] It will appear in the pappers that all of our company did well. It is [portion blotted out]. . . .

This it is [portion blotted out]. . . . Two lives lost and some wounded. Some was wounded a Quarter from the fight by grape shot Gun. Witherspoon's company was not in the fight.[34] When I say this, I mean they did not fire a Gun. George Ashby was shot in the Foot.[35] Mosley in the leg by the cannon.[36] William Wilson was killed, the Parsons son.[37] I have heard that the Arkansas Regiment was in the fight at Manassas Junction. I would be glad to hear the result. I hope Alex will get back safe. Has Tom Ewing got back? It is said that our fight was next to that. The people up this way think the Arkansas Boys good fighters. I don't see how any of us escaped being killed that was in the Battle. We have drilled but very little. Write all the news.

Tell all to write. I will close. T. D. Kingsbury will tell you all I have left out.[38] He made quick time from our camp when the attack was made. Old John says he can go home in two or three days if he can travel as fast as he did when he left camp.

Your son,

Tom F. Spence

Direct your letters to Fayetteville in care of Cap. Flanagan.

• • •

Hog Eye Arks[39]
February 27, 1862

Dear Pa,

We have been in a huddle at this Place for several days. I would say camps, but we have none. Our Picketts have had several fights with the Dutch. They killed eight or ten of our men at Fayettville the other day. We had to go out the next. That is our company. Their was no sleep for the boys. Their come in an express stating that the Dutch were falling back from Fayetteville.[40] I am not able to say what we will be ordered to do, follow, I guess. Mr. Barkman & Kingsbury arrived on yesterday.[41] My Blanket comes in fine time. I will write gain after the Battle. Their is no chance for the Dutch to get out of a fight. They have come to far. Tell Tom Ewing I will write him in a few days. The young men that are around Arkadelphia had better turn out or they will come to Clark soon. Write all news.

Your Son,

T. F. Spence

• • •

At Camp near Van buren[42]
March 19th 1862

Dear Pa & Mother,

We arrived at this place on yesterday. Nothing new. In other words, no news from the Yankees. I suppose they are in camps at Cross Hollows, will move down this way shortly.[43] It is reported in our camps that Gen. Vandorn will give up this part of the state. Do not know whether it is so or not. If it is, our forces will be moved to Mississippi River. I hope that we will stay longer at this place, that is, stay long enough to give them one more fight. I am truly sorry that we were defeated. Nothing more than one could expect of worn out and tired down troops in our Company. James Bridges, Bushnell, M.V. Cole, George May, Sterlin Burton, Clay Ellis are missing, supposed to be Prissoners.[44] Henry Benjamin and P—— Osburne's son are wounded. I guess Benjamin will die. Osburne is slightly wounded in the Back by a Bomb Shell.[45] I reccon the men in Clark that were staying at home until they they were needed surely think it time to show their hand now. It almost seems dishartening to think that our forces are whiped on every occasion hear of late days. I hope the tide will turn in the next *Battle*. Capt. Flanagan is in good health, was not touched with a ball. I wrote to you four or five days ago but was told that Gen. Vandorn would not suffer letters to go off at that time. I was in the fight, got off from my company. I left the field about 1/2 hour by sun for fear that the Northern Cavalry would pick me up. My foot & one leg is almost [swollen?] from walking. Write all the news.
  Your Son,
  T. F. Spence

Chapter 3

"Until endurance ceased to be a virtue . . .":
Shiloh and Corinth

Unlike his brother, Alexander E. Spence was east of the Mississippi in time for the battle of Shiloh. Colonel Fagan posted letters in newspapers on March 4 calling for all of the First Arkansas soldiers enjoying reenlistment furloughs in Arkansas to rendezvous at Memphis by March 15.[1]

After crossing the Mississippi River, Alex Spence and the First Arkansas Infantry were part of Randall Lee Gibson's brigade of the Army of Mississippi at Corinth.[2] That army, under the command of Gen. Albert

James Fagan of Saline County was the first colonel of the First Arkansas Infantry Regiment. He resigned following the battle of Shiloh and returned to Arkansas, where he was promoted to general and earned a reputation as a hard-fighting cavalryman. (Courtesy of the Old State House Museum)

Sidney Johnston, planned a bold attack against Grant, who fresh from his victories at Forts Henry and Donelson, was waiting at Pittsburg Landing on the Tennessee River to link up with a Federal army under Don Carlos Buell. Once Buell's 30,000 Yankee troops joined Grant's 42,682 soldiers, the combined Federal army planned to attack the important Confederate railroad center at Corinth.[3]

Albert Sidney Johnston did not intend to allow these "agrarian mercenaries" to maintain the upper hand in the West. Advancing his 40,335 Rebel troops from his base at Corinth up muddy Mississippi roads into Tennessee, he was in position on the evening of April 5, 1862, to attack the Union camps in the morning.[4] At sunrise, the gray-clad army burst from the woods and slammed into Grant's camps, driving many of the surprised Yankees back toward the Tennessee River. On the Union left, a defensive line formed along a sunken road, including several regiments under Brig. Gen. Benjamin Mayberry Prentiss. Here, they would hold off repeated Confederate assaults, buying time for Grant to reassemble his shaken army.

The initial success of the Confederate assault caused a confusing intermingling of troops, as various regiments became separated from their brigades as they chased the Yankees from their camps. The terrain caused other problems: at one point, the First Arkansas and Fourth Louisiana, tangled in dense undergrowth, actually fired on each other as Fagan screamed to a Louisiana officer "for God's sake to cease firing, that we were killing his men and he was killing ours."[5] Gibson's brigade, with the First Arkansas at its left center, charged Prentiss's troops in their natural fortifications and were met with a withering fire, though they got within close range of the Federal lines. Frank Darnell, the color bearer for the First Arkansas, fell dead with a bullet through his head. Gibson's men recoiled, reformed, and charged a second time with similar results. In a third charge, also unsuccessful, Fagan's horse was shot from beneath him, but the colonel vaulted from the saddle unhurt.[6] The First Arkansas "braved a perfect rain of bullets, shot, and shell," Fagan wrote afterwards. "Exposed, facing great odds, with the enemy in front and on the flank, the regiment endured a murderous fire until endurance ceased to be a virtue."[7] Gibson reported, "Four times the position was charged and four times the assault proved unavailing. The strong and almost inaccessible position of the enemy—his infantry well covered in ambush and his artillery skillfully posted and efficiently served—was found to be impregnable to infantry alone."[8] All along the line of the Sunken Road, throughout the afternoon

This postwar image shows the road to the Hornet's Nest at the Shiloh battlefield, where the First Arkansas Infantry Regiment suffered heavy casualties and Alex Spence sustained a severe thigh wound. (Courtesy of the Old State House Museum)

of April 6, a total of eight head-on Confederate charges were repulsed, leaving as many as twenty-four hundred Rebels dead and wounded in the area they would call "the Hornet's Nest." Among the wounded was Alex Spence, who dropped with a serious thigh wound in a 2 P.M. charge.[9]

Thomas R. Stone of Company G, First Arkansas Infantry, wrote in his diary of the fighting at Shiloh and the attack on the Hornet's Nest:

Sunday our regiment was ordered to charge a battery earlier in the morning. we charged it and took it under a heavy fire of grapes and

Cannister. 4 or 5 men was killed & 8 or 10 wounded. after this we was ordered a little right of center to charge the Enemy in a thicket . . . we charged this thicket three times but the Bushes was so thick and the Yankeys being in the Road which answered as breast-works we could not route him. here it was that nearly all our poor fellows that got killed they were slain here in the thicket and an ugly place it was.[10]

Confederate commanders finally lined sixty-two artillery pieces up some five hundred yards from the Yankee lines and hammered them with a murderous fire.[11] Southern successes on other parts of the field helped to doom the Yankee salient, as Confederate forces flanked the bluecoats and drove many of the surviving troops in the sunken road from their position, eventually capturing between twenty-two hundred and twenty-three hundred Union soldiers.[12]

Their stubborn defense probably saved Grant's army. By nightfall, his surviving troops were formed in a solid line more than three miles long and perpendicular to the Tennessee River at Pittsburg Landing, bringing them under the protection of the terrible rifled cannon of the gunboats *Lexington* and *Tyler*. And by late afternoon the advance units of Don Carlos Buell's army began crossing the Tennessee to reinforce Grant's battered Yankees.[13] The Confederates, on the other hand, were exhausted by their day's exertion, and under the command of P. G. T. Beauregard, who replaced Johnston after the latter's mid-afternoon death.[14] The flamboyant Louisianian withdrew his troops from the firing line to regroup for the next day's battle, but units remained mixed and disorganized as a chilling rain fell upon the thousands of dead and wounded throughout the night.[15] "That night, we slept in the enemy's tents, worn with fatigue, decimated in numbers, but elated that such a hard-fought day had such a glorious close," Fagan wrote.[16]

The next morning, Grant's army, reinforced at last by Buell's divisions, went on the offensive, surprising many Southerners who had expected to spend April 7 finishing off a beaten Union army.[17] The First Arkansas was in the thick of the fighting, first attacking a Union battery on the Confederate left, then moving to the right,

where every inch of ground was being hotly contested, and here the regiment engaged the enemy for some time in the most desperate and determined style, moving steadily on against the serried ranks in front of them, and when broken and temporarily thrown into disorder by the tremendous numbers in front of them, they only retired to rally again and come on with renewed eagerness to the charge. They rallied around their colors and pressed on time and again, until they were forced to retire by the overwhelming numbers against them. Here we suffered severely, losing several commissioned officers in killed and wounded, and leaving many brave men, who had ever been foremost in the fray, dead or dying.[18]

Despite stubborn resistance, Beauregard's army was driven back across the ground that they had taken the day before. By 2:30 P.M., the Rebel commander ordered a general retreat back into Mississippi.[19] The Confederates loaded thousands of their wounded into wagons for a painful, jouncing journey south in the driving rain.[20] Among them was Alex Spence, who would return to Arkansas for weeks of painful recovery from the thigh wound he suffered at the Hornet's Nest. The young infantryman would not travel home alone: his older brother Tom was granted leave to accompany his injured sibling on the difficult journey to Arkadelphia.[21]

The bloody fighting at Shiloh had taken a shocking toll. The combined Union armies suffered 1,754 killed, 8,408 wounded, and 2,885 missing or captured, a total of 13,047 soldiers. Confederate losses were 1,728 killed, 8,012 wounded, and 959 missing, or 10,699 casualties.[22] Gibson's brigade sustained 682 casualties, 364 of which came from the First Arkansas Infantry Regiment.[23] Alex Spence and his comrades had finally seen combat and acquitted themselves well.

The Second Arkansas Mounted Rifles and the rest of Van Dorn's army at last crossed the Mississippi River, too late to participate in the fighting around Pittsburg Landing. The Second Arkansas now bore the appellation "Dismounted," having been forced by lack of transport and forage to leave their horses behind; they would never fight from horseback again.[24] The Army of the West joined Beauregard's army in Corinth, where the Confederates played a waiting game. The Northern army, now commanded by Maj. Gen. Henry W. Halleck, who took field command from Grant following Shiloh, crawled toward the vital Mississippi rail center, throwing up extensive fieldworks after every advance.[25]

The Second Arkansas Mounted Rifles (Dismounted) reorganized during the relatively quiet time in Corinth. Every single company commander resigned, with the exception of Capt. Harris Flanagin of Company E, who was elected colonel of the regiment. The men of Company E chose Tom Spence to replace the popular captain. Company elections were held May 8, to become effective May 23, 1862.[26]

Harris Flanagin was a wealthy Arkadelphia lawyer when he took command of Company E, Second Arkansas Mounted Rifles in 1861. Flanagin was elected colonel of the regiment when it reorganized at Corinth in 1862 and served in that capacity until he resigned after being elected governor of Arkansas. (Courtesy of the Arkansas History Commission)

The two armies skirmished regularly as Halleck inexorably inched toward the Confederate works at Corinth. On May 9, Beauregard ordered an attack against the Federal left at Farmington, Mississippi. Fagan commanded a provisional brigade of the First Arkansas and Second Texas, accompanied by a section of Ketchum's Battery, in this engagement. The First Arkansas lost one man killed and three wounded but captured four Yankees while failing to dislodge the Federal left.[27] Beauregard soon after decided to abandon Corinth and retreat toward Tupelo. In addition to facing a superior Union force, the Confederate commander was concerned about a steadily mounting sick list.[28] Beauregard successfully escaped Corinth by fooling the cautious Halleck into thinking that the Confederate defenders were actually being bolstered: the cagey Louisianian ran empty trains back and forth into town while his troops cheered their "reinforcements." The Southern army reached Tupelo on June 9, but by abandoning Corinth they cleared the way for Union victories at Fort Pillow and Memphis in Tennessee, opening the way for Yankee operations against the Confederate bastion of Vicksburg. Beauregard, never a favorite of Confederate president Jefferson Davis, was replaced with ill-tempered, irascible Maj. Gen. Braxton Bragg assuming command of the western Confederate armies.[29] In Tupelo, the First Arkansas lost its commander, as Col. James F. Fagan resigned to return to Arkansas. Maj. John W. Colquitt of Company I, recovered from wounds received at Shiloh, became the regiment's new commander.[30] Capt. Charles Stark resigned his command on July 4, 1862, and William A. Alexander, Company B's original first sergeant, became company commander.[31]

Alex Spence, meanwhile, was back in Arkansas, slowly recovering from the severe thigh wound that he received at Shiloh. In the months of painful recovery that followed, Alex kept in touch with his friends in Company B and apparently found life on the home front dull after his experiences in the army. Their correspondence offers a view of happenings at Arkadelphia and in Company B during the summer of 1862. By late July, Alex Spence decided to rejoin his company, preparing for what at that point in the war was still a relatively easy crossing of the Mississippi, though his wound probably was not completely healed. He was back in service in time to join his comrades in the invasion of Kentucky.[32]

• • •

Though James Fagan had called on all of the furloughed soldiers of the First Arkansas Infantry Regiment to gather in Memphis by March 15, the date of this letter shows that Company B was running late. This is the last of Alex Spence's letters written before his wounding at Shiloh.

Little Rock, Ark. Mch. 24th 1862
Dear Pa,

I arrived here all safe yesterday Evening. Capt. Stark and the Company are still here. There is a Boat expected here this Evening that will leave for Memphis, but if it does not come, we will leave here in the morning for Duvalls Bluff, White River, and get a boat there Wednesday sometime. The Boats are all pressed into service on this and White River, carrying troops to Pocahontas.[33]

I saw Dr. Jett's son of Washington who was in the fight at Elk Horn.[34] He saw Tommy a few days ago since the battle. He was very well, so he said. I have paid the Editor of the *Democrat* 2$. The Dispatches will be sent you 4 months. We had an awful time on the stage, Walked about 1/2 way. I will write you all from Memphis if I have time. Tell all to write me at Corinth, Miss

My love to all, Your son
Alex E. Spence

• • •

Tom Spence returned to the Second Arkansas Mounted Rifles (Dismounted) after escorting his wounded brother home, learning that he was now the captain of Company E.

Corinth Miss
May 19, 1862

Dear Pa,

I arrived at this place day before yesterday pretty sick. Am able to sit up in my bed now. When I left Memphis, I thought myself very near well but have taken a backsett. Their is no private house in fifteen miles of this place that a man can get to stay at. All have moved off for the fight which is expected every day. You need not be supprised to hear of the *Big Battle* at any time. Our men are *confident* of *success*. The forces are ordered out every day. *Heavy skirmishing* every day. I have been up to our camps once. Capt. Flanagan and the men that were able are now on pickett. I have seen none of them as yet. During my absence, the company reorganized. They elected me Captain for which position I am thankful. Stroope, First Lt., Waldrop, 2nd Lt. Clark Rowe, 3rd Lt.[35] I am sorry that I am not able to lead them in the Battle that is expected every day. Capt. Flanagan is our Col. will make a good one. Sure write me all the news. Alex, I have not seen any of your comp[any] as yet.

Your son,

T. F. Spence

Tell Tom Ewing to come ahead; all will be all right; bring Randle to cook. Tom

• • •

Not even six weeks after suffering his painful gunshot wound at Shiloh, Alex Spence already was growing bored with the pace of life in Arkadelphia.

Arkadelphia Ark. May 28th 1862

"Squire"[36]

Thinking you would be glad to hear the news in "old Clark," I concluded to write you a few lines as several of our Boys leave for Corinth to morrow any way. Every thing is going on here about as usual. People are getting somewhat over their scare about the Federals getting Little Rock.[37] Texas troops are passing here every day for the Rock.[38] Within the last 4 weeks I think there has been at least 10 Regiments passed & more on the way. Col. Bruce is enforcing the Conscript Act.[39] It hurts some of the Boys considerably, but then it takes a great many men who really ought not to go. All the Conscripts leave in a few days for Little Rock. Had I have been well, I could have got any number of recruits, though we got a few any way. There is a good deal of sickness through the Country, not very fatal though. I saw Dave Meadour to day. He says your folks were all well a few days ago.

As for my part, I think I am mending very slowly. My wounds are entirely healed up, but the leaders of my leg are drawn so I have but little use of it. My foot is swollen up very much and is one continual pain. I reckon I will get all right before long. As soon as I get able to go about a little better, I shall start for Camp, for I am getting heartily tired of this place. I am afraid I will be a little lame for a long while.

By this time I reckon you will have heard of the arrests of Revds. Gunter & Langley. They have both been sent to Little Rock where I reckon they will have justice meted out to them.[40]

I am in hopes the health of the Company is good and you all are having a nice time. Will be with you as soon as I am able. I have recd no letters from the Company since I left. Wish you all would write and give the news.

As it is getting late, I will close.

My best Respect to yourself & all the Boys.
Truly yr friend, etc.
Alex E. Spence

• • •

The next two letters in the Spence Family Collection, from Isaac "Babe" Cook and Lt. T. B. Yancey, were written after Gen. P. G. T. Beauregard had successfully moved the Confederate army from Corinth to new positions around Tupelo, Mississippi.

Camp 1st Arkansas Regt Vols Near Tupelo Miss
July 17th 1862

Dear Sister

As Billy Adams leaves to morrow or next day for Arkansas, I will again write you.[41] Have written several letters but received none. Thought it very strang that I did not receive a letter by Billy Adams, but reading a letter from Alex to Yancey, he stated that Brother Dempsy was in the Service, so I supposed you was staying with Sis and did not know when he left. I am very anxious to hear from you. Alex written you had heard of the death of our beloved Brother.[42] I was sorry to hear that Brother Dempsy had gone into the Service.[43] I fear he can not Stand a campaign. He also has a family dependent on him for a support. I would rather remain in the Service five years than for Brother Dempsy to be out one. I think I can stand the campaign very well. My health is good at this time. Has been very good ever since I left Corinth. The health of the Entire Army has much improved. We have been doing nothing Since we left Corinth, only moved to this place a distance of 60 miles. It has been so very dry that it would of been impossible to of moved an Army. It has Rained. I think we will move in some direction soon. Until yesterday we have had no rain in near two months. Crops have suffered a great deal. We had a very nice rain yesterday and last night. Nothing like a season. I think we will have more to night. I received a letter from Tommy two days ago. He was at Chattanooga Tenn in good health. Says he don't think they will remain there a great while. Dont know where they will go. Rather thinks they will go towards Nashville Tenn. Their is some talk of our Regt, of our Regt [sic], being attached to another Brigade and being moved to Arks. We have been over run with the news of Hindman capturing Curtis with eight thousand prisoners which was confirmed in yesterdays papers and contradicted in a day. I remarked that the news was too good when I heard it.[44] I am of the impression that we will have some hard fighting to do yet. Alex written to Yancey of date June 28th

that he would be back in three weeks, that he was going to start to Little
Rock to get a permit from Genl Hindman to return to his company. I
suppose no persons can leave the State without a permit from Hindman. I
wish Alex could get back. We are about destitute of Officers. Capt Stark
has resigned and Lt. Yancey is now at the surgeon to get discharge on
account of his health. I do not know where he will succeed or not. Lt.
Alexander is afflicted with a Braking out of some kind and not able for
duty for a few days past. Liza I dont know when I will try to get home. I
want to name the Baby after our deceased Brother Washington.[45] My
Love to Sis and Charly, Mr & Mrs Spence. Write the first chance.

    Your Loving Brother,
    Babe

• • •

Camp Near Tupelo Miss.
July 17th 1862

Lt Alex. E. Spence
Arkadelphia, Ark.

Dear Alex,

    Your favor of the 28th ult came safely to hand and very glad were we
to hear from you as it was the first news since Bill Gorham arrived and
"you know Bill."[46] Well, as you did not write any news, you must not
expect any. You have hear all about the great Battle in the vicinity of
Richmond.[47] We have just heard that Hindman had captured Genl Curtis
& forces. "God grant that it is so." I believe Hindman is the "man for the
place" and regret to hear that Magruder is sent to take command of the
forces on your side of the river.[48] We are still encamped two miles NW of
Tupelo. We are now under the command of Genl Hardee.[49] Our vacancies were being filled by appointments. Crawford was Lt. Col. "Monro
Capt of Co B" (Capt Stark having resigned), Edward Lt in his Co (H),
Kirk in Co K, but we received an order from Sect. of War stating that
they could not come that game; vacancies must be filled by promotion.[50]
I have not got over my sickness yet. I am now staying about 4 miles from
camp but happen to come in to day and got your letter. I wrote to you
from near Gun Town.[51] Did you receive it? The health of our Company is
pretty good just now, though we have discharged some of *your recruits.*
Cousin Cross Dickerson, Brown (who since died), Hemphill.[52] I am glad
to hear that Fred, McI are doing so well.[53]

    No more news, all the Boys send their best respects to you & all
enquiring friends.

    You better come as soon as you can or send in your resignation, so

Fagan sayes. We have just heard that you have been put to work by Hindman.

Let us hear from you again.

In haste, yours truly,

T. B. Yancey

• • •

This fragment of a letter reveals that Tom Spence was frustrated with the situation following the evacuation of Corinth. It probably was written after July 18, 1862, since John McCabe and Joel Dickinson, who are mentioned in the letter, were promoted on that date.

> . . . This is the first time that you have ever heard me grumble. I will be in this Battle if any chance that is if I can get to the field. I will try & let you hear from me if I get out safe. I have not heard a word from you all since I left. What has become of Alex? Is he getting well? I guess the Yankees will have us cut off from you all in a short time. Tell Tom Ewing to stay at home. You can get nothing to eat for love or money. I was at Mr. Shackelfords fathers while I was sick. Could not get to stay nor any thing to eat. That was my friend's father. We have lost four out of our company since we have been hear sick. If I get wounded, I will try & get to Talladega. Tell Mother if their is any chance for me to get off, I will try & come home in six months. The Yanks can not gard every point of the Mississippi River. Write if you have any chance. I would like to hear from you all. John McCabe is very much mortified at the idea of being third Lieut. of Jo Dickinson's camp.[54]
>
> No more.
>
> Your son,
>
> Tom F. Spence
>
> • • •

Alex Spence's last two letters written during this period find him heading east to rejoin his regiment, though not yet completely recovered from his thigh wound.

Monticello Ark. July 18th 1862

Dear Pa,

We are this far safe "en route to the army." Are getting along very well. The Old Gray stands it fine. There will be no difficulty I think in crossing the "River" as we meet up with some one every day that has just crossed. It is only 40 miles from this place to the Landing and we shall probaly cross to night.[55] Yesterday we met up with a gentleman just from our Regiment who tells us the Regiment left Tupelo last Tuesday was a week for Chattanooga Tenn. We shall have to go by way of Mobile & up through Georgia to get there. I do not know whether I will get to see Col Flanagans Regt. or not. Shall go to see them if they are any where near & I can hear of them. The whole army of Tupelo have left for various places.

We still hear of the Richmond battle. There is no doubt that what we have whipped them badly, but McClellans having surrendered his whole army is all stuff.

If I have another chance, I shall write you again.

Tell all the Folks that want to write to their friends East of the Miss to send by way of Monticello Ark. as there is an agent here making arrangements to carry the mails across the River. You all write and direct yr letters to Chattanooga Tenn.

I am in hopes all are well. My love to all.

Your Son,

Alex E. Spence

• • •

Camp Near Tupelo Miss Aug 1st 1862

Dear Pa,

As I have an opportunity of sending a letter by Dr. Carter thot to write you a few lines.[56] We are still at this place but expecting orders every day for Chattanooga & tis said we will leave here next Tuesday. Nearly all the troops are leaving here for Tennessee. I shall go on with the Regiment when it moves but will probaly resign & go back home, as the surgeon tells me I am unfit for duty & may not be able to stand a march for a long while.

Tell Tom Ewing I saw a man who says his father was at Aberdeen since it was reported he was killed & by Dr. Carter I send his Saddle Bags back to him.[57]

The health of Our Co is very good. I am getting along very well. Think I will be able to stand camp life well, all except marching. As I wrote before, Tommy is at Chattanooga, well at last accounts.

I am in hopes all are well. Tell Mother not to be uneasy about me.

Give my love to all. Your Son,

Alex E. Spence

Chapter 4

"Two faces we shall never meet up with again . . .": Kentucky and Murfreesboro

As Alexander Spence recovered in Arkansas, Braxton Bragg settled on a bold plan for the Army of Tennessee. In late July, Bragg divided his Mississippi army in half. Leaving 32,000 men under Van Dorn and Price to hold central Mississippi, he took 34,000 men and embarked on an ambitious invasion of Kentucky in cooperation with 18,000 Confederate troops under Edmund Kirby Smith in eastern Tennessee. Among Kirby Smith's troops were the soldiers of the Second Arkansas Mounted Rifles (Dismounted), who were members of Brig. Gen. Evander McNair's brigade in J. P. McCown's division, a division to which they had belonged since crossing the Mississippi. The combined force planned to hit Don Carlos Buell's Army of the Ohio, and to welcome the thousands of Kentuckians Bragg was sure were waiting to fight for the Confederacy.[1]

Braxton Bragg led the Army of Tennessee in an invasion of Kentucky in 1862, then through harsh campaigns in Tennessee and Georgia. His inability to get along with his subordinates and to exploit his troops' hard-won victories caused morale problems and desertions throughout his command. (Courtesy of the Old State House Museum)

Beginning on July 23, 1862, Bragg started sending his divisions to Chattanooga along a circuitous rail route via Mobile, Alabama, and Atlanta; the transfer took some two weeks to conclude. On August 14, Kirby Smith left Knoxville and advanced into the Bluegrass State, followed two weeks later by Bragg's forces from Chattanooga. Smith's column bypassed a strong Federal garrison at Cumberland Gap, but on August 29 encountered a Yankee force under Brig. Gen. Mahlon D. Manson at Richmond, located just seventy-five miles south of Cincinnati. The next morning Smith's 10,000 troops—which included the Second Arkansas Mounted Rifles (Dismounted)—attacked Manson's 6,500 green recruits. The Yankees were forced back in a running, seven-mile battle that culminated in the capture of 4,303 Union prisoners. Kirby Smith then occupied Lexington, moving on to the capital at Frankfort by September 3. The Second Arkansas Mounted Rifles took positions well in advance of the main body of troops, marching to Georgetown on September 4 and establishing a camp five miles from Covington on September 10.[2]

The First Arkansas, marching with Bragg's column, headed north from Chattanooga on August 28. The advance Southern units encountered fortified Union troops at Munfordville, Kentucky, on September 14, and were driven back after suffering 288 casualties to the Yankees' 72. Both forces were reinforced over the next two days, but the 4,000 Northerners surrendered on September 17 after their commander witnessed the Rebels' strength under a flag of truce.[3] Bragg advanced toward Louisville, arriving at Bardstown on September 30, but Buell beat the Rebels to that Ohio River town, where he began receiving tens of thousands of reinforcements. With a force of some 60,000 men, the Yankee commander marched against the 40,000 Southerners under Bragg and Smith, disrupting the installation of a Confederate governor for Kentucky on October 4. About 16,000 men on the Confederate left, under Maj. Gen. Leonidas Polk, a former Episcopalian bishop, fell back from Bardstown and took up positions around Perryville on October 7. There, Polk's men fought advance elements of the Yankee army for possession of several pools of the only readily available water in a section of Kentucky that had suffered drought conditions during the summer.[4]

The next day, October 8, the two armies fought a confused, shifting battle in which the Confederate left broke the Federal right and the Union left was victorious against the Confederate right. The First Arkansas saw limited action in an attack against the Union left, but was sent packing through the streets of Perryville by a determined Yankee counterattack.

The Second Arkansas Mounted Rifles (Dismounted), still with Kirby Smith, was not engaged at Perryville. Bragg, belatedly realizing he was vastly outnumbered, retreated during the night to rejoin Kirby Smith, ultimately conducting a difficult retreat through Cumberland Gap into East Tennessee. The cautious Buell did not pursue vigorously and was soon replaced by Maj. Gen. William S. Rosecrans.[5]

While encamped at Cumberland Gap, the Second Arkansas Mounted Rifles (Dismounted) lost its popular colonel. Confederate Arkansas held gubernatorial elections on October 6, two days before the fighting at Perryville. Harris Flanagin had been nominated as a candidate against incumbent governor Henry M. Rector and James S. H. Rainey of Camden. Flanagin received 18,187 votes, easily outpacing Rector's 7,419 and Rainey's 708. Flanagin's resignation was accepted on October 25, and Lt. Col. James A. Williamson assumed command of the regiment.[6] The First Arkansas also saw changes, as it was transferred to Brig. Gen. Lucius Polk's brigade in Maj. Gen. Patrick Cleburne's division, part of the newly designated Army of Tennessee. Under Cleburne, the regiment would endure some of the heaviest combat in the western theater and gain a hard-earned reputation as a fighting outfit.[7]

Following the Kentucky Campaign, Tom Spence, the former sheriff of Clark County, sought a leave of absence to take care of business in Arkansas, a request that Bragg refused. A week later, Tom Spence was dead.

After retreating from Kentucky, Bragg positioned much of his army around Murfreesboro, Tennessee, to protect the important railroad center at Chattanooga from Rosecrans' Federal army at Nashville. Rosecrans moved from Nashville on December 26, 1862, advancing his forces toward Murfreesboro, thirty miles south. Bragg placed his army north of Murfreesboro, in positions on both sides of Stones River, as his cavalry continuously harassed the Yankee columns.[8] The two armies finally confronted each other outside of Murfreesboro, with both commanding generals planning attacks on their opponent's right flank.[9]

Lt. Gen. William J. Hardee's corps deployed on the Confederate left, with Brig. Gen. John Porter McCown's division in the forefront. McCown's troops, including Brig. Gen. Evander McNair's brigade, with which the Second Arkansas Mounted Rifles (Dismounted) served, slept on their arms on the evening of December 30, barred from building fires during the freezing night by their proximity to the Union army.[10] Cleburne's men formed up five hundred yards behind the front lines, and the Spence brothers spent the night before the battle of Murfreesboro within shouting distance of each other.

At 5:30 A.M., the Rebels quietly formed into ranks, loaded their weapons, and moved forward. McNair's brigade slammed into Brig. Gen. Edmund N. Kirk's Yankees, sending them fleeing from the field. McCown's division pursued the routed Yankees, rolling up the remainder of the Union left and driving them back. As at Shiloh, the Confederate success was tempered by confusion. McCown drifted toward the left, leaving Cleburne's division, which thought it was following McCown, exposed to Yankee fire. McNair moved to the right in support of Brig. Gen. St. John Liddell's Arkansas brigade of Cleburne's division. The Second Arkansas Mounted Rifles (Dismounted) charged three hundred yards toward the Union reserves who were facing Liddell, smashing through an intervening split-rail fence and again driving the Yankees from their position in a fight Cleburne described as "short and bloody, lasting about twenty-five minutes." Lieutenant Colonel Williamson wrote in his after action report, "I regret to have to report that Capt. T. F. Spence, an officer and a gentleman, was instantly killed in this charge."[11]

Lucius Polk's brigade, meanwhile, was surprised to encounter stiff Federal resistance in a cedar brake, having believed that they were moving in support of McCown's division. The Southerners drove their foes from the grove but continually encountered stiff resistance as the Bluecoats stubbornly gave way before the Confederate onslaught.[12] The First Arkansas and Fifth Confederate Regiments of Polk's command overran four guns of a Union battery before running into another defensive position in a cedar glade studded with limestone rocks that created a natural breastwork. "The enemy in this place made a most obstinate stand, and it was only after a bloody fight and one repulse that we succeeded in moving them," Polk reported.[13] Moving from there, Polk actually broke through the main Union line but was "driven back in great confusion, and with the heaviest loss we had sustained during the day, their batteries near the railroad and infantry making fearful havoc in our ranks as we retreated." Polk fell back to a line in a cedar glade on a nearby hill, where the exhausted Rebels dug in. The Federal line along the Nashville Pike held. As at Shiloh, a day that had featured great Southern successes ended in stalemate.[14] Neither the First Arkansas nor the Second Arkansas Mounted Rifles (Dismounted) would see further action of note in the battle.

On New Year's Day, the two armies eyed each other warily, but no real combat occurred until January 2, when Bragg attacked Union troops on

Tom Spence's last letter home, written on Christmas Eve, a week before his death at the battle of Murfreesboro, shows he was homesick and depressed after the failure of the Kentucky Campaign and the return of his commander, Harris Flanagin, to Arkansas. (Courtesy of the Old State House Museum) his right. Four brigades of Confederates slammed into the Union left, initially driving the Yankees back but then falling victim to forty-five Federal cannon massed on a hill west of Stones River, which smashed the Rebel assault "with terrible slaughter, fully 2000 of our men being killed and wounded in this attack."[15] The Southern attack accomplished little more than an expanded casualty list. At 11 P.M. on January 3, Bragg's army sullenly fell back toward Tullahoma, Tennessee, thirty-six miles to the south.

Rosecrans's Army of the Cumberland lost 1,730 killed, 7,802 wounded, and 3,717 captured or missing of the 43,400 troops that he commanded at the start of the fighting at Murfreesboro. Casualties in Bragg's Army of Tennessee totaled 1,294 killed, 7,954 wounded, and 1,027 captured or missing of the 37,712 men who went into battle on New Year's Eve, 1862.[16] The Second Arkansas Mounted Rifles suffered 10 killed, 99 wounded, and 11 missing in the fighting at Murfreesboro. The First Arkansas Infantry Regiment lost 11 dead, 90 wounded, and 1 missing in the battle. Among the dead was Isaac W. "Babe" Cook, Alex Spence's friend, who "was literally severed in two, by a cannon ball."[17]

A Clark County newspaper noted the high toll the county paid at Murfreesboro:[18]

Our Heroes

Mr. Henry Waldrop of this place, who was in the battle of Murfreesboro during the entire engagement, says it was perhaps the most desperate battle of the war. He sends us a list of casualties of the soldiers from Clark County. In addition, Mr. Hearn furnishes us, through a letter of Mr. A. Spence, other names from which we make the following list:

Killed.—Capt. Thos. F. Spence, Isaac Cook, ——— McCauley, Erasmus D. Christ [sic].[19]

Wounded.—Capt. W. A. Alexander, in the neck, mortally; James Tarver, Jeff Thompson, Simeon Dunn, W. Gorham, J. Witcher, ——— Andrews, ——— Hemphill, severely; W. H. Tweedle, W. B. W. Brown, slightly.[20]

The news of the death of our gallant and noble young Spence, Cook and others, will fill this community with sadness. The bereaved parents and relatives have the deepest and tenderest sympathies of the people of this county. Well have the gallant sons of Clark borne themselves on every battlefield, in this, the most momentous contest the world has yet witnessed. Coming generations will remember them with gratitude and admiration. Their country can never repay them.

Thomas Spence's body was returned to Arkansas after the war and buried in Arkadelphia's Rose Hill Cemetery.[21]

• • •

Among the soldiers in Kirby Smith's column in Kentucky was Robert E. Hearn, a young trooper in the Fourth Tennessee Cavalry Regiment.[22] Hearn's brother, Alfred, was married to Sallie Spence Hearn, and two of his letters are included in the Spence family papers.

Sept 9th 1862
Miss Sue A Hearn,[23]
Dear niece, I am now seated on the ground, nothing for my horse to eat after marching all night. The boys around me are all sleep. We are now 35 miles south of Louisville and on a march, but I do not know where to; we have been fighting and skirmishing for more than a week. I never saw such destruction as there was at the battle of Richmond. It is needless for me to tell you anything about the fight, for Jack Harlan says he will go to see you all and he can tell you more than I can write.[24] I have nothing to write. Will told you all when he went home and Mr. Harlan can do the same. I have no time to write. I am listening every moment for the horn to sound to start. We are now marching toward Lebanon Ky where we expect to have a fight; there is 1000 Federals and we have only 1500 cavalry, but I believe they intend to fight them.[25] I picked up several things on the battlefield and among them was several types of young Ladies. I only speak of this to show you the Yankees threw ever thing away in there flight. Tell Orin he must come to see me the first chance.[26] I would give any thing to see or hear from home. It is not necessary for me to tell you that we have seen a hard time. Just ask Jack Harlan, Orin or Gran one night come to see me.[27] Sue, you wrote to me about Rufus and I expect you know more about him than I do. This leaves all the days news.
I remain your affectionate uncle,
R. E. Hearn

Kiss mother, Susan and little Orin for me.[28] Give my respects brother Whits family and sister, Rufus and Will & all enquring friends.[29]

• • •

Tom Spence's two letters written during the Kentucky Campaign reflect the changing fortunes of the Confederate invaders, particularly in regard to the availability of food.

Camp near George Town, Ky
Sept. 18th, 1862

Dear Pa,

We arrived at this place on last night on the retreat from Covington. I cannot say where we will make a stand, not far from hear, I hope. This is a fine country, can get any thing that we want to eat. I think if the Regiment was to stop for a few days, I would get well. I have feaver every day. Col. Flanagan has got me a horse to ride. I will keep up as long as I can. Their was but one man killed in our Regiment at Richmond. He was Captain of a company from Hemsted county.[30] I was sick on the day of the fight, not able to partake of it. Capt. Callaway commanded my company. Their was two men wounded, H. L. Cash & D. T. McCallum, slightly.[31] I have not seen Alex. He is with his Regiment under Bragg. Write me all the news the first chance. Tell all to write.
Your Son,
Tom F. Spence
• • •

Cumberland Gap
October 24th 1862

Dear Pa & Mother,

We are now in camp at this place but do not know how long we will stay. This Place is one of the Best fortified places in the world.[32] I have not seen Alex yet but have heard that he has Resigned. Capt. Callaway saw him four or five days ago, says that he cannot walk well.[33] I am not pleased with this place for winter Quarters. Their has been two many Troops camped hear. I had to wash my clothes to day for the first time. It got pretty hard, for I am hardly able to get about anyway. I received a letter from Liza by Capt. Edwards.[34] She wrote all the news. I don't know that I ever read a more interesting on about five lines [sic]. Write all the news. Direct letters to this place. Tell Paynter to sell our land if he can get 25¢ per acre.[35]
I would like for Mother to have me some clothes made this winter. It is almost impossible to get clothing hear. I will try and come home this winter. Tell Sallie I did not get her letter, to write again. Mr. Kingsbury

can tell you all the news about the army. We are short of any thing to eat, the first time I ever suffered for anything to eat in life was this trip.[36]

Your Son,
T. F. Spence
• • •

Having enlisted in the heady days of 1861, Tom Spence abandoned his duties as Clark County sheriff, leading him to seek a furlough in late 1862 to take care of his legal obligations at home.

Camp near Readyville Tenn[37]
December 22 1862

H. S. Bradford[38]
Maj. & A A Genl

I have the honor to ask for leave of absence for sixty days for the following purpose to wit:

I was Sheriff of Clark County Arkansas at the time of my enlistment which was on the 15th day of July 1861. I have not been able to go back and attend to any of my business. There was another Sheriff elected in October last. The Judge of the County Court has ordered me to make a settlement.[39] My business is all unsettled. I am not the only one that will suffer but others that have gone my security if I fail to comply.
I have the honor to be respectfully yours
T. F. Spence
Capt. Co. E, 2d Ark. Reg Dis. Mtd. Riflemen[40]
• • •

Spence's request for leave received approval from his regimental, brigade and corps commanders, but Braxton Bragg overruled them and ordered that he stay with the army, prompting an appeal to the Secretary of War.

Readyville Tenn
December 23rd 1862

Secretary of War,

Enclosed you will find my application for leave of absence which one Brigadier and Major General reccomends. Gen. Bragg Disapproved in the application. You will find that Military and Civil authorities come in

contact shall my securities suffer on account of my not being allowed to
return to Arkansas and Settle with the County Court. My leave will not
interfear with the company in the least for the space of time I ask.

Your Obedient Servant etc.,

T. F. Spence

If you wish to know anything of caracter, I prefer you to A. H.
Garland, Charles B. Mitchell of Arkansas, also to W. P. Chilton and J. L. M.
Curry of Alabama. I suppose they are in Richmond by this time.[41]

T. F. Spence

• • •

A week before his death at Murfreesboro, Tennessee, Tom Spence was
homesick and depressed about conditions in the Second Arkansas
Mounted Rifles (Dismounted).

Readyville Tenn
December 24th, 1862

Sallie

This is a loansome time with me. I have concluded to write to you
once more. I think that you could spare time enough to write me one
letter a year. We have orders to keep two days of cooked Rations on
hand. From this I think that we will be on the line of march in a short
time. It is thought that we will go to Lebinon.[42] Our cavalry reports 15 or
20,000 federals at that Place. I would like pretty well to spend this
Christmas with you all, but times will not admit of it. I guess you all have
a fine time. Of the members of this Regiment all are drunk to night,
Col., Staff, and all. I assure you that we have a very poor set of Field officers. To tell the truth, we have no commanders. I would give anything in
the world to have Col. Flanagan or an other like him. Our Col. likes a
little of what I like a great deal of, that is *sence, hard horse sence.* If he had
justice, he would be in an assilum.[43]

Write all the news.
Your Brother,
T. F. Spence

• • •

Alex Spence wrote home several months after the battle of Murfreesboro
about the death of his brother and his friend.

Camp, 1st Ark Regt. Near Tullahoma, Ten.
Sunday, March 22nd 1863

Dear Sallie

This being Sunday Evening I thought I could not pass off the time more agreeably than by writing home, but it does really seem useless for me to write home as I get no letters. One letter from Mr. Elder is all now I have recd in several months. Why you all do not write I can not imagine—others get letters from Arkadelphia, but I get none though I write some of you every few days. As I know of no opportunity of sending this by hand, I shall mail this and trust to luck in its reaching you all. I have no news to write. Our Army is all at this place quietly resting, awaiting for the Federals to advance. For Several days we have had beautiful weather, ground drying off very fast. The roads are getting very good, and if the Yankees intend advancing, I suppose they will do so in a very few days. Well, Sallie, before I was in the battle at Shiloh, I was very anxious to be in a fight. Since then I have not been so anxious, but I must confess, I am rather anxious to meet the Federals once more. And I suppose in a very few days I shall have my wish gratified.[44] Were I certain this letter would reach you, I have a good many things I would write. I am in hopes, though, I will have an opportunity of sending a letter by hand before the next battle. God only Knows how I will come out in the next battle, but you all need never be uneasy about me in the least. If I get out Safe, I will write you all immediately. If I should fall, some of my friends will write the tale. I should like very much to be with you all at home this Sunday evening, but there is two faces we shall never meet up with again on this earth. I Know you all are troubled enough at home. I have not heard from them since you all recd the news of Tommys & Babes death. I almost dread to hear from there now.

I heard there was a fight near Hot Springs Ark. I hope the last one of those Jayhawkers, Deserters, Traitors were Killed. I am afraid there is a good many of that Kind in Arkansas.[45] I hope since Genl Price has gone to Arks there will be a great change in her prospects.[46] I have about given up all hopes of getting home this spring anyway. I think after next fight our Regt will be consolidated with some Arkansaw Regiment & some of the officers temporarially relieved from duty and Col Collquitt has promised that I shall be one of that number.[47] I don't want to get out of service. Am content to remain for the war.

A few days ago I met up with Henry Morris, the oldest one of Uncle John Morris sons. He belongs to a Cavalry Co. near here. Is 53 years old so he tells me. He has several sons in the army near here.[48]

I shall look for a "big pile" of letters by Mr. Waldrop & McCabe. Am in hopes all of you have written. Capt. Jep. Stansell left here over two months ago. I am in hopes he has visited Arkadelphia and will bring me some letters.[49]

I am in hopes Pa will send me a negro boy on the receipt of this. I want you all to write. I shall continue to write every few days. Has Mr. Hearn, Pete & Miss Sarah Ann forgotten me? It seems they never write me. I am in hopes this will find all well. Does Bettie and Little Lizzie grow much? Tell all the folks to write.

My love to all. Your affectionate Bro.

Alex E. Spence

Direct me—

Col. Colquitts 1st Ark. Regt.

Genl Polks Brigade   Genl Cleburnes Division

Hardees Corps   Tullahoma, Tenn

Tell Mother I *missed* the pound cake she has on Sundays—today.

Chapter 5

"We gained a great Victory at Chickamauga . . .": Tullahoma to Ringgold Gap

Bragg's army established winter quarters between Murfreesboro and Tullahoma, building heavy fortifications at Wartrace and Shelbyville to keep Rosencrans and his army from advancing toward Chattanooga. For months, the methodical Rosecrans gathered supplies and pondered his next move under increasing pressure from Washington to advance.[1]

On June 24, Rosecrans set forth from Murfreesboro against Bragg, sending his four infantry corps and one cavalry corps to traverse different gaps in the Cumberland foothills. Furthest west was Guy's Gap, about six miles west of Bellbuckle Gap, in the Confederate center, which provided access for the Nashville and Chattanooga Railroad toward Wartrace. Liberty Gap, near which Cleburne's division was stationed, lay a mile east of there and Hoover's Gap lay four miles further east. Rosecrans determined to feint toward the east and west to keep Bragg off balance, then hit hardest from the east through Hoover's Gap. Just as the Federals set forth, a rain that one Yankee described as "no Presbyterian rain, . . . but a genuine Baptist downpour" began to fall. It would continue to rain for more than two weeks, increasing the misery of the troops as they struggled through the glutinous mud.[2]

On June 25, as one Yankee column moved toward Shelbyville on the Confederate left and another forced two Rebel brigades away from Liberty Gap, Union mounted infantry armed with repeating Spencer rifles slashed through the Southern defenses at Hoover's Gap. The next day, the Yankees continued assaulting Bragg's right at Hoover's Gap, forcing the Rebels to abandon their center defenses. Cleburne's men fell back from their positions near Liberty Gap on June 27 to avoid being cut off by the advancing Yankees. He reported that "the men had no changes of clothing, no tents, and could not even light fires to dry themselves. Many had no shoes, and others left their shoes buried in the deep mire of the roads." By June 29, the wily Rosecrans had maneuvered Bragg's men into falling back on fortifications around Tullahoma. A day later, Bragg decided that Tullahoma,

William Starke Rosecrans
took his time before com-
mencing his campaign
against the Army of
Tennessee in 1863.
Rosecrans's Yankees
maneuvered Braxton
Bragg's Confederates out
of Tennessee and into the
mountains of north
Georgia in the nearly
bloodless Tullahoma
Campaign. (Courtesy of
the Old State House
Museum)

too, was indefensible and retreated toward Chattanooga itself. Rosecrans's
reliance on strategy instead of head-on assaults yielded a brilliant campaign of maneuver that drove Bragg's Rebels back some eighty miles at a
cost to the Northerners of 83 killed, 473 wounded, and 13 captured or
missing. In addition, the Yankees captured 1,634 Confederate soldiers.[3]

After falling back from Tullahoma, Patrick Cleburne's division and the

First Arkansas Infantry were stationed east of Chattanooga at Tyner's Station, guarding the fords of the Tennessee River.[4] Rosecrans feinted toward Cleburne's troops, but crossed instead in massive force west of Chattanooga. On September 8, Bragg evacuated the important rail center and headed into the mountains of north Georgia.[5]

William Starke Rosecrans, abandoning the caution that was so frustrating to his superiors, eagerly followed Bragg beyond Chattanooga. The Yankee general's three columns became separated in the rugged mountainous region, and Bragg sought to crush them in detail. On three occasions between September 10 and 13, the bilious Southerner ordered attacks on isolated elements of the Union army, but none of the attacks were executed. Rosecrans, however, did conclude that Bragg was no longer on the retreat. In fact, the Southern army was expecting reinforcements: six thousand battle-hardened regulars from the Army of Northern Virginia under Lt. Gen. James Longstreet. Concerned, Rosecrans began consolidating his forces along Chickamauga Creek, named from a Cherokee word meaning "River of Death." On the morning of September 19, the two armies met in what would become the bloodiest battle of the western theater.[6]

The Confederates were hamstrung on the first morning of the battle as corps and division commanders waited helplessly for orders from Bragg to attack the Federals. Instead, Rosecrans struck first, and Bragg began feeding units piecemeal into the action. Around 4 P.M. Confederate troops actually pierced the Union center, but a division-strength counterattack drove the unsupported Rebels back. Other random Confederate attacks also were unsuccessful.[7] Cleburne's division was on the extreme right of the Confederate army and was not brought into action until about 5:30 P.M., crossing the cold, chest-deep water of Chickamauga Creek to promptly run into Union resistance. "Our skirmishers, who were a short distance in advance, soon began a rapid fire, and in a few moments we found the enemy immediately confronting us," Colonel Colquitt of the First Arkansas Regiment wrote later. "We poured into his ranks a spirited fire, before which he quailed and soon began to retire. We continued to move forward until ordered to halt, when we found ourselves some half mile in advance of where our line was first formed. . . . We had thus far captured 1 piece of artillery and many prisoners, who were so eager to surrender and escape our galling fire that they ran through our lines and passed on to the rear, the men taking little notice of them."[8] Cleburne halted his attack at about 9 P.M. and the men of the First Arkansas, still wet from crossing Chickamauga Creek, settled down for a cold night of sleeping by their arms without the comfort of campfires. That night, they listened to the sound of busy Federal axes preparing defenses that the Arkansians would have to face in the morning.[9]

Bragg divided his army into two wings, with Leonidas Polk commanding the right and the newly arrived James Longstreet the left. Bragg planned a coordinated attack to begin at sunrise on his right then roll along the line to fold up Rosecrans's army and cut off its escape route to Chattanooga. Unfortunately for the Confederates, D. H. Hill did not receive his orders that night, delaying and compromising the plan. When the attack did begin, some four hours late, Cleburne's division ran head-on into Maj. Gen. George H. Thomas's troops firmly in place behind log fortifications. The First Arkansas "poured a continued and terrific fire upon them, once or twice causing their fire to become very weak" but after two hours of combat was forced to withdraw after running out of ammunition. While Cleburne's attack failed to crack Thomas's line, it did lead Rosecrans to move troops from his left to reinforce Thomas. This movement caused a momentary break in the Federal line through which Longstreet's men poured.[10] The Union line crumbled and broke, sending thousands of Yankee soldiers, two corps commanders, four division commanders, and Rosecrans himself racing pell-mell toward Chattanooga. Thomas remained firm in Cleburne's front, but began a staged withdrawal after realizing that his were probably the only organized Yankee troops still on the field. The First Arkansas resumed battle at about 4 P.M., just as Thomas was pulling back. "We immediately began a rapid fire, which was kept up about half an hour, when, the enemy appearing to waver, we rushed with a shout to the charge and drove him from his fortified position," Colquitt wrote after the battle. "He fell back to another line of breastworks hastily constructed of rails and made an attempt to check our advance, but it was of no avail. After giving him a destructive fire of a few moments, we again moved forward and drove the enemy in the utmost confusion from this second stronghold. Many of them came running toward us in order to surrender before our galling fire could cut them down."[11] Thomas retreated to a new position on Snodgrass Hill, from which he fended off repeated attacks through the afternoon of September 20 before successfully retiring to Chattanooga with the surviving Federal troops and the nickname "The Rock of Chickamauga."[12]

The fighting at Chickamauga was costly for both victor and loser. Rosecrans suffered 1,656 men killed, 9,749 wounded, and 4,774 captured or missing from his 57,000-strong Army of the Cumberland. Between them, Bragg and Longstreet lost 2,389 killed, 12,412 wounded, and 2,003 missing or captured, a total of 17,804 casualties from an army of some 71,551 soldiers. The First Arkansas, which began the Battle of Chickamauga with 430 men, lost 13 killed, 180 wounded, and 1 missing, close to half of its strength.[13]

Just weeks after being maneuvered out of Tennessee, Braxton Bragg's Army of Tennessee pursued Rosecrans back into the Volunteer State and occupied Missionary Ridge and Lookout Mountain, eminences that dominated Chattanooga and the Union troops huddled there. Reinforcements were on the way for the Yankee army, including two corps from the Army of the Potomac. However, feeding his tens of thousands of men was an immediate concern for the Northern general, who felt that he did not have adequate forces to protect his supply lines. These concerns were confirmed on October 2 and 3, when Joe Wheeler's Rebel cavalry destroyed two Union wagon trains before capturing the Union supply depot at McMinnville, burning other desperately needed goods and capturing 587 men. On October 19, two days after Ulysses S. Grant was given command of everything between the Appalachian Mountains and the Mississippi River, Rosecrans was relieved of command and George Thomas assumed leadership of the Army of the Cumberland. Grant arrived at Chattanooga on October 23 and within a week, using eastern troops under "Fighting Joe" Hooker, seized strategic points on the Tennessee River to establish a secure "Cracker Line" to feed the hungry troops.[14]

After watching the Army of the Cumberland entrench itself at Chattanooga without hindrance from the Rebel army, twelve of Bragg's top officers, including D. H. Hill and James Longstreet, signed and sent a petition to Jefferson Davis calling for their commander's removal. The Confederate president visited the Army of the Tennessee in early October and heard out the angry generals but decided to let his old friend Bragg retain command. In the massive shake-up that followed, the First Arkansas found itself under an old favorite corps commander as the vindictive Bragg cashiered D. H. Hill and brought "Old Reliable," William J. Hardee, back. This dissension among the top commanders did nothing to aid morale in the Southern army, and desertions skyrocketed, with 2,149 reported in September and October alone. On November 3, Bragg disposed of Longstreet by detaching his fifteen thousand veterans to attack Union forces holding Knoxville in east Tennessee, reducing the besiegers' strength even as Federal reinforcements poured into Chattanooga. When the Union struck back at Chattanooga, Bragg's forces would be down to around forty thousand men against Grant's combined total of seventy thousand troops.[15]

On November 23, Grant moved to raise the siege of Chattanooga, bolstered by the mid-November arrival of elements of two corps from Mississippi under Maj. Gen. William Tecumseh Sherman. Grant's plan called for Sherman to take the northern end of Bragg's army on Missionary Ridge, Hooker to hit the southern end of the Rebel lines between Lookout Mountain and Missionary Ridge, and Thomas and his Army of the Cumberland to seize Orchard Knob and demonstrate against the Confederate center atop the ridge. Thomas took the knob on November 23, and Hooker achieved his objective the next day, capturing Lookout Mountain at the same time in "the battle above the clouds." Sherman attacked on November 25. Awaiting him was Hardee's corps, including Pat Cleburne's division. Lucius Polk's brigade, including the First Arkansas Infantry, was guarding a line along the Chickamauga Creek railroad bridge, effectively removing them from the ensuing battle.[16]

Lucius Polk, a nephew of corps commander Leonidas Polk, led a brigade that included the First Arkansas Infantry Regiment. He threw the First Arkansas into a weak spot in the Rebel lines at Ringgold Gap, Georgia, just in time to repel a strong Union attack. An artillery shell maimed Polk in 1864, and his brigade was broken up and dispersed to other units. (Courtesy of the Old State House Museum)

Sherman hit Cleburne hard, but the "Stonewall of the West" held the line on the north end of Missionary Ridge against attacks by six Union divisions. After withstanding repeated Yankee onslaughts, Cleburne's men executed a bayonet charge that drove the Federals from the north end of the ridge. Meanwhile, Thomas's Cumberlanders, perhaps disgruntled by the presence and success of their Northern comrades from Mississippi and Virginia, executed one of the war's grand coups. Ordered to carry a line of Confederate rifle pits at the base of Missionary Ridge, the veterans of Chickamauga continued upward of their own volition, unnerving and driving the defenders of the Confederate center before them. Bragg's line crumbled and the Rebels fled south. Cleburne, on receiving "the appalling news that the enemy had pierced our center," was forced to retreat from the line that his men had fought so hard to protect.[17]

It now fell on Cleburne to save Bragg's army from disaster. The Irishman's division formed a line across Ringgold Gap, intent on allowing their comrades to escape through the mountains into northern Georgia. He placed Lucius Polk's brigade to the rear of his left "with directions to observe my right flank and prevent the enemy from turning me in that quarter." At 8 A.M. on November 27, advance elements of 12,300 Yankees under Hooker struck Cleburne's thin gray line of 4,157 soldiers. As feared, the Federals made a concentrated drive against the Confederate right. Polk rushed the First Arkansas toward the firing line. "Firing commenced before the First Arkansas had formed line of battle and continued during the entire time of bringing the regiment into position," Polk reported. "After a stubborn contest for some half hour, I succeeded in driving the enemy back to the foot of the ridge, where they immediately formed, and being heavily re-enforced, commended to move up the hill again."[18] Cleburne ordered Brig. Gen. Mark Lowrey's brigade to support Polk. Lowrey "found the First Arkansas again heavily engaged, but heroically holding its ground against great odds," Cleburne wrote later. The reinforced line drove back this assault, but the Yankees tried again slightly to the left of their last attack. "I was compelled to move by the right flank to meet them," Polk reported later. "They advanced in columns of regiments and fought stubbornly, coming within 20 yards of my line. They were again repulsed with heavy loss and fell back in the greatest confusion some distance beyond the foot of the ridge. In this attack, the First Arkansas took some 20 prisoners and 2 stands of colors."[19] Union troops next tried to hit Cleburne's line farther along the Confederate right on the rugged slope, but Polk and Lowery anticipated the move. The Yankees attempted to ascend the hill in column of regiments. When they were within forty yards of the Rebel lines, the First Arkansas and Lowrey's troops opened fire. At the same time, Polk committed the Second Tennessee Regiment to an attack against the hapless Yankees' left flank. "They were again driven back to the foot of the hill in great confusion," Polk observed. After four hours of combat, which also included unsuccessful assaults on the Confederate left, Grant stopped the attack and Cleburne successfully withdrew, having bought Bragg time to withdraw his supplies and troops. "In a fight where all fought nobly I feel it my duty to particularly compliment this regiment [the First Arkansas] for its courage and constancy," Cleburne wrote in his official report. "In the battle the officers fought with pistols and with rocks, and so close was the fight that some of the enemy were knocked down with the latter missiles and captured."[20]

The Chattanooga-Ringgold Campaign cost Grant's army 752 men killed, 4,713 wounded, and 350 missing, a total of 5,815 casualties. Bragg lost 361 men killed, 2,180 wounded, and 4,146 captured or missing, or 6,687 of his 40,000-man army. Cleburne's losses, considering the disproportionate share of combat they endured, were relatively light: 62 dead, 367 wounded, and 12 missing, a total of 441 men. The disheartened Confederate troops withdrew into winter quarters, with the First Arkansas settling in at Tunnel Hill, Georgia. In the wake of the disaster at Missionary Ridge, the hated Bragg was at last removed from command, with Hardee assuming command on December 2, Leonidas Polk on December 23, and, finally, Gen. Joseph E. Johnston on December 27, one month after the fighting at Ringgold Gap.[21]

• • •

Alex Spence wrote four long letters home between April and August 1865 that are rich in detail regarding camp life in the Army of Tennessee. It was in this period, too, that Spence began requesting that his father send a slave to tend to his needs.

> Camp 1st Ark Regt. Near Tullahoma, Tenn.
> Saturday, April 4th 1863
>
> Dear Sallie:
>
> Once more I have seated myself for the purpose of writing home, but it really does look like there is but little use in my writing for I get on letters from you all. Some 3 or 4 letters are all I have recd from home since we returned from Kentucky. I mail a letter home every week, then

besides write by every one I hear of going to Arkansas—If you all get my letters you certainly dont answer them—Several of the Company get letters from home regularly by mail—My only chance of hearing from home seems to be through others I reckon, though there is but little use in grumbling—but I must say I do wish you all would write me, and let me hear from home once and awhile. Mail your letters and then send by every one you hear of coming over on this side of the Missippi, and I will certainly get some of them. I have but little to write—Everything is very quiet here with us but I reckon it is only the "Calm before the Storm"— We are having beautiful weather now, if the Federals want to fight us there is nothing to prevent them now. I suppose a few days will tell the tale. I guess Old Rosencrans will find us all waiting for him. Every few days our Cavalry captures a lot of Yankee Prisoners. I saw 750 a few days ago that had been taken by Gen'l Forest.[22] They, like we, are all tired of this War. The health of the Army here is very good, and we are much stronger than we were when the Battle of Murfreesboro was fought. I think we will be able to whip the Yankees at this place very easily. Our troops have been busy digging "Rifle Pits" & throwing up Breast works for the last two months here, but we are all afraid the Yankees will not fight us here, so we can have the advantage for once. Our Regiment is getting very small. If we suffer in the next fight like we usually do the Regiment will have to be consolidated with some other Regiment. Should it be, and any of the officers are relieved from duty, Col. Collquitt has promised that I should be one of them—it is impossible to get a furlough now, nor will they be until Winter again, and then a poor Show. I would like to see you all again very much—Whenever I have any assurance that my resignation will be accepted I shall send it in. While we are stationed like we have been the last 3 months I can do very well, but I suffer when we are on the march. Our Regimental Surgeon is a very particular friend of mine, and when he is along I do very well, but I have little cause for grumbling for I know there is plenty of others in a worse fix than I am.[23] I have made up to take things easy, and am now content with most anything. Several of the Letters the Bhoys have recd from Arkadelphia speak of the nice parties they had Christmas and since. I am in hopes they all had a nice time, presume the Government officials around Arkadelphia, the most of them who are yet to smell gunpowder, cut quite a dash—it looks pretty hard to the young men of Arkadelphia, who are out in the Service, to see our places filled with strangers, but I reckon it is well enough there is some who desire such places. Time, I guess, will show who have been the true patriots in this war.

Sunday, April 5th. Sallie I commence this yesterday but did not finish but will do so this morning. Isaiah Ellis recd a letter from his sister yesterday, date 27 Feby. In it we hear of several deaths in Arkadelphia. Poor

Waldrop, how I pity him. Miss Cora says it was reported Dempsey Cook was dead. I hope it is not so.[24] Tell Liza I have never recd any letter from [her] but expect she is troubled so much she dont write. Well Sallie, Sundays are passed very differently now to what they use to be, it was a generally the big day of week for "reviews & Inspections" now Gen'l Bragg has issued an order prohibiting anything to be done on that day.[25] So it is a day of rest with us. The news reaches us the Yankees are advancing on us, and I am confident ere this reaches you the great battle will have been fought and the fate of Middle Tenn decided—I do not want you all ever for one moment to feel the least uneasiness about me. If I get through safe I will write you immediately.

Sallie when you all receive this I want you to write me and give me all the news. I wrote Pete & Pa a few days ago. Mr. Hearn never writes me. I hear from Rufus occasionally—he is doing very well. I have written Pa about trying to get a negro boy and send me. I suppose he will send him if he can make the arrangements. How does Bettie & Lizzie get along?[26] Do they grow much? I want all to be sure and write often. I shall write every chance. I am in hopes this will find all well. Tell Pa & Mother I will write them again in few days. Give me all the news about Arkadelphia when you write.

> Give my Love to all etc.
> Yr affectionate Bro. Etc.
> Alex E. Spence

Direct me
> 1st Ark Regt Polks Brigade
> Genl Cleburnes Division
> Tullahoma, Tenn.

All be sure and write often

• • •

> Camp 1st Ark Regt Near Tullahoma, Tenn.
> Sunday Evening, Apr. 12th/63

Dear Pa and Mother:

I have just learned of an opportunity I will have in the morning of sending a letter across the Mississippi and so I thought I would write you all a few lines—have no news to write as I have written you all so many letters lately—I hope you will receive them. Still I get no letters from home. Why in the world it is I can not imagine—it does look like you all have forgotten me. Others of the Company get letter but still I get none. I only hear from you all through the letters others receive. It does seem you all might write me oftener than what you do. Sallie never writes.

Our Army is still at this place and Shellbyville. Everything perfectly quiet. News reaches us every few days the Feds are advancing, but if they are it is very slowly. We are waiting very patiently for them to come and will welcome them when they do. We are confident of being able to whip the Federals when they do come. The great battle here certainly can not be delayed much longer. The Roads are in good order and we are having beautiful weather and I suppose when this reaches you the fight will have come off near here. I will write you as soon as it is over, how we all come out.

In the way of living we are having a hard time of it. Corn Meal and bacon is all we get. Any one can buy most anything they want, but it is at enormous prices. Occasionally I get a pass and go to the country and get a dinner—just think, walk say ten miles and than pay *One Dollar* for a meal. Tennesseians know how to make us pay for everything. Sundays pass off with me very slowly, today has been a long, long day. I usually pass it off thinking of home and writing you all. I do not Know when I will be able to go home. No chance to leave now I guess until next fall and then it is rather bad. We all expect to have plenty of marching and hard fighting to do this summer. I do not think we will remain here much longer. Should we move, I'll write you all immediately.

We all expect a great many letters when Messr. McCabe, Waldrop and Cloud return.[27] I hope I will not be disappointed. I am in hopes Pa will succeed in making some arrangement and send a negro boy I wrote about. I hope you all have plenty of provisions and are doing well. Everything must be very high. How many boarders have you? And are you making a crop this year? And what place tending? Did Mr. Waldrop get Tommys trunk home safe? I hope he did. When you all write me give a long letter and all the news how all the Family are getting along and when did you all hear from Texas, etc. I have no idea we will be here when this reaches you but continue to direct your letters to me at this place. Tell Pete, Miss Sarah Ann, Mr. Hearn, Mr. Elder & Sallie to write me, also Liza and Mr. Ewing.[28] I have written them all, but no letters. Does little Lizzie grow much and Keep well? I reckon Bettie has grown a great deal. All of you be sure and write me every chance. I shall write home every opportunity. The health of the Company is very good, and all getting along finely. I am in hopes this will find all in good health. I suppose our forces cleaned out the "Jayhawkers" up in Montgomery—did I know any of the parties engaged?[29] Be sure and have all to write me and give all the news—I do not want either one of you ever to be uneasy about me. I'll always write you should anything happen [to] me. All write soon. My Reports to all inquiring friends.

    Love to all the Folks,
    Your affectionate Son etc.
    Alex E. Spence

direct me
Col Colquitts 1st Ark Regt.
Polks Brigade Genl Cleburnes Div
Tullahoma, Tenn.

• • •

Robert E. Hearn of the Fourth Tennessee Cavalry—the brother of Alfred Hearn, Sallie Spence Hearn's husband—also served in the Tullahoma Campaign, writing to his niece in Wilson County, Tennessee.

Near Chattanooga July 9th/63
Miss Sue A. Hearn,
    Dear niece, I arrived safe to my command after several days travel. Found them in Sequachie Valley.[30] I was very sick when I arrived there, which was caused I think by getting wet. I was perfectly stiff all over and had a high fever. The boys left two mules of mine and two horses at Columbia which the yankees will get. It seems that every thing works against me of late. Tom Dodson has just left here and looks well, but his leg likes a great deal of being well.[31] Rufus & forty of his men was captured at Shelbyville. His Capt also.[32] They carried them in the direction of Murfreesboro, but Rufus give them the slip that night. He fooled along with the guard until he got them before him and then jumped over the fence and made his way back. He caught the army before they crossed the mountain. The yankees got all of his guns but one.[33] I will need my clothes that I left at Mrs. Perries. Mr. Seddeth and Bracket got into a difficulty and shot each other. Bracket died on the spot and Seddeth is thought to get well, but he is shot through the right lung.[34] Tell Mrs. Hankins that Tom came on with me to Chattanooga & Mr. Hankins has moved his negroes and gone down in Georgia.[35] The last I heard from James Bryan, he was waiting on Seddeth and waiting there for me to come. Gran & See is both well. Gran has now gone on a scout across the river. All the boys from our neighborhood is well. Tell Mrs. Sweat that Adolphe has got his horse and sold him for the same that he gave for him, 250$.[36] If the yankees gets those horses over at Columbia, it will be 8 head they have got from me. I would write more, but I haven't time.

You must write every opportunity. Give my respects to all enquiring friends. I am as ever,

R. E. Hearn
• • •

Direct me "1st Ark Regt.
Polks Brigade Cleburnes Division
Genl Hills Corps
Chattanooga Tenn

Camp 1st Ark. Regt. Near Tyners Station
East Tenn. Sunday July 26/63

Dear Sallie,

As I have an opportunity this Evening of sending letters across the Mississippi, I thought I would write you all a few lines, but my letter will be short as I have an awful headache this evening. I have written you frequently lately, and hope some of my letters have been received. The best news I had from home was from you, written 12 June/63. I am afraid our chance for hearing from home will be much worse now since the Yankees have got entire possession of the River.[37] I shall write some of you by every one I see going across & want you all to do the same. Everything is perfectly quiet. Federals a good ways from us. None have yet crossed the Tennessee River.[38] We will certainly not remain inactive much longer. The general talk is we will make a raid in Kentucky Ere long, which I hope is so, for I am certainly getting tired of laying up doing nothing. We are living very hard, a little worse than ever before. I have just got a 5 day furlough and shall start to morrow off. Hardly know where to go. Guess, though, I will go down to see Charley Stark at Griffin Ga.[39] Would go to see Uncle Joe, but there is no show to get where he lives now. Sallie, has Pa ever sent me that negro by anyone yet? Please tell him not to let any safe opportunity pass without sending him. If I had a good negro boy, I would get along very well. If you all have any chance toward fall of sending me clothing I wish you do so. It takes all of our money now a days to buy something to eat, let *alone clothing*. At present prices of things, it will be a hard matter for me to make my wages pay my expenses. I may go to Montgomery Ala tomorrow. If I do, shall try and borrow some money from Judge Chilton, as he told Tommy & me if we needed any money or anything to let him know.[40] The health of our company is very good & all getting along finely. I will not trouble you any about the war but Sallie, times *do* certainly look dark and gloomy. Our army is deserting every day, but thank God no Arkansians are among them. No telling how we will be when this reaches you. I would like to see you all very much, but I do not believe you, mother or any of the family would wish that I would come home now when our country is needing every arm. It was my wish that I come back to the company & here I expect to stay now until our time expires & then we may get home for a short time. By the courier that carries this I send to Fred Greene a statement in regard to our company which I hope will be of some interest to our friends in Clark.[41] My head aches so badly, I shall stop. Tell Mother never to be uneasy about me. Shall I be so unfortunate as to get sick or wounded, the Dr Erskines, who are said to be the best surgeons in our army, have told me to let them know. Besides being good physicians, they hold positions in which they can do a great deal for sick & wounded, one of them being Brigade, the other chief surgeon of Hills Corps.[42]

I hope you all will write me every chance & give all the news. I direct my letters to some particular one always, but they are intended for all.

I am in hopes this will find all well. I trust Pa & Mother have quit Keeping hotel by this time. I will write again in a few days.

My love to all the family.

Excuse haste.

Yr affectionate bro

Alex E. Spence

• • •

Camp 1st Ark. Regt. Near Tyners
Station East Tenn. Aug 5th, 1863

Dear Pa & Mother:

Hearing that we will have an opportunity this evening of sending letters across the Miss, I thought I would write you all a few lines. I have written some of you very often of late & hope my letters have reached you. A letter written by Sallie from home 12th June is the last news I have had from you all. I shall continue writing home every chance whether I get any letters from you all or not. Since my last no move or change has been made in our Army. Everything perfectly quiet, & no prospects of a move soon. We hear but little of the Feds. I believe as yet there are but few on this side of the Tennessee River. One man out of every twenty is now allowed a ten days furlough. The time is so short though it does Arkansaw troops but little good. 2 from my company will get furloughs. I got leave of absence for 5 Days last week & took a trip off to get us some clothes & things we needed. Went to Augusta Ga and considering we have but few acquaintances on this side of the River, spent the time as pleasantly as could be expected.

We are living very hard in Camps, rations scarce, & then not the best when we get them. Everything is very high. Flour 30¢, bacon 1$\frac{50}{}$ & other articles in proportion. Fruit is exceedingly high. Water melons *are only 8 & 10 Dollars* apiece. I am sorry now that I sent that money home last spring, as I may need, and I reckon you all have no use for it, it takes about all my wages to buy something to eat. Tell Pa to keep all the gold he has, not sell or spend it. I have Forty Dollars and was offered the other day 800 for it, but it will be worth twice that much over here, in a short time. If you all have a chance be sure to send me that negro boy, an if you have a chance before winter either send me some clothes or money. Don't think by my writing home for money, that I am spending it by *drinking* or *gambling*— rest easy on that point for these are two vices I believe I am entirely free from. No one can ever say they saw me take *the first Drink or bet one cent.*[43] I write this to Mother, because I know your fears, as you all know the temptations one in the Army is subject to. Our Army here are all in good health, but somewhat discouraged, by our late reserves. A good many are deserting but thank god no Arkansians are leaving from Gen'l Braggs Army. I have no idea when I will be able to see you all. Would like to be at home very much once more but this is no time for remaining there. The President's late call, I guess, will bring out a good many Q. M. & Commissary Assistants into the field. Well it is time got them to come. When you all get this I want you all to be sure and write me. I'll write you all every chance. I am in hopes this will find all. Will have another opportunity of writing this week.

Tell all to be certain to write. I hope both of you continue in good health. My Love to all.

Your Affctate son
    Alex E. Spence
Capt. Co. B 1st Ark. Regt
    Polks Brigade

Please tell Tom Ewing Dr. Erskine told me his Fathers Folks had left Huntsville Ala. He thought they were stopping in Georgia. I dont suppose he has heard from them often.

Alex
    • • •

Alex Spence's letter written following the battle of Chickamauga finds him concerned about conditions at home even as he shares with his parents a list of the casualties Company B suffered in the Georgia fighting.

Camp 1st Ark Regt Before Chattanooga Tenn Oct 14th/63
Dear Pa & Mother,
　　I have just heard of an opportunity to morrow of sending a letter to Ark, so I thought I would write you a few lines, it being the first chance I have had since the battle of Chickamauga. Ere this you have heard of this great battle & its results. It was the hardest fight I have ever been in yet & our Regt suffered more than in any previous battle. I enclose a list of casualities in our Company. I think there is none wounded but what will be able for service again. We have just heard that a "big battle" had been fought at Arkadelphia & the Federals were whipped.[44] I was in hopes they would never reach there but am afraid they will if not already there. For fear the Feds are there as you all have left there, I shall direct this to Dr. Jett at Washington & request him to forward it to you all. Our whole Army is surrounding Chattanooga & the Yankees are there in large force. We are fortified & so are they. A fight may be expected any day. God only know when it will come off. The 2 Armies are not more than 2 miles apart & have been this way ever since 22 Sept. last. We remain in line of battle now all the time & have been this way for over one month. We have been largely reinforced from Va & Miss & so have the Yankees & this will certainly be the next great battle of the war.[45] I doubt very much whether this will reach you all or not. I have written you all every chance lately but have recd no letters from home in a *long long* time. I suppose now you all will have no chance of sending that negro. I would have liked very much to have got him & also for you all to have sent me some clothes or money. I had my valise stolen the other day & every particle of my clothing & any thing of that kind is awful high now.
　　We keep hearing the Yankees have possession of Arkadelphia. I hope it is not so, for I know how they destroy everything as they go. We gained a great Victory at Chickamauga, but it cost many a gallant spirit. Our Regt suffered heavily, half killed & wounded. We were in it both days. We have now just 30 men along in our Co, all well & in good spirits. We live very hard now adays. My health is fine, fatter than I ever was in my life. If you all ever meet up with any chance to send that negro or money, do so, for I need them. It is now raining & we are ordered to go out on picket, so I will stop. I am in hopes this will find all well. Please be sure & all write me soon. Tell all to write & be sure of it. My Love to all.
　　In haste, yr affectionate Son
　　Alex E. Spence

Co B 1st Ark Regt
Polks Brig Cleburnes Division
Genl DH Hills Corps
Chattanooga Tenn

We have just heard the news confirmed that there had been a fight at Arkadelphia & our troops had fallen back. I hope it is not so, if you all have any chance to send me any money, do so, for when my time is up, I want to change my branch of service and try & go home to see you all.

Killed & wounded Co B 1st Ark Regt

19th & 20 Sept 63 Battle of Chickamauga, Ga.

1. killed—Dr. Wilson McCauley [46]

2. wounded—Lt. A. J. Pitner   severely arm   now at home   Rome Ga.

3. Lt. M. M. Sanders   slightly thigh   well & with Co.[47]

4. Sergt. E. G. McBryde   side   since died[48]

5. Priv. E. T. Allen   slightly leg   at hospital   Newman Ga.[49]

6. Corpl. DC Neill   severely ankle   "   "   "   "[50]

7. "   SL Sanders   "   leg   "   "   Atlanta   "[51]

8. Priv. I. D. Ellis   slightly arm   private house at Madison Ga.[52]

9. Priv. Joshua McDaniel   slightly side   now well[53]

10. "   J. L. Newton   "   breast   "   "[54]

11. "   T. B. Norris   severely ankle   at a relatives at Marietta Ga.[55]

12. "   Chas. Trickett   hand slight   about well[56]

13. "   Jas. Hicks   shoulder "   "   "[57]

14. "   A. W. Hughes   thigh & face severely   at a relatives in Ga.[58]

Our wounded have all recd good attention & at last accounts all doing well. None I think are wounded as that it will permanently disable them from service. I have heard from them within the last few days. The health of the Co. is fine.

Alex. E. Spence, Capt
Comdg Co. B 1st Ark Reg

Camp Before Chattanooga, Ten
Oct. 14th 1863.
• • •

Alex Spence compiled this list of casualties from Company B, First Arkansas Infantry Regiment, at the battle of Chickamauga, Georgia. Company B suffered heavily, as did the rest of the regiment in its struggle with Federal troops under George Thomas. (Courtesy of the Old State House Museum)

The relative inactivity in winter quarters at Tunnel Hill, Georgia, allowed Alex Spence time to write home about the hard fighting at Ringgold Gap and the pride he and his fellow Arkansans felt in serving with Patrick Cleburne's division.

Camp 1st Arkansas regiment
Tunnell Hill, Geo. February 1st 1864

Dear Father & Mother,

Hearing of an opportunity we will have in a few days of sending letters across the Mississippi, I thought to commence writing one in time so as to have it ready, though hardly know whether you will ever receive it or not, for I suppose now you all are inside the Federal lines. I have not written you lately. I heard the Federals had possession of Arkadelphia and that you were still there, so I did not think my letters would reach you. The last time I wrote I directed to Dr. Jett, Washington, Ark., requested him to send the letter to you if he had any chance. I recd a few days ago a letter from "Pete" written "1st Nov/63" which is the only letter I have had from "home folks" since 1st July last. Why it is you all do not write I cant imagine. Probably you do and your letters are mislaid on the route. Some of the Bhoys receive letters from Arkadelphia occasionally and through them I hear from you some times.

Well, according to the "old style" of letter writing, let me first begin about health of "self & Company." At present we are all in fine health— not a man sick in camp. I have indeed been fortunate, have not been sick a day in the last twelve months. Disease and battle has done its work with us. I wrote you of the casualties in our Co at Chickamauga. The most of those who were wounded have retd. Some few, though, I fear, will never be able for "Infantry service" again. At Ringgold, Geo on 27th Nov last my company was very unfortunate in battle. Jas. L. Newton of Hot Spring Co was killed & Lt J. G. Robertson & James P. Jones wounded.[59] Both died in a short time from their wounds. No others hurt. Wash Hughes died about 20th Dec. in camp from Disease. So in the last two months 4 of the best soldiers in our company have been taken away. We have gone into quarters at this place which is about 30 miles below Chattanooga, have been here ever since the 1st Dec. Our Division (Cleburnes) is all that is here. The balance of our army are farther down in Geo. near us though. Our Army may be said to be in "tolerable condition." Our reverse at "Missionary Ridge" last Nov is to be regretted indeed. Since then our Army has been gradually lessening. Disease and battle has done its work with us. I am sorry to say there has been a great many desertions.

Yet, strange to say, not as many from the Arkansas troops as from the troops of other States. Arkansaw troops have gained a reputation in this Army of which our state may justly feel proud of. A great many of the troops have reenlisted for the war. Nearly all of our Regiment has done So. They get a thirty day furlough for every ten men that reenlist. None are allowed to cross the Mississippi River though. I hardly know what will become of me, but if there is any chance, you can depend on seeing me in Arkansaw. By some it is thought there will be no reorganization of the Army, that everything will be kept as it is now. If we are allowed to reorganize I will be thrown out, as I am one of the Junior Captains in the Regiment & have not the maximum number for a company, an event I shall not deplore much I assure you as I am anxious to get to Arkansas once more. We can not tell what will become of us until Congress does something. If they conclude to Keep me here, of course, I shall reluctantly Submit. These are "hard and trying times" with us here. Everything is at enormous price. It about takes my wages , 130$ per mo., to get some-thing to eat.[60] For bacon we pay $2^{\underline{50}}$ per lb., 50¢ for flour, 80¢ for beef and everything else in proportion. If things only continue at such prices, God only knows what will become of us. As for clothing, it is almost impos-sible to buy any. A suit coat, pants & vest can not be bought for less than 800$–Boots 200$, Hats 150$–and like prices for everything else. I have been disappointed in not getting any money from home. I can now get a 30 day furlough & would take it and go to Talladega if I had some "nice clothes & money." It does seem to me you all might find Some chance of Sending that money over here. Could you not send it by Dr. Mitchel and let him leave it either at Montgomery, Ala or Atlanta, Geo?[61] I wish you would, as I am very much afraid I will not be able to return home when my time is up. And that negro boy, I do wish you could meet up with an opportunity of sending him. If I get to go home when my time is up, I could hardly raise enough money to pay my expenses, and if I stay here, I shall need it. I do not want you all to discommode yourselves in the least about the money. If you have it to spare, why you can send it. I am writ-ing this as if the Yankees had never been to Arkadelphia. Maybe they have entirely broken you all up, but I hope and trust not. I have seen letters from there written 15th Dec. 63. They said the Federals had done consid-erable damage, but did not mention who too.[62] Said you were living at A. Greenes place, etc.[63] I expect the Federals meet up with a good many Union friends in our part of the State.[64] Gantt & Charley Jordan have done nothing more than what I always expected.[65] Is there anyone else about Arkadelphia who has gone with the Yankees? I would like to know and what has become of most of the people of Clark Co. anyway? I think you all did perfectly right in not leaving. I have seen too many *refugees & exiles* from their homes ever to advise any of my folks to leave. What became of Mr. Stearns family? Why it is Sallie dont write me I cannot think. Mr. Elder, what did he do, leave or not? Pete's family I suppose still remained and how are you all doing, getting along, etc.? In fact if you write, I want you to give all the news. Is everything as high in Ark as it is here? Our Texas relatives, Mr. Stinnetts family & Sis Tam, do you ever hear from them or not? I hope both of you are in good health. You have quit Keeping Tavern I hope.[66] Little Lizzie, is she still with you all yet?

I have written you all several letters since the battle of Chickamauga which I hope reached you. I believe this is the first one since the battle of Ringgold, Geo., on 27 Nov. last because I did not think they would reach you. I shall direct this to Gov Flanagan and request him to send it to you all as I do not Suppose you have any mails to Arkadelphia and shall also write to Sallie & request Genl Fagan to send it to you all. So I hope one of my letters will reach you.

Friday Feby. 5th, 1864

I commenced this several days ago & learn that the gentleman will leave for Arkansas on Monday, so I'll try my hand writing again. Have no news though everything is quiet at the front with us yet. Our Army is all in winter quarters. I do not think from the present signs things will long remain So. Every preparation is being made for a move in some direction, and I suppose ere long the "clash of arms" will again have been heard in Northern Georgia. I have no fears as to the result if the troops will only do their duty. Well perhaps you would all like to know how we pass off the time and get along generally. Our Regiment is doing what is called "Out post duty" and have been ever since we have been here. We are stationed some distance in advance of the main Army, so we are off by ourselves and have a very good time. The Yankees are said to be only 6 or 8 miles from us. I do not think they will come on us very soon. Today I have charge of the "Picket Guard," so am Kept pretty busy. I am very much afraid the Yankees will dash in on us sometime & we will loose all of our Baggage etc. I have been very unfortunate in this respect. I lost everything I had not long since in the way of clothing Stolen out of our waggons. At present I have only 30 men with my company. The bal off sick & wounded. I have only 50 though in all now.

Pa, the gentleman who will carry this is named Mr. Jenkins.[67] He will go to Arks & return. He says he will go to Arkadelphia. He belongs to a Regiment that is near us all the time and is Said to be a responsible man. I shall get him to call on you and if you think he will do *to trust,* you can Send me Some money by him. I shall not direct this to Gov. F as I said, as the gentleman says he will go to Arkadelphia. If you can possibly spare it, do not forget to *send me Some money.* What ever became of Tom Ewing? & Bill?[68] Did Tom every pay off that note? I shall not close this until I see Mr. Jenkins and will mention it to him about bringing that negro and will write you what to do. I wish I could hear from you all. It does seem you might have written me. Others have been getting letters from Arkadelphia. Has Sallie forgot how to write? It really looks like it. I reckon there is no use in grumbling, but then it does look hard when others are getting letters for me to get none.

Febry. 6, 1864

I still have not finished my letter, but will do so now. I have not seen the gentleman who carries this, but I do not suppose he would like to be bothered bringing that negro. We understand that all men and officers belonging on this side of the River have been ordered back to this commands by Genl Kirby Smith.[69] I suppose you will have an opportunity of sending what you want across to me by some of our Clark Citizens, at least I hope you will do so. I am still unable to say what will become of us. Congress has done nothing and it does not seem she will. The general belief is that we will all be Kept on this side of the River, but if there is *any possible chance,* I am going to cross the Mississippi.

I shall expect a long letter when this gentleman returns and want you all to be certain and write every chance. Give all the news how everybody is getting along, what doing, etc. for the benefit of those who have friend & relatives in our Co. I send a list of those present. All are for duty except Isaiah Ellis who was wounded in the arm at Chickamauga, but will be all right ere long. I will now close this and will promise to write you all every chance and want you to do the same. Tell Mother we live pretty hard, but I have got used, so don't mind it much. Ask Sallie to write me & all be certain to write me. Direct your letters as given below. Hoping this will find you "all well" and doing well. I am

Your Affectionate Son,

Alex E. Spence

My love to all the folks, respect to all friends & everlasting hatred to those who have proved traitors to our Cause in Clark Co.

Direct "Me"

1st Ark. Regt. Polks Brigade

Cleburnes Division Hardees Corps.

Army of Tenn. Dalton, Geo.

Chapter 6

"There has been some hard fighting . . .":
The Atlanta Campaign

The First Arkansas went into winter quarters at Tunnel Hill, Georgia, where the regiment was resupplied and the local resources made the stay relatively comfortable.[1] Cleburne held classes in military sciences for his brigade commanders in a rough log hut, urging them to share the information with their regimental commanders. This classroom instruction found practical application on March 22, after a five-inch snowfall when Cleburne led Lucius Polk's brigade in a massive snowball attack on Daniel C. Govan's Arkansas brigade. The division commander was captured, paroled, captured a second time, and threatened with the traditional punishment of carrying a fence rail before being released again. When the snowball fight ended with Govan victorious, Cleburne showed that there were no hard feelings, authorizing a ration of whiskey for all of the combatants. Cleburne also took time to reflect on what was perhaps the biggest problem facing the Confederacy: dwindling manpower reserves.[2] The Irishman's solution was a radical proposal to emancipate Southern slaves and enlist them as combat troops, which Cleburne felt would provide desperately needed soldiers, burnish the Confederacy's image overseas, and remove the abolition plank as a Northern war aim. Both Govan and Colquitt were among thirteen of Cleburne's brigade and regimental commanders who signed the proposal, which was swiftly and unceremoniously suppressed by Pres. Jefferson Davis. While Cleburne's proposal may have eclipsed his star in Richmond, he remained hugely popular with his troops.[3]

In late February, Cleburne and his men were ordered to Mississippi, an order that was quickly remanded when Federal troops began probing the Rebel lines in Georgia. The division was stationed on Mill Creek near Dalton, Georgia, to await developments. Sherman, now in command of the Union's western armies, brought 98,797 men and 254 artillery pieces against Johnston's 55,000 or so troops. The ensuing campaign would be one of maneuver, with Johnston attempting to draw Sherman into battle

Patrick Ronayne Cleburne, an Irish-born former British soldier who later moved to Helena, remains widely respected as one of the Confederacy's finest division leaders. His controversial proposal to arm slaves to replace Southern combat casualties may have been a factor in his not being promoted to higher levels of command. (Courtesy of the Old State House Museum)

Joseph E. Johnston led the Army of Tennessee in a series of retrograde movements that ended on the outskirts of Atlanta in the summer of 1864. His attempts to husband his strength and lure Union troops into attacking fortified positions proved unpopular in Richmond, and he was soon removed from command though he would lead the army again in its final months in 1865. (Courtesy of the Old State House Museum)

against strong defensive positions and Sherman working around the Southern flanks to force the Rebels to continuously fall back toward the bastion of Atlanta.[4]

Sherman's Union army began its offensive on May 4, while Johnston's Rebels awaited their approach from fixed defenses on Rocky Face Ridge, about twenty-five miles south of Chattanooga. Sherman here showed the strategy that he would pursue throughout the campaign, sending two of his armies to confront the entrenched Rebels while the third swung to the right. In this case, it was James B. McPherson's Army of Tennessee that made the swing, plowing through Snake Creek Gap on May 9 to confront the lightly defended Confederate works at Resaca, fifteen miles to Johnston's rear.[5] Cleburne's division was entrenched at Mill Creek when this movement began and was dispatched through the sweltering heat to Dug Gap in Rocky Face Ridge, where Hooker's corps was assailing a small Rebel force that included the Second Arkansas Mounted Rifles (Dismounted). "They had gallantly repulsed every assault," Cleburne reported. "The fight was still going on, and some anxiety was felt . . . lest the overwhelming numbers of the enemy might carry the position before my command could ascend the hill." The Confederate line held, however, and the Union attack petered out at nightfall.[6] The armies then spent three days skirmishing and probing to no great advantage. The experience of Cleburne's division, which moved into line on a ridge near Resaca on May 14, was typical: "In the course of the afternoon, he [the enemy] made several attempts to charge, but uniformly they were unhappy failures," Cleburne wrote. "In front of Brigadier-General Govan, one of his officers, supposed to be a general officer, was heard to address his troops, endeavoring to incite them to a charge. He told them amongst other things that they were the men who had taken Missionary Ridge, and that they could take this. But his eloquence was of no avail. His men came but a few paces into the open ground of the valley, whey they retired precipitately under our fire."[7] On the 15th, Cleburne was ordered to Calhoun, just south of Resaca on the railroad, to face another Union probe. The next day, he sent Lucius Polk's brigade, which included the First Arkansas, forward. "Polk became briskly engaged with the enemy's skirmishers after advancing but a short distance," Cleburne reported, but the Confederate soon withdrew his troops to stem another advance on Calhoun, which never developed into a full-scale attack.[8] The Irishman's division continued retiring and entrenching, retiring and entrenching, reacting to continued Federal movements to the south. On May 17, Sherman again sent McPherson around the Confederate left, forcing Johnston to fall back on Cassville to protect the railroad to Atlanta. The Southern commander planned to strike Sherman from Cassville, but the normally bellicose John Bell Hood failed to press the attack and Johnston again retreated, this time to slave-constructed earthworks across the Western & Atlantic Railroad at Allatoona Pass. The wily Sherman declined to attack the strong positions there, instead making another sweep to the right, forcing Johnston to rush to Dallas and throw up works there, near New Hope Church, where the two armies fought on May 25 and 27. Cleburne's division on the Confederate right at Pickett's Mill was heavily engaged in the fighting at New Hope Church, inflicting heavy casualties on attacking Union forces. Polk's brigade and the First Arkansas were in a quiet section of the line, "but it was a source of strength and confidence to the rest of the division to know that [Polk] had charge of the weakest and most delicate part of our line," Cleburne noted. The two armies were now only 20 miles from Atlanta.[9]

Over the next several weeks, Johnston and Sherman sparred and parried but never came to grips. On June 14, the Episcopalian bishop and Confederate general Leonidas Polk was struck and killed by Union artillery fire as he observed Sherman's positions with Johnston and Hardee from

William Tecumseh Sherman used superior numbers to flank the Army of Tennessee out of a series of fortified positions, to the very outskirts of Atlanta. He finally captured the Georgia capital after cutting the railroad line between Atlanta and Jonesboro, Georgia. (Courtesy of the Old State House Museum)

atop Pine Mountain. The next day, the bishop's nephew and Cleburne's friend Lucius Polk was severely wounded by a Union shell that ripped away part of his left calf, causing the leg to be amputated and ending his military service.[10] Polk's veteran brigade, reduced by years of combat and hard living, did not survive the loss of its commander: the various regiments were broken up and moved to other units. The First Arkansas Regiment was consolidated with the Fifteenth Arkansas Infantry and became part of Brig. Gen. Daniel C. Govan's regiment of Cleburne's division. Colquitt retained command of the consolidated unit. The Rebel lines continued to ease back until they were astride the railroad in strong positions along Kennesaw Mountain and its spurs, and the two armies settled in opposite each other.[11] On June 27, a frustrated Sherman abandoned maneuver and attempted a full-scale assault to bludgeon the Rebel army out of his way.[12] The attack in one-hundred-degree weather failed miserably, but was marked amid the savage combat by an act of humanity on the First Arkansas's front. The fierce rifle and artillery fire had ignited dry leaves and undergrowth below the Confederate entrenchments. As the flames crept toward the helpless Yankee wounded, Lt. Col. William H. Martin of the First Arkansas waved his handkerchief at the Federal lines and called for a cease-fire until the stricken men could be moved to safety. Rebel soldiers leaped from their trenches to help Union men pull the injured from the path of the flames, then the combat continued unabated. Martin's action so impressed Col. John I. Smith of the Thirty-first Indiana that the Hoosier presented the Confederate with a brace of pistols.[13] The fighting at Kennesaw Mountain resulted in an extremely one-sided Southern victory. Total Union losses were around 1,999 dead and wounded and 52 missing, compared to 270 Rebel dead and wounded and 172 missing. The Yankees attacking Cleburne's division lost around 300 dead and 500 wounded. Incredibly, Cleburne's well-entrenched Confederates lost only 2 killed and 9 wounded in the savage fighting.[14]

Sherman returned to his earlier strategy and again moved to his right, forcing Johnston to abandon the Kennesaw line and retreat to prepared lines on the Chattahoochee River. Sherman, chastened perhaps by his disastrous attack on Kennesaw Mountain, declined to hit the Rebels' elaborate fortifications and instead swung two corps to the left, crossing the Chattahoochee on July 8. Johnston retreated across the river the next day and took up positions in strong works only four miles from downtown Atlanta. Faced with a Union army on the outskirts of the critical Georgia capital, Confederate president Jefferson Davis reached the limits of his

Alfred Waud's sketch provides an eyewitness account of the removal of wounded Union troops from in front of the positions of the First Arkansas Infantry Regiment in the 1864 fighting at Kennesaw Mountain, Georgia. (Courtesy of the Library of Congress)

patience with Johnston's retrograde movements. On July 13, Braxton Bragg, who served as a military adviser to Davis after his removal as commander of the Army of Tennessee, arrived in Atlanta to assess the situation. Hardly a Johnston supporter, Bragg recommended that the Southern commander be replaced, but not by Bragg's old enemy, the senior corps commander William J. Hardee. Instead, thirty-year-old John Bell Hood, a combative general whose arm was crippled at Gettysburg and who lost a leg at Chickamauga, was on July 17 given command of the Army of Tennessee for the climactic battles for Atlanta.[15]

John Bell Hood was every bit as aggressive as Johnston was cautious, and his army charged out of the Atlanta defenses on July 20 to attack "Fighting Joe" Hooker's Twentieth Corps as it crossed Peachtree Creek on the Confederate left. After four hours of heavy combat, the Rebels retreated back within their works after suffering some twenty-five hundred casualties, compared to around seventeen hundred on the Union side. The First and Fifteenth Arkansas was not involved in that day's fighting: just as

Cleburne's division was about to join the attack on the left, a desperate message arrived warning that Yankee troops threatened to roll up the Rebel right, and Cleburne was sent to hold the line. Replacing Joe Wheeler's cavalry in the early hours of July 21, the infantrymen hurriedly threw up earthworks in the dark while enduring Federal cannon fire. Throughout the day, Cleburne's undersized division withstood artillery fire, sharpshooters and full-scale infantry assaults in what Cleburne later called the bitterest fighting of his life. Around 10 P.M., the Irishman's division was withdrawn into Atlanta to prepare for an attack on July 22 in which Hardee's corps would attack the Yankee left and rear while Frank Cheatham's Confederates would hit the Union lines north of them. Daniel Govan's brigade, including the First and Fifteenth Arkansas, was on the left of the attacking elements of Cleburne's division when the attack commenced at about 1 P.M. The Second and Twenty-fourth Arkansas Infantry Regiment, forming the right of Govan's brigade, fought their way up to the first of three lines of Yankee fortifications and the Union troops asked to surrender. However, on seeing how few assailants they actually faced, the Federals changed their minds and instead took the Rebels prisoner. As the Union center charged against Govan's Fifth Arkansas Infantry, Colquitt's First and Fifteenth Arkansas slammed into the Yankee left, capturing a battery of six Napoleon guns. Govan then ordered Colquitt's men to wheel left and liberate their fellow Arkansians from their captors. "This was promptly and opportunely done, and compelled the immediate surrender of all [the Yankees] who did not take flight in the confusion," Govan reported. "This timely success rescued those of the Second and Twenty-fourth who had been entrapped, and the officers of this command now received the swords of their late captors. The First and Fifteenth Arkansas took the two guns which were placed upon the road." Govan's men continued to a second line of Federal entrenchments and were stymied there until Capt. Thomas Key's Helena Battery was brought up to pound the Yankee lines from within two hundred yards. The Union troops broke when Hiram Granbury's Texas regiment struck their left, falling back to yet a third line of fortifications atop Bald Hill. The attacking Rebels could not surmount this final line, and with the approach of night the exhausted Confederates fell back to the second line, which they had captured earlier. The next day remained a stalemate, though the opponents did allow a truce at midmorning to remove the dead and wounded from between the lines. The achievements of Cleburne's division were the high point of the day for the Confederate army, and the exploits of the First and Fifteenth

Arkansas were among the most noteworthy. Colquitt's regiment captured the entire Sixteenth Iowa Infantry Regiment, as well as two guns of the Second Illinois Battery and the six Napoleon cannon of Company F, Second Regular U.S. Artillery. This limited victory came at a high price, however. Govan's brigade lost 86 men killed, 322 wounded, and 91 missing. Among the dead was First Lt. Andrew J. Pitner of Company B, First Arkansas Regiment, a close friend of Alex Spence. John W. Colquitt was wounded; the former schoolteacher lost a foot and would no longer lead troops in battle. Lt. Col. William Martin also was wounded in the fighting, and Capt. Felix G. Lusk took command of the consolidated regiment. Total Confederate losses for the day, including those of Cheatham, were between fifty-five hundred and eight thousand compared to thirty-eight hundred for the Yankees. Hood's army dwindled as the Federal noose tightened around Atlanta.[16]

John Bell Hood replaced Joseph E. Johnston in command of the Army of Tennessee and commenced sharp attacks that caused heavy casualties among irreplaceable Confederate troops but garnered few strategic advantages in the fighting around Atlanta. Hood led the army to its virtual destruction in battles at Franklin and Nashville, Tennessee, in late 1864. (Courtesy of the Old State House Museum)

After the battle of Atlanta, Sherman once again began maneuvering around the Confederate left, this time attempting to cut the Macon & Western Railroad, the last open railroad out of Atlanta. Hood sent two divisions to halt the attempt. The Confederates were roughly handled at Ezra Church on July 28, losing 4,642 troops compared to 700 Yankee casualties, but managed to keep the rail line open. Hood, after suffering 15,000 casualties in eight days while inflicting only 6,000 on his foe, took a page from his predecessor's book and awaited the Yankees from behind his strong fortifications surrounding Atlanta. Sherman patiently continued sidling to his right to threaten the Confederate supply line. Finally, on August 29, the Yankee commander decided to force the issue, leaving one corps to face Atlanta and sending the other five under the command of O. O. Howard to Jonesboro, an unfortified area twenty-six miles south of Atlanta. Hood dispatched a two-corps strike force under Hardee to face this new threat. On August 31, Hardee attacked, with a corps under Cleburne on the left and Lt. Gen. Stephen D. Lee's corps on the right. Lee's veterans quailed before the Federal entrenchments, many surrendering or refusing to charge the Union lines. Cleburne was equally ineffective in his debut as a corps commander. His own division, under temporary command of Mark Lowrey, wandered off to the left after a diversionary force of Yankee cavalrymen while John A. "Black Jack" Logan's division of Federal veterans repulsed his remaining troops. Total losses for the day were 1,725 Confederate casualties compared to less than 300 for the Union. Cleburne's division lost 28 killed and 147 wounded.[17]

As Hardee and Howard fought at Jonesboro, Union general Jacob Cox's division of the Army of the Ohio hit the Macon & Western Railroad south of Atlanta at Rough and Ready. The blue-clad infantry immediately began wrecking Hood's lifeline. The Southern commander ordered Lee's corps back to face an anticipated attack on Atlanta, leaving Hardee's corps under Cleburne to withstand two full Yankee corps and parts of two others. Cleburne placed his corps in a fish hook–shaped formation, with Govan's Arkansians at the bend in the line. At 3 P.M. on September 1, 1864, the Yankees attacked in a mass six ranks deep, smashing into Govan's thin lines. The Arkansians fought desperately, ferociously, but were overwhelmed by the sheer number of Northern troops. Govan and his six hundred or so survivors became prisoners of war, and the battle flag of the First and Fifteenth Arkansas was captured by the Fourteenth Michigan Infantry Regiment. The Arkansian and his men would be taken as far as Nashville, then released in a special exchange of two thousand prisoners on September 9. Govan's sacrifice enabled Cleburne to cobble together a

The flag of the First and Fifteenth Arkansas Infantry Regiment was among the many Confederate banners seized when the majority of Daniel C. Govan's Arkansas regiment was captured at the battle of Jonesboro. (Courtesy of the Old State House Museum)

new line to withstand the Union juggernaut. As darkness fell, the Union troops withdrew with their prisoners and allowed Cleburne to slip away to the south. John Bell Hood abandoned Atlanta that same night.[18]

Between Sherman's departure from Chattanooga in early May and Hood's abandonment of Atlanta in September, the Confederate Army of Tennessee lost some 30,000 men from its maximum of approximately 70,000; 20,000 of those casualties occurred during Hood's short tenure as army commander. The Federal armies, numbering around 110,000 men, suffered around 37,000 casualties during the Atlanta Campaign. The Atlanta Campaign, and the fall of the Georgia capital, not only cost the South thousands of irreplaceable soldiers, but the Union victory also stiffened Northern resolve and helped Abraham Lincoln win reelection, virtually eliminating any chance of a negotiated Southern independence.[19]

• • •

Alex Spence's letters written between February 28 and August 14, 1864, show the high morale the Army of Tennessee maintained throughout the Atlanta Campaign, including faith in the leadership of Gen. John Bell Hood.

Camp 1st Ark Regiment
Sunday Evg. Febry 28th, 1864

Dear Father & Mother,
     Having an opportunity of sending letters to Arks. this evg, I thot to write you a few lines. Must be brief though as the gentleman leaves in a few moments. Genl Johnston has agreed for one man from every Company from Arks. to go home on a sixty day furlough. I will start one from my Co. in about 8 days, unless "active operations" commence between the 2 Armies here. I do not know when I will be able to visit home. According to the late act of congress, all the troops are Kept in service just as they are, so I suppose there will be no changes in our Regt. & it will be impossible for me to get off unless our Regt is consolidated & I am relieved—then I will return to Arks. Our Army has been in line of battle for 4 days here, expecting the Federals to advance, but they do not & this Evg tis reported they are falling back, so I suppose we will have no fight for some time yet. The health of my Co is very good, but few of us though left now to represent old Clark. I have recd no letters from home in a *long long time*. Why it is I can not imagine? I have been disappointed in receiving no money from home. I suppose you can send me some & that negro boy by the one that goes back from my company, at least I hope you will do so. If you can not raise the money, you can send that note on Tom Ewing & I will try to get the money from his Father. I will write you again when the one from my Co. gets off. I hope this will find you all well. I have written you frequently of late. Hope some of my letters were recd. I wish you would all write me often. It does seem you have forgotten me. I am hurried & must stop. My love to all. I'll write again soon.

Your Affectionate Son
Alex E. Spence
Direct Co. B 1st Ark Regt. Polk's Brigade
     Cleburnes Division
     Dalton, Geo.
          • • •

Dalton, Geo Feb 28/64

Mr. Flanagan,

Excuse me for troubling you, but I am very anxious my people should hear from me at home, so please will you have the Kindness to send this to my Father's family at Arkadelphia. I have written to them repeatedly, but recd no letters from them, so I suppose my letters did not reach them. But little news here. Our Army has all reenlisted for the war. "Arks troops" were among the first. The Army is in fine health & the best of spirits. We have been in line of battle at this place for 4 days, expecting a general attack from the Federals, but I do not believe they will make it. There has been considerable skirmishing. I think we will be able to whip the Federals very easily when we fight. I hope the Federals do not occupy Arkadelphia.

Very respectfully yours, etc.

Alex E. Spence, Capt
Co. B, 1st Ark Regt

• • •

Camp 1st Ark. Regt. Near
Dalton, Geo March 7th, 1864

Dear Sallie,

As Mr. Carter of our Company leaves for Arkadelphia direct this evening, I thought to write you a few lines.[20] Have written Pa & Mother, but my letters to any of the family are intended for all. I want to write so much I hardly know what to begin with & suppose I had better make my letter short. I have but little in the way of news. Everything is perfectly quiet here. God only knows when we will have a fight here, no prospect now of one soon. I suppose active operations will commence before a great while and then we may expect "hot work" for awhile. I shall put my trust in Providence. I have escaped so far. May be I may get through all safe yet. Soldiering is pretty hard just now. We live on pretty scant rations sure, but we are use to it. "Arkansaw Troops" have all reenlisted for the war and I among them.[21] Arkansaw and Texas troops have the best reputations of any troops in this Army. "Pat Cleburnes" Division composed of Texians & Arkansains mostly is noted for its fighting qualities. The fact is our Division never has been whipped yet, and we are fools enough to believe it will take the whole Yankee Army to do so. We all glory in the name of Arkansians & of belonging to "Cleburnes noted Division." Our troops have all been comfortably clad during the winter & had good winter quarters, but the Yankees made a raid on our lines while our Division was at Montgomery, Ala., on its way to reinforce Genl Polk in Miss & destroyed our quarters so we are now in "tents, etc.," doing tolerable well.[22] We had a fine trip on the Cars. I believe the Ladies of Alabama are more patriotic than in this state. When the Yankees advanced here, we were ordered back in a hurry, but the Yankees doubtless hearing "Pat Cleburne" & his command was coming "thought discretion the better part of valor" & left for Chattanooga again.

I hope they will let us rest quietly here awhile. It makes me mad to think of affairs in Arkansas. I think our Army over there might as well be disbanded for the good they do. Arkansas has been given up almost without a struggle.[23] I hope something will be done over there soon. Well, Sallie, I have sent out an application to go to Arks on 60 day furlough. Have not much idea I'll get it, but concluded to try it anyway. If I am successful, I will be in Arkadelphia by the time Mr. Carter reaches there. Sallie, I have not heard from home or any of you in a long time. Why it is you all do not write I can not imagine. Mr. Hearn is in service, I heard.[24] What has become of Pete & family, Mr. Elder, Liza & all? I would like to hear & do you ever hear from Texas from our folks? I want you all to write me by Mr. Carter and give all the news. Tell Pa I have been disappointed in not getting some money & that negro from home. Suppose though he has no opportunity of sending. He can now do so by Mr. Carter. He will bring anything and is a very reliable man. *Be certain* and send me the negro boy. If Pa has not got one, get Pete to let one of his come. A negro I think is safer in the Army than anywhere else now, and as for the money, I am actually needing it. Pa can send any kind he thinks best, Confederate money, "old Issue" is worth but little here. After 1st Apl next, probaly Pa can get bonds & send. 4 per cent bonds I believe is the best, but he can tell & let him do as he thinks best.[25] If he has a *surplus* of gold, I would not care if he would send me a few dollars of it. It takes all my wages to get something to eat & unless I can get some money & fix up and go like an officer should I shall resign and take my place in ranks where it is not expected of a man to dress much. I suppose it will be impossible for you all to send me any clothes, but I want that negro boy and money sent certain and that over coat of mine if Mr. Carter can bring it. I would like to have it, but fear it will be too much trouble to bring, but he will bring anything you all wish to send me. I shall expect many letters from home and Arkadelphia when Mr. Carter returns. Would write to some of the Young Ladies, but have heard nearly all of them have married. I understand a good many about Little Rock have married Federals. Hope none about Arkadelphia have done so. I believe nearly all of our Regiment have concluded to *marry in Georgia* as we claim this to be our home now. I believe I wrote you last Summer about meeting & forming the acquaintance of such a nice young lady from Va. Like a great many of them over here, she wants to marry pretty bad! & as I was not in that notion, we did not exactly get along.

Sallie, I expect I have written enough. Tell Mother I have got so I can live on "nothing." Breakfast this morning "meal, coffee & corn bread" & good prospect of dinner being the same. This is what we get *very often,* but still there is no grumbling. I would give anything to be at home once more and see you all. Don't know though when I shall have that privilege. Our Regiment has been consolidated and I am still retained.[26] Suppose I will have commission here as long as the war lasts. May get a chance to visit you all some of these days. Have but little hopes of my furlough getting through this time. I hope you all are well. Pa & Mother have quit Keeping Hotel. Well, I am glad of it. Did the Yankees interrupt any of our things and how did Pa get along with them? Write everything, for it will be news to me. Does Pa & Mother live at Al Greenes place yet? I hope you stay with them a good deal. Little Lizzie & Fannie, how do they get along? Have both grown a great deal I reckon? Write what has become of *every body* of Arkadelphia I Know. Tis no use in my writing about members of my Co, Mr. Carter will tell all. He will be to see you all.

I might write a week but it would be the same thing over & over. I shall count on that negro & money *certain.* I expect to have to stay here and want to try & live, so I hope I will not be *disappointed.* Pa can send the money he thinks will be best over here. I am owing some, borrowed money and want to pay it. Tell Pete, Mr. Hearne, Mr. Elder & all to write me. Never be uneasy about me. I have never been sick a day yet & hope to get through this war safe yet.

Give my best respects to all friends about Arkadelphia & I would be glad to hear from any of them.

I hope you will all write me and in everything that has happened and I want you all to write me every chance you have. I have written you all very often of late. Write what has become of Mr. Ewing & Liza.

I hope I will not be disappointed in receiving the things (negro, etc.) expected from home. Should Mr. Carter need any assistance, tell Pa please to help him.

Write often. Give my love to all.

Your Affectionate Brother,

Alex E. Spence

Direct "Me"
Co. "B" 1st Ark Regt Polks Brigade
Cleburnes Division Army of Tenn.
Dalton, Geo

I want Mother to give you all a scolding about not writing me & have you all to write me & tell her I shall depend on her & Pa sending me the *money* & *negro*. Sallie, I never heard, did you all ever get Tommy's things I sent home, his ring & money? You must *all write* long letters & often. Alex

Now all need not expect me as I have no idea my furlough will be approved. If it was to be, I would beat Mr. Carter to Arkadelphia.

• • •

Near Marietta Ga.
Tuesday Evg. June 7th/64

Dear Father & Mother,

As I hear of an opportunity tomorrow of sending letters to Arks, I thought to write you a few lines. Do not know whether it will reach you or not, hope it will. I dislike very much writing you all when we are situated like we are now, but maybe you will be uneasy about me after hearing of the battles in North Geo. By the caption of this, you will see the Army of Tenn. have once more been on the retreat. For thirty days now, we have had stirring & exciting times, been but little use for the wicked soldiers of Genl Johnston's Army. On the 7th day of May the Federals moved on us at Dalton & after being whipped in every direct assault they made on us, they concluded to flank us & as they had a much larger force than ours succeeded. Not a day has passed since 7th May last but what there has been some hard fighting & I am happy to say in every instance have we been very victorious. We halted & offerd Genl Sherman & his following battle but in every instance they would refuse to advance on us direct. We have now been near this place some ten days & as it is a place the Federals cannot "flank," they will be compelled to advance on us. All of North Georgia is a line of fortifications. The Yanks fortify & so do we. Our "line of battle" extends for over 20 miles & is some 28 miles Northwest of Atlanta. Our loss in the recent battles has been very small, the Federal loss very heavy.[27] Notwithstanding, we have been retreating. I never saw our Army in better spirits. All are confident we will whip the Yankees. If they ever advance near here, they will certainly be the worst whipped set of men the sun ever shone on. Tis said one of Genl Johnston's principal motives for falling back was so as to be able to gain a complete victory when we do fight the Federals. At Dalton a victory would not have amounted to much. The Federals could have fallen back on Chattanooga & we could not have done here much pursuing them as it was too mountainous a country. Here we will have a "full sweep" for miles. "Cleburne's" (Our) "Division" of Texians & Arkansians have fully done their part in these fights so far. Trans Miss troops are particularly relied on in this Army. We always occupy the "post of honor," *the front*. Our Regt has suffered some in Killed & wounded.

Charles Trickett of my Co was slightly wounded in a skirmish the other day, the only man who has been hurt. So far the Yankees have acted very cowardly. It is almost impossible for the officers to get their men to move forward on us. Have been out skirmishing with them several times & often heard officers trying to get their men to move "forward," but all in vain. They hardly come, when they do, they are drunk. They know what to expect from the "Rebels." Our Division is now behind "good breast works" where we expect to fight the Yankees & all of us are confident we (our Division) alone can whip *half* of Sherman's Army. We have to Keep pretty close behind our works to keep Yankee Sharpshooters from "hitting our heads." It is expected they will make a general attack along our whole line tomorrow or next day. If they do, they are badly whipped certain. Have no fears about me. So far thank heaven I have escaped unharmed. Should I be so unfortunate as to get wounded, I have some good friends in Georgia & will be well cared for. The fate of North Geo. will certainly be decided in a very few days. Our news from Va is encouraging. Genl Lee has been successful every day as yet.[28] People need have no fears about this battle. Our retrograde move to this place will prove "all for the best" yet & Genl Joe Johnston will yet achieve one of the greatest victories in this struggle. We have as many men as we need to whip out Sherman & will do it. The news from Arks, Texas & La lately is certainly encouraging to the troops from those places who have been struggling for over two years now & their homes overran.[29] I am in hopes by this time Arkansas is entirely free from the presence of the hated foe. Mr. Carter reached us all safe some time ago. You may know we were all glad over news to get letters from home. I was truly glad to hear the Feds had dealt so leniently with you all. Truly you were fortunate. Accept many thanks for the money, but the *gold* he had to use to get across the River. It takes a pile over here to buy a negro. They are worth from *4,000 to 6,000* dollars. I wish to buy much. You could have sent me one. I still renew the request if you get your Boys back from Texas & have any possible chance, send me one. Mr. Moreland is over in Arks.[30] Maybe you can send one by him. I shall stow away my money for harder times. The new "currency bill" has as yet done but little good for prices and now everything is as high as ever & the prospect pretty fair for things remaining so for some time yet.[31] Tell Sallie & Mr. Hearn I saw Rufus the other day. He was safe & well. Made his escape from Knoxville some time ago when he had been wounded.[32] Also please tell Miss Sarah Ann I saw Lt Col Ben Sawyer yesterday.[33] He was well & his folks at last accounts. Miss Sarah Ann's mother is dead & I reckon she has heard of it. She died last Oct. I believe. I also saw Uncle Ben's youngest son a few days ago. He is a Lieut in the "29th Ala Regt," here and seems to be doing finely.[34] What's the reason Pete & Miss Sarah Ann did not write me? I expected more letters that I recd. Please return for me to Mrs. Sallie Greene my most sincere thanks for her long letter. Tell her I shall write her as soon as "this thing" is decided here—at last accounts her brother was at Madison & well. Tell Miss Billie her brother has a very good situation at Madison Ga.[35] My Company is very small. I will only have about 28 in the coming fight. I am in fine health though some sickness with us. We have gone through the subbers lately, but hardships seem to agree with me nowadays.[36] No telling when our big fight will come off. When it does, I will try & send you a list of casualties in Co. B very soon. I hope we will all be fortunate, but of course *all* cannot expect it. Was any of our "Clark Boys" killed or wounded in the late fight across the Miss?[37] If so who were they? Write me & when you all do have a chance of writing, give all the news. Tell me what has become of all of my old friends—Marty Randolph went with the Feds, about what I expected. I guess he thot it would pay. Maybe he will find out one day he was mistaken. I would like very much to meet up with my old school mate on the field as he has choosed to go with the Federals.[38] Did you know Humphrey Peake has gone to the Yankees. I understand he is a surgeon in the Federal Army.[39] What has ever become of Tom & Bill Ewing? Are they still in Clark & what doing? Mr. Elder, he is still with you all. Tell him I need his letter & will write before long. When I write home, I intend my letter for all the family. Geo. Ashby & Bill Lindsey, what has become of them? Mr. Hearn & Pete, how do they stand service? I am in hopes both stand it fine.[40]

I was truly glad the health of all was so good & you all are in such fine spirits. God only knows when I will be able to visit home. Maybe one of these days before long. You all need never be uneasy about me. I hope to spend many a day at home yet. I want you all to write me every chance & I will do the same. Do not be uneasy about me in the coming fight. I hope I will come out all right yet. I am "cooped up" so I can hardly write. It is raining & I am "under my blanket stretched over a pole." It has rained very hard for several days, so we have had no pleasant time, but everything is born cheerfully for the sake of our Country. We are now in a beautiful country, but everybody has run from the Yankees.[41] I suppose most of the Arkadelphia refugees will return now. I am in hopes they will never have to leave again. Who proved traitors to us while the Yanks were at Arkadelphia?

Be sure *for all to write me very often.* Maybe I will get some of your letters. The Texas folks, send them my address & tell them to write me. Always direct my letters as given below & they will be sure to reach me. I am in hopes this will find you all in good health & getting along finely. Have you any crop gardens, etc.? What a treat a few vegetables would be now. All be sure & write. Excuse all defects & give my love to all.

Your affectionate son,

Alex E. Spence

Direct   Co. B. 1st AR Regt

Polks Brig.—Cleburne's Division

Hardee's Corps—Army of Tenn.

My respects to all enquiring friends if any.

Alex E. Spence

Co. B 1st Ark Regt

• • •

Trenches near Atlanta, Ga[42]

August 10, 1864

Wednesday Evening

My Dear Father and Mother:

As Smith Johnson and young Norris of my Company have been discharged and will leave for home in a few days I thought to commence my letters so as to have them ready by the time they start.[43] I have written you all several times lately and do hope some of my letters have reached you. We have had hard times on this campaign and it is not over. We may expect to go "the elephant" again.[44] I will write you a list of casualties of my Company in this campaign which I wish, if possible, you would have published for the benefit of our friends and relations. Lieutenant Pitner, who was mortally wounded the 22nd of July near Atlanta, died on the morning of the 8th instant at Griffin, Georgia. Poor fellow, he was as brave a man as ever lived and one of the best men I ever knew. How I have escaped unharmed through this "furious game of death," that is what I have been saying for the last three months, I hardly know. On this campaign of 90 days our Regiment has been under fire for over 50. We are getting used to being shot at but you may guess there is no fun in it. The casualties in the Regiment have been very heavy. We have lost two-thirds of our men. I expect you all think by our falling back so far our army has been whipped, but such has not been the case. We have whipped the enemy in every fight on this campaign and think ourselves able to do so every time. The troops regretted the removal General Johnston but now they are perfectly satisfied with Gen. Hood. They know he will fight—the Federals will never be able to get Atlanta. We will hold it at all hazards. On the 22nd of July we were in the most desperate battle I was ever engaged in. Our Division got in the rear of Shermans army and you may guess we had some hard fighting to do. We charged the Yankees and drove them from their lines of thin ditches, capturing 16 pieces of artillery and any number of prisoners and small arms. We had a hand to hand fight—killing a good many Yankees with bayonets. Since the fight we have been resting until a day or two ago. Now we are in the trenches and the Federals are near us—may come on us at any moment but we are all ready and waiting for them. Texas and Arkansas soldiers are head and shoulders above any troops in this army. Our Division is the main prop of Hoods army. We have a good name and reputation but it took hard fighting to get it and now takes harder fighting to sustain it. I am truly glad to see our troops in the "Trans-Mississippi Department" have been doing such good service lately. I hope Arkansas and Texas will soon be freed of all Yankees.[45] I suppose you have learned ere this that Mr. Carter reached here in safety—brought me the money except the gold—which he had to pay to get across the Mississippi. A few days ago Mr. Moreland reached the camp in safety—brought my letters from home written 4th July and you may believe I was truly glad to hear from you all. Once more I have written you all. Very frequently every man I hear of going to Arkansas I write by him hoping that some of my letters will reach you. I hardly have any idea I will get to Arkansas in the course of the next 12 months or not. Maybe I will. What do you all think—would there be any chances of making up a company—proving I could get the authority to come over for that purpose? My company is getting small and I fear we will have to consolidate before long, probably with another company. I assure you all I would like to be with you all once more. I was indeed glad to hear you all were doing so well and were living in a land of [illegible].

August 14, 1864.

Johnston and Norris will leave this afternoon. Nothing of interest has happened. The Yankees are trying to flank in on our site and we have been moving to the right to prevent them. The Federals will never be able to reach Atlanta. Pa—If it is convenient, I wish you could send me that negro boy. Sometime when good safe opportunity. I have had Johnsons negro Simon, but will give him up now. Today is Sunday. I wish it was so I could spend the day with you all. I hope you are in good health and doing well. This evening we will have plenty of watermelon to eat. We get a few vegetables and occasionally some fruit. Pa—by Smith

Johnston I will send you Tommys sword belt. I would send his sword and rifle but fear they might lose them. I shall take care of them. Tell Mother never to be uneasy about me. If I am ever so unfortunate as to get sick or wounded I have some good and kind friends in Georgia who will take every care of me. This time I am writing all of you and I want all of you to write me. Send by mail. Frequently letters come that way.

CASUALTIES IN COMPANY B. CAPTAIN ALEX E. SPENCE.
From 7th May to 14th August, 1964.

Killed:

Private W. T. Witcher	June 2, 1864[46]
" R. L. Davis	July 20, 1864[47]
Sergeant B. F. Blacknall	July 21, 1864[48]
Private Joshua McDaniel	July 22, 1864[49]

Wounded:

Lieutenant A. J. Pitner	July 21, 1864, mortally, died Aug. 8[50]
" M. M. Sanders	July 21, 1864, slight chest wound[51]
Sergeant S. D. Smith	July 22, 1864, slight chest wound[52]
Private Charles Trickett	May 20 and July 22, slight shoulder wound.[53]
Private William Graves	June 10 , severe side wound[54]
Pri. William V. Hughes	June 11, severe arm wound[55]
" Walter Norris	June 16, severe side wound[56]
" Joseph Pierce,	June 25, severe left arm wound, arm amputated[57]
" Zack Pierce,	July 7, severe left arm[58]
" Marion Pierce,	July 22, slight hand wound[59]
Private F. H. Stafford,	July 22, Slight arm injury[60]

• • •

This letter fragment probably was written around August 13, 1864, the date of the Hood order to which Spence refers.

Genl Hood has just sent around an order that Atlanta will be held at all hazards & we will do it certain.[61] We are strongly fortified & it will be impossible for the Feds ever to take *our* works—altho we can take theirs. On the 22nd July we took three lines of their ditches, but I can assure you it was no easy job. Johnston and Norris can give you all the news. I shall write you all every chance & hope that you will all do the same. A few days ago I recd a letter from Sis Tam. Will write her by Mr. Johnston. Let me hear from the Texas folks every time you write. I do hope this will

find you & Mother in good health & doing well. I enclose a list of casualties in our Co which if possible please have published for the benefits of friends & relatives. I want to write Sallie so I will close this. Kiss Little Lizzie for me, & be sure and write often.
My Love to all
Your affectionate son
Alex E. Spence
• • •

Trenches around Atlanta Ga
Sunday Evg. Aug 14th, 1864

Well, Sallie, I have written all the letters to Arkansaw I intend sending by "the Bhoys" but *one,* and that one is to *yourself,* so this evening I will write you provided I can keep from "dodging the bullets" that are flying around us long enough to do so. Let me tell you something about our situation. "Our Brigade" is now stationed on the extreme left of our Army. We are strongly fortified & just fronting us distant about 1/2 mile, the Yankees are Strongly fortified & both parties seem to be waiting on the other to assault their Works. Our skirmishers & the Enemy's are very close. Consequently, "Sharp shooting" is an every day occurrence in some places & our works and the enemy's are within 250 yards of each other. "Our line of battle" & fortifications is Some 12 or 15 miles long & extending around Atlanta. We are now some 6 miles south west of the place. This Evening it is reported the Federals are moving east of Atlanta, so I guess about tonight we will shift our position to the Extreme right as "Cleburnes Division" are charged with protecting the flank of the Army. The troops have the utmost confidence in Genl Hood's ability as a commander, and all are satisfied to go where he says go. I have no idea Sherman or any of his Northern hordes will ever reach Atlanta, only as prisoners of war. The citizens have nearly all left the place. The Federals "shell the city" at a furious [rate] at times. Several Ladies have been Killed. I was down there the other day & while "Shells" were flying thick, I saw a good many Ladies on the streets.[62] I guess you knew Atlanta was once *my home.* Have Staid there about 3 months, in 1863, when I was on Post duty. My acquaintances though now have all left the place.

Sallie, in my letters home I expect I have written enough about "wars," so to some other subject. I have met up with a good many old Talladegians in the Army. Pa's old friend Jno. T. Morgan is a "Brigd. Genl." They say he is a perfect drunkard & I believe does not stand very high as an officer.[63] What do you think? You recollect Miss Martha Stone? She is now Mrs. Mickle. I heard from her a few days ago through a friend. She lives in South Ala. She sent me her best respects and a very pressing invitation if I ever got a "furlough—sick or wounded" to be certain to visit her, as she is a "young widow" and very wealthy. *Probaly* I will visit her. Her husband Capt. Mickle was killed in the battle of "Chickamauga" last fall.[64] The Yankees have been to Talladega, but I suppose did but little damage. Miss Sarah Ann has heard long ago of her mother's death. She died some time last year.[65] I wrote her once about it & I believe I have also written you about meeting Uncle Ben's youngest son. He is a Lieut in an Ala Regt. here. I do not Know whether he has got thro our recent battles safe or not. I have not met up with Rufus Hearn in a good while. Suppose though he will write you by Smith Johnston. Rufus is said to be the best soldier in the Battery. Why don't you & Mr. Hearn write him? I guess the "Artillery" have had about the easiest time of any Company that ever left the place. We have been "through the subbies" I do assure you.[66] Sallie, ere long there will be a couple of officers from our Regt over to Arkansas after the men belonging to the Regt. They will be in Arkadelphia after some of my Company who are there. Do not say anything about this until they get the men. I want you if you please to try and send me two or three nice white Shirts, or any kind of nice ones. They will be but little weight and any of my Company will bring them. I have met with the misfortune a short time ago to loose my clothes. It is a very difficult matter to keep anything on a campaign like this. I tried very hard to get on the job of going to Arks but could not as I only have one officer now left. May be one [of] these days I will be able to visit home. If I get through this campaign safe I intend trying to resign again as I have so few men probaly I will succeed this time. I would like to be with you all once more very much This is Sunday Evg. Do you spend Sundays down at home like you used to. I hope you go down there often for I know Pa and Mother have a lonesome time in the old house. I reckon Sundays are not like they used to be in Arkadelphia. Does not the place look desolate. You will have heard of the death [of] Lieut. Pitner. I regret his death very much. He was my best friend & a brave & gallant soldier. For over 3 years now, we have been mess mates and shared the same blanket—poor fellow his relations live in this State but they were not able to visit him. He died at Griffin, Geo and Mrs. Starke Charley's mother had him buried at her family burying ground.[67] Ben Blacknall a most excellent man was Killed also. The fact is the best men I had have been killed. I have written Mr. Blacknall in regard to his death. Tell Mr. Hearn if he pleases to tell Mr. J. B. McDaniel to inform Joshua McDaniels folks of his death. Would write them but I have not time. Joshua McDaniel was killed on the 22nd July in a charge we made on the Enemy's works. A minie ball struck him in the head, killing him instantly. He fell in 40 yards of the Enemy's works. He was a good man & splendid Soldier.

Sallie, I have written about sending me the negro boy—again if he ever meets up with a good opportunity of and can do so without putting himself to too much trouble. Cooking goes most too hard with us & the Shirts you can attend to if you ever have a chance of sending me. I want you all to write every chance. Try some of your letters by mail. They come to us frequently that way. I shall write you all by mail & every other chance my letters by mail. If I hear there is no mail to Arkadelphia I will direct care [of] Dr. Jett, Washington Ark. Request him to forward them to you. This letter is intended for both Mr. Hearn and yourself & both answer. How does Bettie and little Tommy get along?[68] Do they grow much and does Bettie go to school? learn fast, etc? When you write, give every thing what has happened. It will be news to me. The letters by Mr. Moreland I destroyed. We were going into an engagement in a day or two after they were recd so for fear they might fall in Federal hands, I burned them up.

All be certain & write me often. Johnston & Norris will go to see you all, tell all the news how we are getting along, etc. I do hope this will find all well. Tell Mr. Hearn I shall expect a letter from him. Give my love to all.

Your affectionate Brother,
Alex E. Spence

• • •

Though obviously demoralized by the loss of Atlanta and the Confederate defeat at Jonesboro, Georgia, Alex Spence's last letters from this period reveal a tough, professional soldier prepared to continue fighting despite the Army of Tennessee's recent setbacks.

Line of Battle near
Jonesboro, Georgia
Tuesday Sep 6th 1864

My Dear Father & Mother,

I have just heard of an opportunity of sending a letter to Arks & have time only to write you a line as I know you will all be anxious to hear from us after the late battles. Well, contrary to my expectations, we were not able to hold Atlanta. Old Sherman flanked us out of the place. We are now some 30 miles below there on the Macon Rail Road. Genl Hood has been completely "out generaled" by Sherman. Genl Johnston would have done much better with this Army than Hood has. On the 31st ulto & the 1st Inst. "we (our Division) had a desperate fight. On the 31st, we were victorious. On the "1st Inst." we were beaten.[69] Our Brigade was completely overpowered. We fought about ten to our one & of course were driven from our trenches. Nearly all of the Brigade "Govans" were killed and captured. Our Regt suffered heavily. I was in the worst place I was ever in before in my life. Gib Peeples of our Co was Killed.[70] Please tell his mother about it. I have not time to write her. He was shot through the head by a minie ball & died instantly. He was a brave & gallant soldier. Sergt S. D. Smith was wounded. Private Jas. Baxley, Tom S. Carter & Robt. McDonald were captured.[71] I will enclose you a list of all those now with the Company, which please let their friends know as none of them have a chance of writing. My Co has been consolidated, but I do not get off as nearly all of our officers have been Killed or wounded & I am afraid I will not as our Field officers are all wounded & now I am "second" in command of the Regt, "am playing Lieut Col." We have only about 90 men in our two Regts, the "1st & 15th Ark" & only about 350 now in the noted "1st Arkansas Brigade." The Yankees pursued us to this place we fortified & last night they retreated toward Atlanta, which place it is supposed they will now make their base of operations. I have just retd from a "Scouting" expedition among their camps & works. I do not Know what we will do, but we are hardly in a condition to make an advance move. Some of our Army are much discouraged. Georgia troops more than any others. Arkansas & Texas troops are *never whipped. They* will be Killed or captured, but not whipped. I have lost all my "clothing, papers, etc.," but I had the pleasure the other day of making two Yankees "bite the dust" & got me a fine hat.

I have written you all very often of late & do hope some of my letters reached you. I understand another courier will leave for Arks in about ten days. Will then try & write you a longer letter. Have recd no letters from any of you in a long time. Write me every chance & be sure & have all to do so.

Tell Miss Sarah Ann I saw George Armbrester yesterday. He was well & said their folks were well last accounts.[72]

All be sure & write me every opportunity. I must close as I am hurried. I do hope this will find all of you in good health.
Give my Love to all.
Your affectionate Son,
Alex E. Spence, Capt

Direct all letters:
Co. B 1st Ark Regt
Govans Brigade Cleburnes Div.
Hardees Corps
Army of Tenn

• • •

Camp 1st Ark Regiment
on the Atlanta & West Point R. Road
Near Palmetto Geo Sep 25th 1864

My Dear Father & Mother,

I have just learned of an opportunity of sending letter to Arks & have
only a few moments to write in. The last letter I wrote home was on 5th
Sep, which I hope reached you but for fear it did not reach you I will
give you some of the news. We were in no battles after Johnson & Norris
left us until 31st Aug & 1st Sept. On the 31st Aug no one of my Co was
hurt. On the 1st Sep. S. G. Peeples was killed. S. D. Smith slightly
wounded. Tom. S. Carter, Jas Baxley & Robt McDonald captured. The 1st
Sep was an unfortunate day for our Brigade. We had hastily thrown up
some temporary Rail works at Jonesboro Geo when the Enemy charged
us with some Eight lines of battle. We repulsed them twice, but the third
time our works were carried. Over one half of the Brigade were captured. Those that did make their escape run out after the Yankees were in
the works with them. There were in the ditches with us when I left. I had
no notion of being captured. Most of the prisoners captured on that day
have been exchanged & retd. All will be here in a few days. Our Army is
now fortified 25 miles west of Atlanta. No Yankees nearer than 8 miles of
us & no prospect of any fighting soon. We have done no fighting since 1st
Sept. I have been out on several scouting expeditions & came very near
being captured the other day. The people over here are much discouraged, but the Army is in fine spirits. All they want is a leader. I fear Genl
Hood's "not the man for the times." Mr. Sherman out generaled him &
flanked him out of Atlanta. The courier is waiting & hurrying me, so I
must close. I wish if you ever get that negro boy back & have an opportunity, you would send him over to me. I have no idea when I will be able
to get home. If any chance, will be there this winter. My Co. has been
consolidated, but I do not get off.[73] The other Captain is off badly
wounded.[74] Write me every chance. This courier is named Ellis & lives in
Washington. You can write by him.[75] All be certain & write me every
chance. I do hope this will find all well. Please be so kind as to inform
Mrs. Peeples of the death of her son. Poor Gibb, he was a good fellow & a
brave & gallant soldier—but he has met the fate that has fallen to thousands of others. I will write you all every chance I hear of sending letters
to Arks. Capt Cloud reached here the other day & brot me "Petes" letter
of 8th Aug. Why did you not all write? Be certain of sending me the
negro boy if you ever meet with an opportunity of doing so, as I want
him if it will not put you all to too much inconvenience. We do not

expect anything to be down here for several days. I must close. All be certain & write every chance.

Give my love to all. In haste

Yr affectionate Son

Alex E. Spence

Co "B" 1st Ark Regiment

Govans Brig Cleburnes Div

Hardees Corps

Army of Tenn

Chapter 7

"Now I shall have something to live for . . .": Franklin

After the fall of Atlanta, John Bell Hood and his forty thousand survivors fell back to Lovejoy's Station, about forty miles from the Georgia capital, and then to Palmetto, twenty miles west of Atlanta. The Army of Tennessee headed north on September 29 to disrupt Sherman's long, vulnerable supply line. On October 13, Cleburne's division, including the First and Fifteenth Arkansas, arrived at Dalton, where the U.S. 44th Colored Infantry occupied a small fort. The garrison of 751 men surrendered, and after being robbed of their shoes many of the black soldiers were put to work destroying the railroad line to Atlanta.[1] The Rebel army, pursued by the bulk of the Union troops, then headed west and south into northern Alabama. Cleburne confronted the Federal garrison at Decatur on October 28, but after skirmishing with the Yankees Hood elected to bypass the town and move on to Tuscumbia. The limited action around Decatur cost about 200 Confederate casualties and Union losses of 155 men.[2]

Both Hood and Sherman now made momentous strategic decisions. The latter, convinced that it would be a waste of men and time to try to maintain his tenuous supply lines to Tennessee, decided to ignore Hood entirely and embark on a march to the sea, living off the land in a campaign to dissect the Confederacy and "make Georgia howl!" before joining Union operations in the east. The former devised a plan to march to Kentucky, where he expected to pick up twenty-thousand recruits to help him strike Union general George Thomas's army in Tennessee before heading east to join Robert E. Lee's army against Grant and Sherman. Sherman's strategy proved wildly successful; Hood's resulted in the virtual destruction of the Army of Tennessee.[3]

Amid the movements of armies over the past two years, Alex Spence had met a young woman in Madison, Georgia, perhaps while visiting a member of his company who had been wounded at Chickamauga and sent to Madison to recuperate. Spence and Amanda Willson fell in love, and in September 1864, he asked her to be his bride.[4] She responded in October, and his reaction shows that the clerk turned soldier remained a romantic after nearly four years under arms:

Camp 1st Ark Regt.
Near Tuscumbia Ala.
Nov 3 1864

My Dearest Friend,

We have just been informed that we will have an opportunity of sending letters off to morrow, so I thought to write you a few lines this
Evening. I wrote you last from Gadsden Ala. 21st Oct. which letter I hope
reached you. The last letter I have recd from you bears date "5th Oct" &
words can hardly express *my feelings* upon reading the contents of *that* letter. It does Seem I can hardly realize that I am the person whom you
have one day promised to make *happy.* Now I shall have something to live
for & hope that soon the day may come when I can call you "all my
own." When shall that day be it is now for you to say—I hope you will
not decide like a great many to wait until "the war Ends." Shall it be
whenever it is possible for me to get a leave of absence to visit M[adison]
for that purpose. Times are not like they used to be. We have others to
consult besides ourselves about affairs now. Before you name the day, let
me tell you I shall be compelled to visit my home in Arks first. We expect
this campaign to be ended in 6 weeks. Then I am promised a 60 days furlough to visit Arks. As soon as I return, then I expect to call on you to
fulfill that promise—let me ask you, does yr Father & Mother know anything of this? Had I better write to them or can I rely [on] you getting
their consent? God knows that I shall never do *anything* to cause you in
the least to regret your decision. It does seem an age almost since I heard
from you. We are expecting a mail in to day. I hope to receive several letters from you. Do you write me often? I hope so. I am a very exacting
correspondent. Will write you every chance & shall expect to hear from
you very often. Why did Miss Matt send such a message to me as she did
in Mr. B letter? I hope she dont think I am going to relinquish all my
claims on her as my friend. If she does, she will be disappointed, for I shall
still claim her as one of my friends. When Mr. Bourland recd her note of
Enquiry I never flattered myself for one moment that she was particularly
anxious to hear from me. I guessed at whose instance the note was written. My friend Mr. B seems "bent on" corresponding with Miss M. She
must recollect he is a young man & *very susceptable.*

Well, what is the news about M? Have the Yankees ever made any
more raids to the place? I hope not. I suppose they have as much as they
can do *watching* our movements up here. What do you think of Genl.
Hoods move? Has he succeeded in forcing the Federals to leave Atlanta
or not? We seldom hear any news from Geo. Have, though, heard various
reports about Atlanta being evacuated.[5] Since we left Newman Ga. 8th
Oct., we have had a pretty hard time.[6] Since then we have marched about

350 miles. "Our Regt" has been in but one fight. That was at Decatur Ala 5 or 6 days ago. Then, owing to some mismanagement, we suffered considerably & accomplished *nothing*. We could have taken the place, but it would have cost more than it was worth. The Federals were very strongly fortified there & were in considerable force. I have stood the trip so far fine—"hard marching, short rations, etc" suit me very well. For a few days on "Sand Mountain" & around Decatur, "rations" were pretty scarce with us.[7] "Parched Corn" was in considerable demand. Now we are living fine & expect better times when we get into Tenn. We find but few people living in this part of North Ala. Nearly all have become refugees. What few that are here are "not much Secesh."[8] Had about as soon see a Federal as a "Reb." "Our Confederate funds" wont begin to "buy a chicken or a canteen of *sorghum*." The Army reached this place two days ago. All are now resting preparatory to another forward move. Our Pontoon Bridges are now completed across the Tenn River at this place. A part of the Army are crossing to day. I suppose from what I hear our Corps (Cheathams) will cross to morrow.[9] From here tis said our destination will be Columbia Tenn., but I fear very much we will not be able to reach that place as the Federals are said to be concentrating their forces in Tenn very fast.[10] I think we intend to make a raid in Middle Tenn, mainly to get supplies for the winter, for we certainly can not stay up there this winter without some hard fighting & I dont think Genl Hood intends fighting much now a days. The belief is here we will "winter" some where near Corinth Miss. I never saw our Army in better spirits & we are much stronger in numbers to day than when we left Jonesboro Geo, but enough about "Army Moves." I have never yet recd that "package." I wrote to a young friend of mine at Griffin to get it & I suppose he has done so, though I have never heard from him. As soon as we get settled, I hope it will reach me.

 We are to have an "inspection of our Command" in a few moments, so I will have to close. In yr last, you promised to write a long letter in a few days. I am expecting *that* letter now. Before closing this, I must again ask you to write me very often. Yr letters will reach me some time & then they will be *welcomed*. I will write you every chance. My next I suppose will be written from Tenn. Present my kindest regards to all. As Ever,
 Sincerely Yours,
 Alex E. Spence
"Write Soon"[11]
 • • •

In addition to his fiancée, Spence also wrote to his parents, though he did not inform them of his betrothal:

Camp 1st Ark. Regt.
Near Tuscumbia, Ala
Nov. 5th 1864

Dear Father & Mother,

We have an opportunity this Evening of sending letters to Arks. so I thought to write you all a few lines. Have not written to you before in sometime because I have not had a chance of sending a letter. My last was written about 1st Oct. from Newman, Geo. Since then our Army has been on "the move." The "Seat of War" has been transferred from Georgia Soil. Genl Hood has been conducting a "grand flank movement"—which so far has been entirely successful. In the first place after leaving our Camps near Jonesboro, Geo, the Army moved on the Rail Road from Chattanooga to Atlanta & succeeded in tearing up about 40 miles of the "track" besides capturing several places and a great many prisoners on the Road. Among the places captured were Calhoun, Dalton, Tunnel Hill & Ringgold, Geo. For the want of supplies we were compelled to move back from Dalton to Gadsden, Ala.—at this place we got an outfit for another raid. The Army crossed Sand Mountain & moved on Decatur, Ala. We surrounded that place & Kept the Yankees in their fortification for three days—could have taken the place but it would have cost more than it was worth. "Our Regt" skirmished with the Yankees two days—we lost some men but none of our Company. From Decatur we moved to this point reached here last Monday & have been expecting to cross the Ten. River every day. Our "Pontoon Bridges" have been across the River at Florence for several days. I guess we will cross about tomorrow. Tis said then we move towards Nashville via Columbia, Tenn. I can't think we will remain in Middle Tenn long because the Feds are concentrating their forces there very fast & Genl Hood sure does not intend to fight a battle on this campaign. The general belief is that we will only make a raid up in Middle Tenn to get supplies & we will "winter it" somewhere near Corinth, Miss. The cars are now running to this place via Corinth, Miss. While we were at Decatur I was in Six miles of "Uncle Joes" but he was in Yankees lines & I could not visit him. This country up here is about entirely deserted, not a half dozen farms between this place & Decatur in cultivation. What few people that live here had about see a Federal as "A Rebel." We have had a very hard time on this campaign.

Have done no hard fighting though—but plenty of "hard marching." I have stood the trip fine, "hardships" agree with me pretty well. Our Field Officers all being about—I have been acting as one on this trip, "consequently" am mounted. We are having some very cold weather—but our Boys are all pretty well clothed. We have enough clothing, Blankets etc. stowed away down in Geo. if we can only get them. If nothing happens I will be at home this winter, if we go into "Quarters" near Corinth I shall try for a furlough. If I can not get that I *shall* resign. There is some talk of all the "Trans Miss troops" being furloughed this winter, but I have but little confidence in it. If they do not get furloughs I fear a great many will desert & go anyway, though I do not think a single man of *my Co* will go without leave. I have not rec'd any letters from you all written since about 1st Aug. Rec'd one the other day from Tom Ewing written 27th Sept. In it he writes you all had heard that I was wounded. I do not see how such reports start, as I have not been "scratched" on the campaign. We have heard that Gen'l Price was recently defeated in Mo. I do hope it is not so.[12] We hear no news where we are. Do not Know whether the Yankees have left Atlanta or not.[13] Have heard they had evacuated the place, but I do not believe it. I suppose they will be compelled to leave there shortly. I am on duty to day & must close this. Will write you all every chance & all of you must do the same. I do hope this will find you all well etc.

My Love to all,
Yr affectionate Son
Alex E. Spence

please direct   Co. "B" 1st Ark. Regt.
Govans Brigade
Cleburnes Division
Cheathams Corps
Army Tenn.
• • •

Camp 1st Ark. Regt.
Near Tuscumbia Ala. Nov. 11th 1864

Dear Father & Mother—

    Mr. Barksdale the Courier for Reynolds Ark Brig has just arrived bringing letters from Arks—& says he will wait here one hour for us to write back, so by being brief I can write you.[14] I expected some letters from you all by the courier, but am disappointed—he says he goes to

Arkadelphia, & why it is you all do not write me, I cant account for. The last letter I rec'd from any of you was written by "Pete" in August. I have written you all very often—wrote you only 4 or 5 days ago & I trust some of my letters will reach you. Ere this reaches you you will have learned our Army has left Georgia. We reached this place about 2 weeks ago & have been expecting to cross the Tenn River every day, but owing to a want of supplies have not yet crossed—Everything is now in readiness & I guess we will cross tomorrow or next day. Tis said our destination is Nashville, Tenn. I can't think we will remain in Tenn long—because the Federals are moving nearly all their forces there the general belief is we will only make a raid in Middle Tenn to draw our supplies for the winter & that we will get back to Corinth & go into winter quarters. Of one thing certain we are going to have a hard trip. It is getting pretty late for us to start, but may be it will pay. We are having some very disagreeable weather. It is very cold & then rains every day or two. I am pretty well fixed for the trip "a new pair of boots & a good suit of clothes." Genl Hood has got the Army in good fighting trim "marching trim"—only one wagon allowed to carry two Regiments, consequently every one is required to "carry his all." Our Baggage was all sent off last spring & summer & has all been "captured or lost." If there is any possible chance I will be at home this winter. You may look for me. Do not be too certain on my coming. I may not be able to do so. If chance to get a Furlough I am pretty sure I can resign & will do so if possible. I will certainly be able to get some one off from my Company this winter. If I do not get to go home I suppose I can hear from you all oftener when we get to Miss. We were in about six or 7 miles of Mooresville Ala where Uncle Joe lives not long since.[15] The Yankees were in there. I was not able to go to see him. This part of Alabama is about deserted. Very few people living between here & Decatur & what few that are here don't rejoice much at our coming. We hope for "better greetings" though when we get to Tenn. My Company is pretty small. 21 is "all told" of those along with us now. We were consolidated for awhile with another Company but there was some objection & I got it broke up. What few of the Boys that are present are all in good health & have stood the trip fine. We have never yet learned whether Norris & Johnston reached home safely or not. I hope they did. I am on duty today, besides my time is about up, so I must close. My Kindest Regards to Mr. Hearn & Sallie, Mr. Elder, Pete & Miss Sarah Ann—and tell them I write *to all* in *one letter* & think they could all write me much oftener than they do. The Gent who carries this makes regular trips to Arks & back—you can write by him. Will write you all every chance. Write me all the news, how you are getting along etc. I hope this will find you all well. This is written in great haste & you must excuse it.

My Love to all,
Yr affectionate Son
Alex E. Spence

Co. "B" 1st Ark. Regt.
Govans Brig. Cleburnes Div.
Cheathams Corps, Army, Tenn.

• • •

The courier Barksdale also carried letters home for another Arkadelphia resident, James M. Candler of the Second Arkansas Mounted Rifles (Dismounted). The presence of these letters in the Spence Family Collection may indicate that they were never delivered to Candler's father.

Nov 11th 1864
Camp Near Tuscumbia Ala
My Esteamed friend,
It tis with the greatest of pleasure that I seat my self to day to drop you a few lines to let you know that I am well at this time and I hope when these few lines gets to hand, they will find you enjoying the same blessing. You, I have nothing that would interest at this time, But the army is in good spirits at this time. Mr. Spence, Alex Spence was over to see me a few days ago. He is well. We have had a hard campaign of it. General JB Hood did tear up the Rail Road up from Kenneesaw Mountain to Dalton. Burnt all the cross ties and Bent all the iron And captured 700 hundred negros & 800 hundred yankees and Kill 7 negros and a Bout 600 yankees in the forts on the road and mules and wagons and men. It tis reported that we will go in to Tenneesee, But I dont think now that we will go. Sherman is Brought some of his force Back to Chattanooga Tenn. I think we will go in to winter quarters soon. Mr. Spence I have writen 2 or 3 letters to you. I have not recived 1. I want you to take the letters out of the ofice for me and keep them till you See father. I dont Know Who to write to. I think you will Be the Best one to write too. I have writen 1 to Cousin Nancy Hawkens, a Bout 12 miles from Arkadelphia. I want her to get the letter.[16]

I have not much to write this time and so I will bring this to a close for this time. I remain your friend till death. You will direct your letters to James M Candler in Co. F, 2nd Ark Reg, Reynolds Brig.

James M Candler[17]
To Mr. Spence

• • •

Nov 11th 1864 Camp in the field

A few lines to father. If you see him, you will please give this to him for
me.
My Dear father and Mother and Sister,
    I take this great oportunity of wrighting you a few lines to let you
Know that I am well at this time. I hope when this gets to hand, they will
find you all well. I Recived a letter from you. I did not get 1 this time by
Barksdle. Father, I [know] nothing that would interest you at this time,
But we had a hard march a Bout 400 hundred miles. We captured a hundred negros and 700 hundred And a great many of wagons and men. Kill
7 Negros and a Bout 600 hundred yankees.
I think Sherman lost was a bout 115 thousand kill and wounded. From
Dalton [page 2, at top is written, "Reynolds Brig. Walthall Div.] to Atlanta
Ga. Our lost a bout 10 thousand kill. We have had a great many
wounded. I have writen a letter to cousin William Candler in few days to
go. General forest has captured 14 transports and 4 gunboats and 4 barges
loaded with clothing for the yankees.[18] If you see cousin Nancy
Hawkens, tell her if she will go to Arkadelphia, she will find letters there
from me. I have written 2 or 3. I have recived 1 from you and uncle
William freman all so.[19] We will move in a few days as it tis Reported that
we will go in to Tenneesee, But I dont think so. I think we will go in to
winter quarters soon. I will bring this to a close. After this time I will
write again. I think I will Get a furlough this winter.
    James M. Candler
To JS. N Candler[20]

Direct to Co F 2nd Ark
    • • •

Hood's army headed north in a sleet storm on November 20, and four
days later Cleburne visited his old friend, the First Arkansas's former
brigadier Lucius Polk at the general's "Hamilton Place" plantation in
Tennessee. Hood sought to get between thirty thousand Union troops commanded by Maj. Gen. John M. Schofield and an equal number of Yankees
under George Thomas at Nashville. Schofield fell back from Pulaski,
Tennessee, to Columbia on the Duck River, and Hood sent two divisions,
including Cleburne's, to hit his rear and cut him off from Nashville. At
Spring Hill, on November 29, the Rebels encountered two divisions
Schofield had rushed there to stymie Hood's plan. As the Rebels formed up
for the attack, Cleburne was warned that the Yankees appeared to be preparing to charge. "I'll charge them!" the general roared. Govan's brigade, along

Gen. John Schofield slipped his Federal army past the Army of Tennessee at Spring Hill, Tennessee, then occupied strong fortifications on the Harpeth River at Franklin. Schofield's successful maneuver enraged Confederate commander John Bell Hood, who ordered a full-scale frontal assault on the Yankee position. (Courtesy of the Old State House Museum)

with Mark Lowrey's, moved against Federal brigadier general Mark Bradley's Yankees on the Union right between 3:30 and 4:00 P.M. Despite being hammered by Yankee artillery, the Southerners slammed into Bradley and sent the Federals fleeing, the pursuing Rebels shouting, "Halt, you Yankee sons-of-bitches!" By the time Granbury's Texans had run off two

This view from Winstead Hill shows the wide plain that the Army of Tennessee had to traverse to assault the heavily fortified Union army at Franklin. After viewing the field, Gen. Daniel C. Govan told Cleburne, "Well, General, there will not be many of us that get back to Arkansas," to which the Irishman replied, "Well, Govan, if we are to die, let us die like men." (Courtesy of Carter House Museum)

particularly troublesome cannon and Cleburne had reordered his lines, darkness fell and the attack was called off. The inconclusive fighting at Spring Hill cost the Rebels around 500 casualties, the Yankees about 350. Hood's troops failed to block the Franklin and Columbia Turnpike, and Schofield slipped the remainder of his troops past the Confederate camps that night, falling back to entrenchments protecting crossings of the Harpeth River at Franklin.[21]

Hood was enraged at Schofield's escape from his trap and intended to crush the Union army on the banks of the Harpeth before it could link up with Thomas at Nashville. The Confederate commander determined to conduct a full frontal assault on the entrenched Yankees. Cleburne, who had received much of Hood's ire for the previous day's failure at Spring Hill, told his leader, "I will take the enemy's works or die in the attempt." The works were formidable, completely surrounding the town of Franklin with both ends anchored on the Harpeth River. To reach them, the Confederate army would have to cross one and one-half miles of flat, open ground, all the while under artillery and rifle fire. Govan told Cleburne, "Well, General, there will not be many of us that get back to Arkansas," to which the Irishman replied, "Well, Govan, if we are to die, let us die like men."[22]

By 3 P.M. on November 30, the Confederates were in formation, some twenty thousand soldiers in nine brigades forming a line two miles wide, their flags flying and bands playing martial airs. Cleburne's division formed the center of this host, with Govan's Arkansians, including the First and Fifteenth Arkansas Regiment, marching between the regiments of Granbury and Lowrey. Cleburne told his men to hold their fire, close fast, and "use the bayonet." At 4 P.M., the Army of Tennessee moved forward with brigade bands playing "The Bonny Blue Flag" as they approached the twenty-two thousand Federal troops and their three lines of entrenchments.[23] Union artillery began slamming into the advancing Rebels, tearing great holes in their lines. Cleburne halted his division when about four hundred yards from the enemy, moving them into line from their column formation. The Rebels charged, driving the advance line of Yankees before them as Cleburne cried, "We will go into the works with them!" The fleeing Yankees and charging Confederates became intermingled as they approached the Federal lines in front of Fountain Branch Carter's house and cotton gin. The Union defenders held their fire for fear of hitting their own men but finally let loose a volley. Cleburne, with two horses shot from beneath him, charged forward on foot, waving his sword over his head. The Arkansians and Texans of Govan's and Granbury's brigades crashed into the Yankee earthworks, climbing over them and closing with the men of the 100th and 104th Ohio Infantry, who broke under the attack of the howling Southerners. Cleburne rushed toward the breach and fell dead fifty yards short of the Yankee lines, a bullet through his heart.[24] Cleburne's men seized the cannon of the First Kentucky Battery and attempted to turn them against the Yankees, but the fleeing gunners had taken their primers with them, rendering the guns useless.[25] The Union brigades of Col. Emerson Opdycke and Brig. Gen. James W. Reilly launched a slashing counterattack and the fighting became a furious, hand-to-hand battle for the breach in the Federal lines.[26] Granbury fell dead, a Yankee bullet blowing out the back of his head. The Rebels were forced to the outside of the earthwork, the Yankees held the inside, and the men continued firing at each other at point-blank range until around 10 P.M., when both sides fell back from the carnage at the breach.[27] Furious fighting elsewhere along the Federal entrenchments also petered out with no substantial gains being realized by the attacking Confederates. Schofield's men again slipped away in the darkness, leaving the field to Hood.[28]

The Battle of Franklin was an unmitigated disaster for the Confederacy. More than seven thousand of the twenty thousand or so

Rebel soldiers who took part in the grand assault on Franklin were dead, wounded, or missing. Govan wrote after the battle, "Our div. was decimated—losing one half of its officers and men. That I am left alive . . . is due alone to a 'Special Providence.'" Capt. Samuel T. Foster of Granbury's brigade wrote in his diary of Franklin's aftermath: "Our Brigd and the Ark. Brigd are so badly cut up that we can't move. Some officers have no men, and some companies have [no?] officers—So we have to reorganize and consolidate, a Captain has to command the Brigade. . . . the wails and cries of widows and orphans made at Franklin Tenn Nov 30th 1864 will heat up the fires of the bottomless pit to burn the soul of Gen J B Hood for Murdering their husbands and fathers at that place that day. It can't be called anything else but cold blooded Murder." In addition, to Cleburne and Granbury, four other Confederate generals died in the battle. Among the Rebel casualties were sixty-five division, brigade, or regimental commanders, including fourteen within Cleburne's division. Schofield, on the other hand suffered only 2,613 casualties, of whom only 189 were listed as killed.[29]

Like so many of his comrades in Govan's regiment, Alex Spence, too, lay dead on the field at Franklin.

Writing years after the battle, Lt. M. M. Sanders of Company B, First Arkansas Infantry Regiment, remembered the horrors of the battlefield at Franklin and shared those memories with the readers of the *Arkadelphia Southern Standard:*

> At the dreadful battle of Franklin, Tenn., the fearful loss of life here, beyond the most terrific scenes of battle array, almost forbids us to call it a battle. Our last Captain, the young, the brave, the high toned Alex. Erskine Spence, was a victim of this memorable field of strife. . . . It was said that the Company only bore one gun from this awful carnage. The destruction was so great, yet it must be remembered, our dear old company did not lose many men in this, of all battles, the most terrible. The crimson from chivalrous sons, simply stained the field with color so heart rendering it can never be forgotten by those present.[30]

Epilogue

"Many painful reminiscences are connected . . ."

With the death of Alex Spence, this story draws to a close. The remnants of the First Arkansas continued the 1864 Tennessee campaign, remaining under Govan as part of a brigade comprised of the survivors of five regiments, counting only 534 in its ranks men when it attacked George Thomas's lines at Nashville on December 15.[1] In fighting the next day, Govan's luck ran out as he was hit in the throat and his brigade disintegrated, as did the Army of Tennessee as an effective fighting force.[2] The First Arkansas's survivors wintered in Mississippi, as Spence had conjectured. The next spring, the regiment was in South Carolina, once again under the command of Joseph E. Johnston. Johnston's army moved into North Carolina, colliding with Sherman at Bentonville on March 19, 1865. Retreating to Smithfield, the First Arkansas was consolidated with ten other skeletal Arkansas regiments that were placed under the command of Col. A. E. Howell.[3] Finally, on April 27, 1865, at Greensboro, North Carolina, Johnston surrendered his army. The long journey of the First Arkansas was at an end.[4]

Tom Spence's old unit, the Second Arkansas Mounted Rifles, also saw much action after his death at Murfreesboro, participating in twenty-four battles, sieges, and campaigns. The unit was consolidated with the First Arkansas Mounted Rifles (Dismounted), the Fourth Infantry Battalion, and the Fourth, Ninth and Twenty-Fourth Infantry Regiment at Smithfield, North Carolina, on April 9, 1865. The Second Arkansas's few survivors also surrendered at Greensboro on April 27, 1865.[5]

Alex Spence left a grieving family behind in Arkadelphia, but also a fiancée in Georgia. Two years after his death, Amanda Willson wrote Alex's sister, Sallie Hearn:

Madison Nov. 30th 1866
Mrs. Hearn,
    My dear friend,
    I don't know that you would care to hear from me, but I cant refrain from writing. I have written frequently to you but no reply. It may be your silence is from the fact that you have failed to receive my letters.

That knowledge would be much pleasanter that to think I had been forgotten by you. I have been in my room alone all day, vainly dreaming of the past. With the 30th of Nov., many painful reminiscences are connected. Two years ago today has it been since that dark *dark* shadow crossed my pathway and I was left with a blighted heart to mourn the loss of one whom I had learned to idolize. It is wrong in me to indulge painful memories, but it is a feeling I cannot if I would dispell. As long as life shall last, my mind will revert to the past. I have just taken from my trunk a bundle of letters and read them over as I used so often to do when I was sad. Some of my friends have wondered why I keep them, but these dear mementoes will ever occupy their accustomed place in my trunk. While reading them, I thought perhaps you would like to read one among his last, so I have concluded to enclose the one next to the last. It would be such a great pleasure for me to see and talk with you all. I have a brother who is going to your state soon. Mother has given her consent for me to go to see you, but father thinks it too far. I hope at some time in the future I may be permitted to make you a visit.

Mrs. Pharr (an acquaintance of yours, I presume) is now living here. She was once a resident of your town. She has joined the church since her removal to Madison. She has a bright little boy and seems to be doing well.[6] How is Mr. Ellis of your place coming on? We have often thought of him and wondered where he was. If you have ever met him, I imagine he has given you a description of your unknown friend.[7] I hope it will not be long before I have the pleasure of hearing from you. Remember me very kindly to your father, mother and family.
Believe me truly,
    Your aff. friend,
    Amanda Willson[8]

Alex Spence's body was recovered after the Battle of Franklin and returned to Arkadelphia, where it rests today next to that of his brother, Tom, in Rose Hill Cemetery.[9]

Alex Spence's body was recovered after the battle of Franklin and brought home to Arkadelphia. The Spence brothers, Alex and Tom, are buried side by side in Arkadelphia's Rose Hill Cemetery. (Courtesy of the Old State House Museum)

Appendix 1

The Poison Spring Letter

Neither Alex nor Tom Spence wrote one of the most significant letters in the Spence Family collection. In fact, its signature is torn from the last page. The letter recounts, from someone who was there, the battle of Poison Spring near Camden, Arkansas, in 1864.

Poison Spring was one of the major battles that occurred in the Camden Expedition, an ill-fated attempt by Maj. Gen. Frederick Steele's Federal army in Arkansas to pass through the southwestern portion of the state to link up with another Union army under Nathaniel Banks in Louisiana and establish a free soil cotton-growing colony in Texas. Steele's army left Little Rock on March 23, 1864, into a region ravaged and picked clean of forage by three years of war and the hungry Confederate army in southwest Arkansas. After skirmishing on April 10 through 13 with Rebel troops at Prairie D'Ane near present-day Prescott, Steele, joined by a separate column out of Fort Smith under Brig. Gen. John M. Thayer, abandoned his drive south and occupied Camden on the Ouachita River. Banks was equally unsuccessful in his attempts in Louisiana.[1]

On April 17, 1864, Steele sent a detail under Col. James M. Williams, commanding officer of the First Kansas Colored Infantry, with 198 wagons to seize five thousand bushels of corn located sixteen miles west of Camden to feed his hungry army. Though Confederate troops destroyed half of the corn, Williams seized the remainder, and his 1,170 Kansans, Iowans, and Hoosiers headed back toward Camden on the morning of April 18. Brig. Gen. John Sappington Marmaduke, commanding a force of more than 3,600 Arkansians, Missourians, Texans, and Choctaw Indians, deployed his troops near Poison Spring on the Upper Washington Road to stop them. Marmaduke deployed his Arkansas troops to block the road to Camden, placing his Texans, Missourians, and Choctaws south of the road in position to strike the wagon train in the flank. Discovering the road blocked, Williams rushed the First Kansas Colored to the front of the column, where they established an L-shaped line to protect the head and south side of the supply train. After fighting off two Confederate attacks, the First Kansas fell back before a third and joined the other survivors of Williams's command in a fighting withdrawal to the north and eventual retreat toward Camden.[2]

With the retreat of the Union column, the nightmare began for the wounded and captured soldiers of the First Kansas Colored Infantry. The Southerners, already angry about former slaves taking up arms against them, were enraged to find the Yankee wagons filled not only with corn but also "stolen bed quilts, women's and children's clothing, hogs, geese, and all the *et ceteras* of unscrupulous plunder." In addition, at least one Rebel unit, the Twenty-ninth Texas Cavalry, had faced and been defeated by the Kansas unit the previous summer at Honey Spring in the Indian Territory. The Confederate victors now roamed the battlefield, shooting the wounded blacks and calling out, "Where's the First Nigger now?" "All cut to pieces and gone to hell by bad management!" Many Southern soldiers recounted the aftermath of the battle in chilling detail in the days and years following the battle, and the casualty list bears witness to the fate of the hapless First Kansas: Of 301 Union casualties at Poison Spring, 182 were from the First Kansas Colored Infantry, and 117 of them were killed. Such a high proportion of fatal casualties as opposed to wounded was highly unusual in Civil War combat.[3] Steele's army suffered the loss of another supply train at Marks' Mills a week after Poison Spring and soon abandoned Camden, fighting a sharp battle at Jenkins' Ferry on April 30 while escaping across the swollen Saline River to retreat to the safety of Little Rock.

George May (right) of Company E, Second Arkansas Mounted Rifles, was captured by Union troops at the battle of Pea Ridge, according to Tom Spence's letter about the battle. May served with the unit until 1864, when he deserted and returned to Arkansas. He was soon under arms once again and was killed at the battle of Poison Spring, Arkansas, in 1864. (Courtesy of the South Arkansas Regional Archives)

Among those writing of the battle of Poison Spring was a correspondent of Sallie Hearn, whose husband and brother were among the Arkansians who fought there:

Camp 9 miles E of Camden
Ouachita Co April 20th

Dear Sallie,

Its now night and have just learned that a Mr. Moore would start home in the morning soon, so I write by the fire light. We have been annoying the Feds ever since leaving Arkadelphia. The day after I wrote you last, we were (that is, our Co) marched up in the Prairie to support a battery. No one in the Co hurt, one man killed and few wounded near us, some fifty yards off. The cannon balls would strike the ground in front of us and bound over the company. Could see them for a hundred yds before they struck the ground. The Feds the night after moved in direction of Camden and now occupy the place with a large force, the number I have had no reliable means of ascertaining, but they have reinforced since they came through Arkadelphia.[4] On Monday last, the 18th, we had a fight at the Poison Springs on the Camden and Washington road, 15 miles from Camden. A forughing [foraging] party variously estimated from 2 to 4 thousand we attacked at 12 Oclock by cannonading and then by small arms which lasted for three hours in the enemy was completed routed. Capturing 200 waggons and about 1250 mules and killed from 4 to 6 hundred and captured about 100 hundred prisoners. It was running fight. They were chased by the souldiers that we were with about three miles on foot and then the cavelory took them in hand and dont now know how far they pursued. I have said Fed yes of deepest dye negroes. I think there were 10 negroes killed to one white Fed. Just as I had said before, they made the negroes go in front and if the negro was wounded, our men would shoot him dead as they were passed and what negroes that were captured have, from the best information I can obtain, since been shot. I have seen enough myself to know it is correct our men is determine not to take negro prisoners, and if all of the negroes could have seen what occured that day, they would stay at home. What I have seen reminds me of the talk I gave Henry and John. They may have been there as I have had no information as yet from home. If so, they are convinced by this time. (I cant believe that either went.)[5] Among the killed was Dr. Rowlands Clabe and Kyles Berry and old man Edwards' boy was captured.[6] I have told how they were disposed off. From the best information, we lost about one hundred & sixty killed and wounded. A small portion killed; among them was George May, all the one that I knew.[7] None of our company hurt its quite fortunate yet we were in the fight all

the time and boys done well. Some few of them sick; none dangerous.
None that we Know except Ed. Hicthcock [*sic*], nothing cerious with
him.[8] We have been reinforced by infantry estimated at from 10 to 12
thousand. They are now in striking distance and there will be a move
soon I predict to try Mr. Steel. Three days rations ordered to be cooked.
This is done at the waggons and sent us. Would not be supprised we
started by daylight in the morning. This I only have to judge from
extreme circumstances, Although I am almost certain they will make no
attack in Camden, owing to fortifications made by our own men last
winter and faul. It is said to be well fortified and, of course, there will be
no attack against works.

Read this to Henry and John and it will remind them of what I told
them. This leaves me in fine health. Am quite anxious to hear from you,
to learn all the news about Arkadelphia. Take it for granted . . . [portion
illegible] . . . destroyed a great [?] of property as they had feather beds
and all the comforts about ones house in their waggons. Clothing, etc.
Now is the time . . . [page torn] . . . theives to in that country since both .
. . [page torn] . . . miss are gone. I expect [steeling?] . . . [page torn] . . . on
at a rapid rate. It is not . . . [page torn] . . . to tell you [portion illegible and
page torn] . . . [V? C.?] would . . . [page torn] . . . it has been talk . . . [page
torn] . . . for me it . . . [page torn] . . . since I left . . . [page torn].

The remainder of the letter, including the signature, is torn away.

Who wrote this letter to Sallie Hearn? By late April 1864, Tom Spence
had been killed in battle and Alex Spence was fighting William Tecumseh
Sherman's Yankees in the mountains of Tennessee and Georgia. However,
two members of the extended Spence family remained in Arkansas
throughout the war: Alfred G. Hearn, Sallie's husband, and Dudley Spence,
her brother. Both men enlisted in Confederate service later in the war than
did the younger Spence brothers, perhaps in part because they were considerably older than Alex and Tom. (Dudley Spence was thirty-nine in
1860 and A.G. Spence was thirty-four.) They joined a cavalry troop that
was raised in Clark County in late 1863, serving in Capt. Reuben C. Reed's
company of Col. Robert C. Newton's Tenth Arkansas Cavalry, a unit that
is not included in the National Archives' Compiled Service Records. When
Steele invaded South Arkansas in 1864, this unit was attached to William
"Old Tige" Cabell's cavalry regiment, which was within the command of
Alex Spence's original colonel, James F. Fagan, now a brigadier general of
cavalry. Reed's company was present at Poison Spring, and both Dudley
Spence and Alfred Hearn probably would have been present.[9] However,
postwar records of the Freedmen's Bureau provide evidence that Hearn

was the probable author of the letter. There are two references to "Henry and John" and the author's admonitions toward them about the dangers of military life for black soldiers, indicating the two men mentioned were family slaves. On January 1, 1866, Freedmen's Bureau records show that Justice of the Peace P. M. Carmichael married John Hearn to Tempy Spence. Given the practice that many ex-slaves took the last names of their former masters after emancipation, this John Hearn could be the same John mentioned in the Poison Spring letter, indicating that Alfred G. Hearn wrote the October 9, 1864, letter to his wife, Sallie.[10]

Regardless of who wrote the Poison Spring letter, it provides testimony to one of the darkest chapters in Arkansas's involvement in the Civil War.

Appendix 2

Thomas Spence's Eulogy

On June 18, 1875, the *Arkadelphia Southern Standard* reprinted a lengthy eulogy delivered ten years earlier when the body of Capt. Thomas F. Spence, Second Arkansas Mounted Rifles (Dismounted) was reburied at Rose Hill Cemetery in Arkadelphia.[1]

As we had no Decoration Day at this place, there being but few Confederate soldiers who lost their lives during the war buried here, we give place today to the very eloquent and touching eulogy delivered by Hon. H. B. Stuart on the occasion of the reburial by the Masonic fraternity, in this city, of Capt. THOMAS F. SPENCE, in December, 1865. Capt. Spence was a brave and true soldier of the "Lost Cause," and was killed while gallantly leading his men to victory at the battle of Murfreesboro. At the request of the many friends of the heroic dead, we re-produce this feeling tribute to his memory, having been kindly furnished with the only copy known to be extant by the venerable mother of the deceased.[2]

Eulogy on Capt. T. F. Spence[3]
Arkadelphia, Ark., Dec 30th, 1865
Hon. H. B. Stuart:
    Dear Sir and Brother:—the undersigned committee on behalf of Arkadelphia Lodge No. 19, would respectfully ask of you a copy of your Eulogy delivered on the funeral occasion of Bro. T. F. Spence, for publication.
    Yours Very Respectfully,
    And Fraternally
W. SMITH
JOE H. THOMAS
P. M. CARMICHAEL

Arkadelphia, Ark., Dec. 30th, 1865

Brothers:—Your note requesting a copy of the remarks made by me on the funeral occasion of Brother T. F. Spence is before me. (The subject and circumstances alone induce me to comply with the wishes of the Lodge, and I herewith place a copy at your disposal.)

Fraternally Yours

H. B. STUART

I. W. Smith, Joe H. Thomas and P. M. Carmichael. Committee

Friends and Fellow Citizens—The circumstances that have convened and called us together today are of such a sad and mournful character that every heart in this community must be touched and moved with the deep solemnity of the occasion.

Divines tell us, and truly so, that upon all funeral occasions, that whatever our actions may be in performing these funeral rites it can not alter the condition of the dead. The orator on these occasions may stir the living by his eloquent and sympathetic appeals, but it stirs no emotion of the dead, the dead still sleep on. He may heap eulogy after eulogy, mountain high, up on the character of the deceased and still the dead sleep on. The winter's wind may sigh and howl its mournful requiem and still the dead sleep on. The gentle summer breeze sprinkled and softened by the sweetest dews of heaven passes by and still the dead sleep on. Strains of martial and soul-searching music may be brought into requisition, it falls upon a listless ear, and the dead still sleeps on. "The night winds sigh, the breakers roar, and shrieks the wild sea mew," it disturbs on ocean-sleeper, and the dead sleeps on. The thunder of the cannon's roar and the cloud's fire shock of the warring element may meet in high carnival, it disturbs not death's sleeper, the dead sleep on. "The lightening may flash and the loud thunder rattles, the hero lies still, he fears them not, he heeds them not, he is free from all pain he sleeps his last sleep, he has fought his battle, no sound can awake him to glory again."

Nor do we of the Masonic Fraternity propose to alter the condition of the dead; our object should be and is to testify our regard for departed worth, and if possible to benefit the living. And in connection with the community at large, the fraternity of masons, as an order, claim it as a priviledge to meet to-day and to share in paying a last tribute of respect to a good citizen, a gallant gentleman, a brave soldier, and a worthy mason. Few men of his age were more generally known in this community than

Capt. Thomas F. Spence, to whose memory we have met today for the purpose of testifying our sincere regard and whose mortal remains we are soon to return to their mother earth. As a child and boy he made early and lasting impressions of his superior endowments, and his respectful demeanor while a youth to his superiors in age, strongly indicated his excellence in manhood. As a man young in years, he met the expectations of his friends, and demonstrated what his youth had promised, a useful and honorable member in society. Free, just generous and liberal in manhood's early dawn, he was surrounded by a circle and host of friends ready to share any adversity and with all their means and ability to aid his promotion and prosperity. Few indeed are the men in this life at his age that have had the honor to enjoy the confidence of old and young, rich and poor, so completely as did Capt. Spence, and as a man and citizen without spot or blemish, his name, his memory, his character will ever be remembered, while there is gratitude in the hearts of his countrymen. As a civil officer, the mass of people of this Clark County, more than once expressed their confidence and admiration of his superior abilities as an executive and civil officer, and I can only refer you to his acts, and those now living who came in contact with him in the discharge of his duty as an officer. Prompt, punctual and candid, kind and generous, he soon won the confidence of the people, by the faithful and impartial manner he acted to each and every citizen in the discharge of the duties of his office. And he left the Sheriff's office of Clark County, perhaps the most popular man that ever held it; such at least, is my impression

As a soldier, his rank, his name is written, and will continue to be written, with "the bravest of the brave." Napoleon the Great, who was seldom mistaken in his judgement and estimate of the character of men, in passing one of the highest compliments to a scar-worn veteran of a hundred battle fields, and perhaps the highest compliment ever heaped upon the character of a brave and gallant soldier, did it in the few words that I have just quoted: Marshal Ney was in his opinion, and with his opportunity to judge the thousands and tens-of-thousand soldiers that rallied beneath the eagles of the Mighty Emperor, "the bravest of the brave." And in forming our estimate of character, we are to consider, weigh well all the circumstances connected with each individual case, and then to see what are the evidences to be deduced therefrom. Marshal Ney, "the bravest of the brave," according to the Emperor Napoleon's standard of judging, remained a private in the French Army for a considerable period of time and rose slowly to distinction in the beginning of his military career. Capt. Spence, in this respect, made more rapid strides, than "the bravest of the brave" in his profession of arms.

The brave are always just generous and as such never fail to win the confidence love and respect of their companions in arms. The army of all other places and positions, is said to be the severest ordeal the character of man passes through, to test his integrity for truth, veracity and honor, and if he undergoes the trial of the camp life, which all its scenes subject him to, he is said to be truly tested.

The battle field had no terrors that could daunt Capt. Spence—the thunder of the cannon's roar only stirred the inner man and nerved him to the onset, as a volunteer citizen soldier, he proudly and heroically led his command in the blaze of every battle. Exempt from military service by the commission he held as a civil officer, but when he believed his country needed, and demanded soldiers, there was no sacrifice that he was not ready to make, and as a private he entered the Confederate Army. Soon the courage of the young soldier was to be tested upon the bloody and hard fought battle of Oak Hill; there for the first time, he was to witness the rush of hostile armies; there for the first time, he met the battle shock; there for the first time, he heard the cannon's roar; the cries of the dying and wounded, the shouts of victory, the battle won. During the long hours of this battle, Capt. Spence seemed to bear a charmed life, at the head and in front of his command, by word and deed, he powerfully aided in holding his comrades on to the contest until the last turned foe disappeared from the contest. At Elk Horn he gallantly sustained his former reputation. When ordered to the Cis-Mississippi Department, without reluctance or murmur, he rendered cheerful obedience to the demands of his Government. Unscathed and unhurt, he passed through the battles of Richmond and Farmington. Soon, alas, the battle of Murfreesboro was to be fought. And with it, the young and gallant soldier's career on earth terminated, and his spirit fled upward to meet the God of battles.

As ever in the battle leading his men in the thickest and hottest of the fight he fell mortally wounded; in his expiring moments, in the last agonies of death, upon the threshold of eternity, unable to articulate a single word, with his finger he pointed his fellow-soldiers to the ranks of the enemy. Not a word of farewell to father or mother was allowed him, not a word he could utter to his grief stricken comrades, who crowded around him to take a last farewell look at the warrior in death. Truly may we say of him "that he asked no stone to be sculptured in verse, he asked not that fame should his merits rehearse," but it was him that could truly ask that his countrymen might know "that he fell like a soldier, he died at his post." Thus in the vigor of manhood's early dawn, in its bud and bloom, Capt. Spence passed from earth to eternity. The earth will soon claim its own, "Let the dust return to the dust and the spirit of God who gave it." I have briefly and imperfectly referred to Capt. Spence as a youth and citizen in the social circle, as a civil officer in the discharge of his duty, and as a soldier in the camps and upon the battle field; I have done so, in terms not satisfactory to myself; and, I fear not at all so to this enlightened and sympathizing audience. I come not to apply the square, the compass, the gavel and the plumbline, to speak of him as a Mason. In the brief review I have made of his character and memory as a citizen and soldier, I have done so in simple and plain language, and without partiality or prejudice, and I have been unable to discover a solitary blot, defect or blemish. As a Mason, his certificate of respectability and standing is endorsed by every heart here today that loves the great principles of virtue and morality taught in Masonry. And the presence of the Order today, draped in mourning, is abundant proof upon this point and that every Mason present feels that he has lost a friend, brother and a true Mason.

The Masonic Fraternity, as an Order, have ever professed to act with candor, avoiding hypocrisy and deceit, and this means besides many other things that we are not to withhold our admiration and praise wherever it may be due, and in the same spirit of candor, we are to censure and point out the faults and fallings of an erring brother, and hence our coming together today, that they may testify to the world that Masons delight to honor a brother, who has left no trace on earth that he was ever unfaithful to the trust confided in him as a Mason. Truly, we may say of Capt. Spence, not only as a Mason, but in all the relations of his life that he was "often tried, never denied," and on all occasions "found worthy and well qualified" for the various positions assigned him in life. Every Mason, every good citizen here today must feel proud of the character of a man and brother who through life sustained all the principles of truth and honor that characterize the gentleman, soldier and Mason. True to one of many virtues that the first lessons of Masonry teaches and nothing could be more beneficial to the community at large, the race of man than to always observe the truth. Speak the truth, speak no evil of thy brother behind his back or before his face; would that we could ever recollect and feel this important injunction we should then live in peace and dwell in harmony, and like Capt. Spence, whose example we should remember and imitate, we should be respected in life and our memory cherished in death as one of the benefactors of the human race. Speak no evil of thy brother; how this should ring upon our ears, and touch and move every heart. Does this injunction apply alone to thy brother of the mystic tie? If so, the teaching of the time honored and ancient institution of Masonry that has been and still is respected by the purest and best men of every land and clime would not have reached us in its original purity and simplicity. Speak no evil of thy brother. This injunction is closely allied to the command of Christ, the searcher of all hearts. "Bless them that curse you," says Christ. Then, we are to speak no evil of a brother, but to speak no evil of them that hate and despitefully use us, for if we love those only that love us, we have no promise of any very great reward for such lover. Speak no evil of thy brother, and like Capt. Spence, your countrymen will love your memory, relish your deeds and imitate your example, and like him, your names may be written in character of light among the stars of heaven and thy memory, indelibly impressed upon the hearts of thy country's men.

Capt. Spence's life was short, and his young hopes blasted in the prime of youth, still, young as he was he has left a brilliant record behind, such as few of us may hope to be able to attain in the goodness of God's providence, our days may be protracted to the longest period of human existence.

When this war and blood drenched earth of ours shall have become quiet and peace and harmony prevail and our civil and political rights restored and all unnecessary excitement passes away, as it soon will, the historian, impartial and honest in recording the deeds of valor and renown of the living and the gallant dead of our unfortunate and unhappy struggle, will place thousands of names for heroism and gallantry, side by side with the father of his country and the hero of hermitage, and in that splendid gallaxy of names, the name of Capt. Thomas F. Spence will not be forgotten, but will appear in the same rank, in the same line of "the braves of the brave."

The scene we are now passing through forcibly impresses us with the certainty of death, and that death is constantly around and about us; the air we breathe and that constantly surrounds us, contains the elements of death, for the poet tells us that "death rides upon every passing breeze." The flowers that grow, and that are scattered along our pathway to animate and gladden the heart with their beauty and fragrance are also said to contain the elements of death; for the same poet tells us, that death not only rides upon the passing breeze, but "lurks within the bell of every flower." How sad my friends is the reflection that we too, soon, like the corpse before us, must sink into the arms of death, and in our cold and lifeless forms, forever slumber in the house of clay.

I cannot close my remarks, without saying to the citizens, that this occasion very naturally calls to our reflection, the scenes we have passed through the last four years. My advice to all citizens and Masons is to submit without a murmur, to the government you live in; it is our duty to do so and especially is the duty of every Mason to submit to the laws of the government in which we live, his obligations require it and we should never dishonor that obligation.

And now, in conclusion, what can I say to console the aged and venerable parents? I can say all that can be said of the good and upright man, all that is noble and pure, and how gratifying it must be to your hearts to see such a large and respectable audience in attendance, to share in the last tribute of respect to one you loved so well. If I had the divine power that Christ had, when he knelt at Lazarus' tomb, what a shout would ascend from this room; what a meeting here on earth; indeed it would be a heavenly scene. Then how consoling the thought that you may in the spirit land, see and live forever with your dear child that has gone before you. And now, as the sun has nearly gone down on your pathway, and the twilight of your years have come, had I the power, I would bedeck the firmament of heaven with "stars so thick and bright, that your souls would sing and forget it's night."

Appendix 3

Solomon Spence's Obituary

The Spence Family Collection included a handwritten obituary marking the death of Solomon Spence Sr., who died on September 16, 1872.

Obituary

Died in the place on the 16th Sept, Solomon Spence in the 80 year of his age. He was born in Granville Co Va, 1793, emigrated to Ala when a teritory. United in marriage to Miss Frances Carethers in 1819 and in 1849 removed to Ark. Settled in Arkadelphia where he spent the remainder of his days. He was a soldier in the War of 1812. A man of strong predudices and firm principles. He never wavered. Lively and pleasant in social intercourse, ever a true friend of man.

A wife the companion of his early manhood and four children are left to mourn their loss. Indeed, he was a kind, affectionate husband, an indulgent, tender father. He endured his long afflictions with uncomplaining fortitude and patience, and when emaciated and wasted by disease with but little physical strength, he knew his end was nigh, earnestly began to trim and light his lamp and with it all ready, stood tottering on the verge of eternity until "his Savior, smiling, bid him come up higher." He was a member of the Methodist church, conscientious in all his acts.

The father of eleven children, seven of whom sleep in the tomb, two noble sons he laid upon the Southern alter and we alone of all, stood by to smooth his dying pillow, but now we can look up with joy and say my father's home in Heaven for "The light of God" shone from his face in an expression of peace & serenity as he talked about his pleasant home beond the Jordan of death and bid us all meet him in the kingdom of heaven.

Appendix 4

The Places They Fought

The First Arkansas Infantry Regiment and Second Arkansas Mounted Rifles fought at battlefields in Arkansas, Missouri, Mississippi, Alabama, Tennessee, Kentucky, Georgia and Virginia. Many of these places have been preserved as national, state, or local parks that now welcome visitors to sylvan scenes where once great armies clashed. Some of the battle sites where members of the Spence family fought are listed below.[1]

Arkansas
(For Arkansas tourism information, call 1-800-NATURAL.)
Pea Ridge National Military Park, P.O. Box 800, Pea Ridge, Ark. 72751-0700, located on Highway 62 about ten miles north of Rogers, Arkansas.
Poison Spring State Park, Highway 76, Bluff City, Ark. 71722, located on Highway 76 near Bluff City.

Georgia
(For Georgia tourism information, call 1–800-VISIT-GA.)
Pickett's Mill Battlefield State Historic Site, 2640 Mount Tabor Road, Dallas, Ga., 30132, located off Highway 92 via the Dallas-Acworth Road.
Chickamauga and Chattanooga National Military Park, P.O. Box 2128, Fort Oglethorpe, Ga. 20742, located on U.S. Highway 27 near the Tennessee state line.
Kennesaw Mountain National Battlefield Park, 905 Kennesaw Mountain Drive, Kennesaw, Ga. 30152, located off Interstate 75.

Kentucky
(For Kentucky tourism information, call 1-800-225-TRIP.)
Perryville Battlefield State Historic Site, P.O. Box 296, Highway 1920, Perryville, Ky. 40468-9999, located on state Highway 1920 .
Cumberland Gap National Historical Park, U.S. Highway 25E South, P.O. Box 1848, Middlesboro, Ky. 40965.

Missouri

(For Missouri tourism information, call 1-800-877-1234.)

Wilson's Creek National Battlefield, 6424 West Farm Road 182, Republic, Mo. 65738, located southwest of Springfield, Missouri.

Tennessee

(For Tennessee tourism information, call 1–800-TENN-200.)

Chickamauga and Chattanooga National Military Park/Lookout Mountain, Point Lookout Visitor Center, Lookout Mountain, Tenn. 37350, located on East Brow Road off State Highway 148 at Chattanooga.

The Carter House, 1140 Columbia Avenue, Franklin, Tenn. 37065, located off State Highway 31 South at Franklin.

Stones River National Battlefield, 3501 Old Nashville Highway, Murfreesboro, Tenn. 37129, located on Old Nashville Highway near Highway 41 at Murfreesboro.

Shiloh National Military Park, Route 1, Box 9, Shiloh, Tenn. 38376, located on Highway 22 north of Corinth, Mississippi.

Virginia

(For Virginia Civil War tourism information, call 1-888-CIVIL-WAR.)

Manassas National Battlefield Park, 6511 Sudley Road, Manassas, Va. 22110, located on Virginia Route 234, twenty-six miles southwest of Washington, D.C.

Notes

Introduction

1. Among the earliest settlers of the region were Jacob Barkman and John Hemphill, who settled in 1811 in Clark County. Barkman would establish a thriving shipping operation, carrying cargo back and forth to New Orleans via the Ouachita River; he also ran a vast cotton-growing operation. Hemphill would become the region's first industrialist, establishing a saltworks around 1814. The city originally was called Blakelytown, named for William Blakely, a blacksmith. The name was changed to Arkadelphia in the early 1840s, a name combining the words Arkansas and Philadelphia, by some accounts, or "arc" and Philadelphia, a "brotherly circle," by others. Arkadelphians gave a barbecue on April 2, 1842, the day of the vote for the location of the county seat, which may or may not have played a role in their city becoming the county seat. The courthouse was erected two years later and served Clark County for more than fifty years. By 1860, Baptists, Methodists and Presbyterians all had churches in Arkadelphia. The Arkansas Institute for the Blind was incorporated the same year and the people of Arkadelphia raised sixteen hundred dollars to establish it after state funding failed to materialize. Barbara Caffe, "Antebellum Arkansas 1800–1850," *Clark County Historical Journal* (spring 1980): 63–64, 66–67; John Gladden Hall, *Henderson State College: The Methodist Years 1890–1929* (Kingsport, Tenn.: Kingsport Press, 1974), 11–12; Wendy Richter, ed., *Clark County Arkansas: Past and Present* (Arkadelphia, Ark.: Walsworth Publishing Company, 1992), 59, 167; Clyde W. Cathey, "Slavery in Arkansas, Part 4: Fugitives," *Arkansas Historical Quarterly* 3, no. 2 (summer 1944): 163.

2. The Spence Hotel stood on Main Street between Fourth and Fifth Streets until it burned in 1872. *The Goodspeed Biographical and Historical Memoirs of Southern Arkansas* (Chicago and St. Louis: The Goodspeed Publishing Co., 1890), 173; Hall, *Henderson State College*, 13; Richter, ed., *Clark County Past and Present*, 155; Population Schedule [Free] of the Eighth Census of the United States, 1860, Arkansas, National Archives Microcopy No. 653, Rolls 25, 39 (cited hereafter as Arkansas 1860 Census); Population Schedule [Slave] of the Eighth Census of the United States, 1860, Arkansas, National Archives Microcopy No. 653, Rolls 6, 53 (cited hereafter as Arkansas 1860 Slave Schedule).

3. The Spence family had a tradition of serving as county sheriffs. Solomon Sr. served as sheriff of Talladega County, Alabama, for three years beginning in 1841. His son Solomon Spence Jr. was Clark County sheriff from 1854 until his sudden death at age thirty-one in 1858. Thomas F. Spence replaced his older brother in that position. *The Goodspeed Biographical and Historical Memoirs of Southern Arkansas*, 117, 173.

4. Arkansas 1860 Census, 21, 25, 29, 62; Arkansas 1860 Slave Schedule, 6, 9.

5. South Carolina seceded on December 20, 1860, followed soon after by Alabama, Florida, Georgia, Louisiana, Mississippi, and Texas. Carl Moneyhon, "1861: 'The Die is Cast,'" in *Rugged and Sublime: The Civil War in Arkansas,* ed. Mark K. Christ (Fayetteville, Ark.: University of Arkansas Press, 1994), 1–4.

6. Moneyhon, "1861," 2–3. Clark Countians showed considerable internal disagreement about leaving the Union, with different political meetings in the county yielding resolutions that both supported establishment of a secession convention and strongly opposed secession. Jack B. Scroggs, "Arkansas in the Secession Crisis," *Arkansas Historical Quarterly* 12, no. 3 (autumn 1953), 195–96.

7. Moneyhon, "1861," 4–6.

8. Michael B. Dougan, *Confederate Arkansas: The People and Policies of a Frontier State in Wartime,* (Tuscaloosa, Ala.: The University of Alabama Press, 1976), 45; Moneyhon, "1861," 6.

9. Moneyhon, "1861," 7; Gov. Henry M. Rector replied to Lincoln's request thus: "In answer to your requisition for troops from Arkansas to subjugate the Southern States, I have to say that none will be furnished. The demand is only adding insult to injury. The people of this commonwealth are freemen, not slaves, and will defend to the last extremity their honor, lives, and property against Northern mendacity and usurpation." Dougan, *Confederate Arkansas,* 61.

10. Moneyhon, "1861," 8. Murphy stated: "I have cast my vote after mature reflection, and have duly considered the consequences and I cannot conscientiously change it." His vote was greeted with shouts of "Traitor! Traitor!" and "Hang him!," but Little Rock widow Mrs. Frederick Trapnall threw him a bouquet of flowers as a gesture of respect. Dougan, *Confederate Arkansas,* 62–63.

Chapter 1: "The ball I expect will open before long . . .": The First Arkansas in Virginia

1. In presenting a flag to a company of volunteers at Des Arc, a Miss Whitney asked, "When marshaled before the booming cannon and exposed to the solid sheets of liquid death, may it inspire your souls and nerve your arms and lend new courage to your drooping souls." The company commander replied, "While contending for our cherished rights we will plant this flag triumphantly on our soil or find a grave beneath its verdant sod." Dougan, *Confederate Arkansas,* 72.

2. Another Arkansas unit formed by Helena's Patrick Cleburne was designated as the First Infantry Regiment of State Troops and the First Infantry Regiment of Arkansas Volunteers, but it ultimately was designated the Fifteenth Arkansas Infantry Regiment. Daniel E. Sutherland, *Reminiscences of a Private: William E. Bevens of the First Arkansas Infantry, C.S.A.* (Fayetteville: The University of Arkansas Press, 1992), xxviii. Any hard feelings over the cachet of being the "First Arkansas" likely were gone by the time attrition led to the consolidation of the First and Fifteenth Arkansas in early 1864. Stewart Sifakis,

Compendium of the Confederate Armies: Florida and Arkansas (New York: Facts on File, 1992), 67.

3. The other nine volunteer companies in the First Arkansas were the El Dorado Sentinels (Company A), the Camden Knights (Company C), Clan McGregor from Pine Bluff (Company D), the Saline County Volunteers (Company E), the Ettomon Guards of Little Rock (Company F), the Jackson Guards of Jacksonport (Company G), the Crockett Rifles from DeWitt (Company H), the Monticello Guards from Monticello (Company I), and the DeWitt Guards from DeWitt (Company K). John C. Hammock, *With Honor Untarnished: The Story of the First Arkansas Infantry Regiment, Confederate States Army* (Little Rock, Ark.: Pioneer Press, 1961), 8–9, 14.

4. Sutherland, *Reminiscences of a Private,* 22; Hammock, *With Honor Untarnished,* 16.

5. Holmes's brigade was in reserve at First Manassas but was called up just as the precipitate Union retreat began. Holmes did order his artillery to fire on the fleeing Yankees and sent his cavalry to chase them. "The fire of the former was exceedingly accurate, and did much execution, and the pursuit of the latter was very effective, taking many prisoners and capturing much property," he reported after the battle. *War of the Rebellion: A Compilation of the Official Records of the Union and Confederate Armies,* 70 vols. in 128 books and index (Washington, D.C.: Government Printing Office, 1880–1901), Ser. 1, 2: 565–66, in *The Civil War CD-ROM* (Carmel, Ind.: Guild Press of Indiana, 1996), (hereafter cited as *OR;* all references are to Series 1 unless otherwise noted); Hammock, *With Honor Untarnished,* 37.

6. William Bevens of Company G, First Arkansas Infantry, wrote that "we built batteries to blockade the Potomac, which was only a mile and a half wide at this point. We built three batteries in one mile and mounted large siege guns. The enemy was greatly astonished on the morning we cut the pine thicket and laid our guns open to view." Sutherland, *Reminiscences of a Private,* 45.

7. Bevens remembered that "we built huts out of logs, placing them in the side of the hill and roofing them with a foot and a half of dirt to keep out the rain. A few of the boys had tents, but I think our log huts were more comfortable, for we covered the floors over with straw." Sutherland, *Reminiscences of a Private,* 49.

8. "Confederate money was good and we could grab things cheap with it," William Bevens wrote of the regiment's new situation. "Fifty cents a gallon for shelled oysters; twenty-five cents a pound for butter; pies and cakes every day. Think of such grub for a soldier!" Sutherland, *Reminiscences of a Private,* 54.

9. In February, the *Washington (Arkansas) Telegraph* wrote that "we learn from Mr. S.H. Williams that about five hundred of Col. Fagan's regiment have volunteered for the remainder of three years or during the war, and that it is estimated that 600 or more of the regiment will join the organization." Wiley Washburn noted, "At that time we reenlisted for the war to a man. One old man

was discharged. We were given 60 day furloughs to go home, and we were a jolly set too, but we were not allowed but 1 month, and ordered to rendevous at Corinth in March." *Washington (Arkansas) Telegraph,* February 12, 1862, p. 2; James L. Nichols and Frank Abbott, eds., "Reminiscences of Confederate Service by Wiley A. Washburn," *Arkansas Historical Quarterly* 35 (spring 1976): 53.

10.   Fagan told his men, "We will not return to our old camp on the Potomac, but will march at once to the soil of Tennessee to aid in expelling the invader from the land of Andrew Jackson." Hammock, *With Honor Untarnished,* 51.

11.   Alex Spence's service records show that he reenlisted for two years on January 26, 1862; however, in letters written in late February, he explicitly states that he had not signed on for a new term of service. Since the majority of the other original members of the company show January 26 reenlistment dates, that was likely the effective date for all of them. In any event, Spence would serve in the First Arkansas Infantry Regiment for the remainder of his life. Compiled Service Records of Confederate Soldiers Who Served in Organizations from the State of Arkansas, National Archives Microcopy 317, Roll 51 (hereafter cited as Service Records).

12.   Information on the First Arkansas camp experiences in Virginia comes from Hammock, *With Honor Untarnished,* 37–51 *passim;* Bell I. Wiley, *The Life of Johnny Reb: The Common Soldier of the Confederacy* (Indianapolis: The Bobbs-Merrill Co., 1943; reprint, New York: Book-of-the-Month Club, 1994), 60; Sutherland, *Reminiscences of a Private,* 55.

13.   The Camden Knights under Capt. William L. Crenshaw contained seventy-nine men enrolled in Ouachita County. Hammock, *With Honor Untarnished,* 8.

14.   James C. Monroe was appointed as lieutenant colonel of the First Arkansas Infantry on May 8, 1861. He was transferred to Arkansas in spring 1862, and was replaced by John B. Thompson, the First Arkansas's major who would die before the Hornet's Nest at Shiloh, "his body having been pierced by Seven bullets while at the head of his regiment leading it in a charge." Monroe later would again serve as lieutenant colonel under James F. Fagan, this time in the First Arkansas Cavalry Regiment. Monroe was made colonel of the regiment to date from October 24, 1862, after Fagan was promoted to brigadier general. Service Records, Rolls 5, 50, 52; Sifakis, *Florida and Arkansas,* 50–51. Charles S. Stark, twenty-seven, was a farmer before raising Company B of the First Arkansas Infantry and serving as its first captain. He reenlisted for two years on January 25, 1862, but resigned on July 11 of that year. Service Records, Roll 51.

15.   In the week before this letter was written, President Lincoln had issued a call for 42,034 three-year volunteers; feverish meetings of Unionists and secessionists were held and pronouncements were made in Maryland, Virginia, and Kentucky; U.S. ordnance stores were seized at Kansas City, Missouri; secessionist forces occupied Fort Arbuckle in Indian Territory; both Arkansas and Tennessee passed secession ordinances; the Confederate Congress passed and Jefferson Davis

signed a declaration of war between the Confederacy and the United States; pro-Union and secessionist militias gathered in St. Louis; opposing mobs rioted in Knoxville, Tennessee; Union troops began pouring into Washington through Maryland; and the U.S.S. *Yankee* and Confederate shore batteries exchanged fire at Gloucester Point, Virginia. It is understandable that Alex Spence foresaw "big fighting, and plenty too." E. B. Long with Barbara Long, *The Civil War Day by Day: An Almanac, 1861–1865* (New York: DeCapo Press, 1971), 69–72.

16.　John M. Bradley seized the steamboat *Arago* at Pine Bluff on May 9, 1861. He then sent Governor Rector a telegram reading, "Steamboat Arago is owned by her papers in Pittsburg, Pa. and has one hundred tons provisions, belonging to owners. Shall we confiscate her here. Plenty of good Southern Steamboatmen to take her where you want her, free of charge." The author of the article states that Rector declined the boat's seizure and allowed it to return to Pittsburgh, but Alex Spence's letter indicates that the *Arago* was indeed brought to Little Rock. David Wallis, "The Steamboat Affair at Pine Bluff," *Jefferson County Historical Quarterly* 6, no. 1 (1975): 4–5. The *Arago* was a side-wheel packet built in 1860 in Brownsville, Pennsylvania. She normally ran between Pittsburgh and St. Louis and was owned by partners in St. Louis and Memphis when she was burned at Dog Tooth Bend near Commerce, Missouri, on February 6, 1865. Frederick Way Jr., comp., *Way's Packet Directory, 1848–1994: Passenger Steamboats of the Mississippi River System Since the Advent of Photography in Mid-Continent America* (Athens, Ohio: Ohio University Press, 1983), 26.

17.　Alex may be referring to John M. Ashby, thirty-five, an Indiana native who worked as a saddler and lived in Arkadelphia with his wife and child. Ashby owned six thousand dollars in real property and four thousand dollars in personal property in 1860; among his holdings were five slaves. Arkansas 1860 Census, 25; Arkansas 1860 Slave Schedule, 5.

18.　Marcha was Martha Elder, Alex Spence's sister who was married to Joshua Elder.

19.　The steamer *Kentucky* under Capt. John Scott was a 375-ton side-wheel packet built at Cincinnati, Ohio, in 1856. The vessel achieved a measure of infamy later in the war. Impressed into U.S. war service in 1864, she was chartered in June 1865 to move eight hundred former Confederate soldiers from Shreveport. The *Kentucky* hit a snag on the Red River and quickly sank, with many of her passengers drowning. Some suspected afterward that the accident may have been deliberate. Way Jr., comp., *Way's Packet Directory,* 269.

20.　The companies of the First Arkansas gathered at the Memphis Fairgrounds, about a mile away from the Mississippi River city. They stayed in Memphis for four days before departing for Virginia. Sutherland, *Reminiscences of a Private,* 16–21.

21.　The El Dorado Sentinels under Capt. Asa S. Morgan contained eighty-nine men enrolled in Union County. Hammock, *With Honor Untarnished,* 8.

22.　Illinois troops occupied Cairo, Illinois, on the evening of April 22, 1861, taking possession of the key point at the convergence of the Ohio and Mississippi Rivers. By June 1, it was well fortified and armed with artillery capable of throwing a thirty-two pound ball down the Mississippi River. Long, *The Civil War Day by Day*, 64, 81.

23. On May 10, 1861, Capt. Nathaniel Lyon, commander of the St. Louis Arsenal, led as many as seven thousand U.S. Army regulars and Home Guard units against around seven hundred pro-secession state militia troops at Camp Jackson in St. Louis. The militia troops surrendered without a struggle. A crowd gathered as the militia troops were being led away, and some of the Unionists opened fire. Ultimately, twenty-eight or twenty-nine people were killed, mobs roamed the city through the night, and all of the saloons in the Mississippi River city were closed. Long, *The Civil War Day by Day*, 72–3.

24. John S. F. Callaway, forty-four, a schoolteacher, enlisted as a private in Company B, First Arkansas Infantry Regiment, on May 19, 1861, at Lynchburg, Virginia. He was discharged for disability on May 29, 1861. Service Records, Roll 46. Stamp Jones is probably one of two soldiers of that name in Company B. James P. Jones, a twenty-five-year-old brick mason joined Company B as a private on May 19, 1861, at Lynchburg. Jones, a native of Mecklenburg County, Virginia, would suffer wounds at Ringgold Gap on November 27, 1863, that would prove fatal; he died at Gilmer Hospital in Marietta, Georgia, on December 23, 1863. Wesley D. Jones, twenty-six, a lawyer, enlisted at Little Rock on March 5, 1862, and died in a Chattanooga hospital on November 12, 1862. Service records provide no guidance on which Jones was known as "Stamp." Predictably, there were a number of soldiers named Jones in the First Arkansas Infantry Regiment: Allen and Martin C. Jones in Company A, James P. and Wesley D. Jones in Company B, Joel and Nathan Jones in Company C, Enoch and Joseph H. Jones in Company D and Thomas H. Jones in Company H. Service Records, Roll 48.

25. Thomas M. Ewing, a twenty-three-year-old farmer, is listed in the service records as "not mustered in Service being absent sick on 19th May/61 discharged." Ewing owned a 320-acre farm, with 200 acres under cultivation, when the war broke out, and was credited with $25,000 in real and $25,000 in personal property in 1860, including twenty-five slaves. Though he never served with the First Arkansas, he did serve as a clerk with the quartermaster's department in Arkadelphia and at Marshall, Texas, during the war. After the war, he served Clark County as a justice of the peace, county surveyor, circuit court clerk, and county judge in addition to his farming enterprises. Tom Ewing would have a more personal connection to the Spence family as well, marrying Mary E. "Liza" Cook Spence, the widow of Solomon Spence Jr., on November 19, 1862. Service Records, Roll 47; *The Goodspeed Biographical and Historical Memoirs of Southern Arkansas*, 138–39; Arkansas 1860 Census, 35; Arkansas 1860 Slave Schedule, 11; Richter, ed., *Clark County Past and Present*, 71; Pauline Williams Wright and Barbara McDow Caffee, *Clark County, Arkansas: A Genealogical Source Book* (Baltimore, Md.: Gateway Press, 1982), 65.

26.   The Kingsbury brothers, natives of Massachusetts, were prominent merchants in Arkadelphia. T. D. Kingsbury, thirty-eight, was married with one child, while brother George, thirty-six, lived in Arkadelphia with his wife and three children. T. D. Kingsbury was the wealthier of the two, with $25,000 in real and $11,000 in personal property, including thirteen slaves, in 1860. George Kingsbury owned only $600 in real and $200 in personal property in 1860. He enrolled in Company F, Second Arkansas Mounted Rifles, on July 27, 1861, at Camp McRae, Arkansas, and was elected second sergeant. He was discharged on October 24, 1862, "by virtue of [the] conscript act [and] being over 35 years of age." The native of Springfield, Massachusetts, was thirty-nine years old when discharged. He was five feet, nine inches tall and had a dark complexion, gray eyes, and dark hair. Bobby Jones McLane, *Clark County, Arkansas, 1860 United States Census* (Hot Springs, Ark.: Arkansas Ancestors, 1988), 50; Service Records, Roll 19; Arkansas 1860 Census, 20, 25; Arkansas 1860 Slave Schedule, 7.

27.   R. C. Davis was an Arkadelphia lawyer before the Civil War. Arkansas artillerist Thomas J. Key would encounter him east of the Mississippi River nearly four years after this letter was written and describe him as "well read, polished in manners, and a true specimen of Southern gentleman." According to Key, Davis served in McNeil's Virginia Partisan Rangers. McNeil's Rangers were organized in early 1863 from Second Company E of the Eighteenth Virginia Cavalry Regiment and fought in eight battles and raids before surrendering May 8, 1865, near Romney, West Virginia. Wirt Armistead Cate, ed., *Two Soldiers: The Campaign Diaries of Thomas J. Key, C.S.A. and Robert J. Campbell, U.S.A.* (Chapel Hill, N.C.: The University of North Carolina Press, 1938), 36–37; Stewart Sifakis, *Compendium of the Confederate Armies: Virginia* (New York: Facts on File, 1992), 145.

28.   Andrew J. Pitner, twenty-five, enlisted in Company B of the First Arkansas Infantry Regiment on May 19, 1861, and was elected second sergeant. He was promoted to second lieutenant on July 25, 1862, then to first lieutenant on January 30, 1863. Pitner was severely wounded in the arm at the battle of Chickamauga but returned to the company. He was fatally wounded at Atlanta on July 21, 1864, dying of his wounds at Catoosa Hospital in Griffin, Georgia, on August 8, 1864. Service Records, Roll 50.

29.   The First Arkansas was sent to Richmond in late May, spending about three days at the Confederate capital before moving again to Brooke's Station. The regiment established Camp Jackson at Brooke's Station, located about five miles west of the mouth of Aquia Creek, which is an estuary of the Potomac River. While at this camp the First Arkansas received drill training from cadets of the Virginia Military Academy. Hammock, *With Honor Untarnished*, 23; Sutherland, *Reminiscences of a Private*, 30.

30.   The First Arkansas would not actually move to Manassas Gap until July 17, 1861. Sutherland, *Reminiscences of a Private*, 37.

31.   John Letcher (1813–1884) was the first of Virginia's two Civil War

governors. He served four terms in Congress in the 1850s, where he opposed talk of secession but supported Southern traditions and rights. After his election in 1861 he attempted to cool the passions of Virginia's secessionists but reluctantly called a secession convention. As in Arkansas, the first convention did not approve secession, but a second did so following President Lincoln's call for troops. He personally recruited Robert E. Lee and Thomas Jonathan (Stonewall) Jackson to command Virginia troops and was an enthusiastic supporter of Pres. Jefferson Davis. Letcher also willingly surrendered much state autonomy to the Confederate government in Richmond. In 1863, he for the first time in his life lost a political race when incumbent John B. Baldwin defeated him in a bid for a seat in the Confederate Congress. William Smith replaced Letcher as governor in 1864. F. N. Boney, "Virginia," in *The Confederate Governors*, ed. W. Buck Yearns (Athens, Ga.: The University of Georgia Press, 1985), 216–31.

32. The First Arkansas was armed with .58-caliber rifled muskets. They received these weapons because Col. Thompson B. Flournoy, appointed by Governor Rector to form the regiment but replaced by James Fagan when the men elected permanent officers, refused to accept obsolete muskets seized from the Little Rock Arsenal. Hammock, *With Honor Untarnished*, 16.

33. Spence is referring to Col. Archibald Yell's First Arkansas Cavalry Regiment and its actions at the February 23, 1847, Battle of Buena Vista in the Mexican War. In that battle, some of Yell's 479 Arkansians were stationed on the American army's left flank but broke and fled the field after firing only one round at attacking Mexican cavalry. John S. D. Eisenhower, *So Far from God: The U.S. War with Mexico, 1846–1848* (New York: Random House, 1989), 183, 188; William W. Hughes, *Archibald Yell* (Fayetteville, Ark.: University of Arkansas Press, 1988), 127–28.

34. Spence probably is referring to Michael Bozeman, a wealthy landowner who lived in Caddo Township in Clark County. He represented Clark and Montgomery counties in the Arkansas General Assembly in the 1852–53 sessions. Bozeman owned twelve-thousand acres and nine slaves in 1850 and was recognized for decades later as "a very prominent man" in the county. Population Schedule [Free] of the Seventh Census of the United States, 1850, Arkansas, National Archives Microcopy No. 432, Roll 25 (cited hereafter as Arkansas 1850 Census); Population Schedule [Slave] of the Seventh Census of the United States, 1850, Arkansas, National Archives Microcopy No. 432, Roll 32 (cited hereafter as Arkansas 1850 Slave Schedule); *Goodspeed Biographical and Historical Memoirs of Southern Arkansas*, 127; Janice Wegener, ed., *Historical Report of the Secretary of State, Arkansas, 1978* (Little Rock, Ark.: Secretary of State, 1978), 414.

35. The First Arkansas Infantry Regiment moved to camps at Evansport, Virginia, after the first battle of Manassas. Evansport, which is now called Quantico, lies on a bluff above the Potomac River about ten miles north of Aquia Creek and four miles southeast of Dumfries. The camp of the First Arkansas was dubbed Camp Holmes, though Alex Spence and Isaac Cook call it Camp

McGregor in some of their letters. Sutherland, *Reminiscences of a Private*, 44; Hammock, *With Honor Untarnished*, 37.

36. This likely is the business run by the Kingsbury brothers, probably run in partnership with J. E. M. Barkman of Arkadelphia. Barkman, forty-one, a farmer, lived in Arkadelphia with his wife and five children and owned $30,000 in real and $35,350 in personal property in 1860, making him one of the wealthiest men in Clark County. Barkman also owned twenty-eight slaves in 1860. Arkansas 1860 Census, 20; Arkansas 1860 Slave Schedule, 8.

37. David R. Meadors, a thirty-seven-year-old farmer, enlisted as a private in Company B on May 19, 1861. The service records list him on the company rolls until January 1862, after which there are no further records. It is possible that Meadors did not reenlist with most of his comrades. Service Records, Roll 45.

38. Randle may have been a slave belonging to Tom Ewing. Tom Spence also refers to him in a letter of May 19, 1862, when he writes as a postscript: "Tell Tom Ewing to come ahead; all will be all right; *bring Randle to cook*" (emphasis added).

39. Liza is Mary E. Cook Spence, widow of Solomon Spence Jr. and sister of Isaac "Babe" Cook, Alex Spence's close friend. Dr. Ward may be Pvt. Bryan B. Ward, thirty-one, a dentist serving in Company C, First Arkansas Infantry. Ward, who served as an orderly to General Holmes in the fall of 1861, went to Arkansas on furlough in July 1862 and never returned to the regiment. Wright and McCaffee, *Clark County, Arkansas: A Genealogical Source Book*, 129; Service Records, Roll 52.

40. "Cass" is likely a reference to either cassimere, a thin, fine twilled woolen cloth that was lighter in weight than broadcloth, or cassinette, a cheap fabric with a cotton warp and a weft of fine wool or wool and silk; Jonathan Callaway of the Second Arkansas Mounted Rifles also refers to having clothing made from cass. Frederick P. Todd, *American Military Equipage, 1851–1872: State Forces*, vol. 2 (New York: Chatham Square Press, 1983), 1313; Jonathan Callaway to J. H. Thomas, September 4, 1861, Civil War Letters and Papers of Jonathan W. Callaway, C.S.A., Arkansas History Commission, Little Rock.

41. In the holiday atmosphere surrounding the First Battle of Manassas, crowds of politicians and civilians accompanied the Union army to watch the anticipated battle. In the rout that followed, many civilian carriages were abandoned as the mob of soldiers and civilians streamed back toward Washington. At least one carriage, that of Massachusetts senator Henry Wilson, was left behind after a Confederate soldier unloaded a shotgun blast into it as the senator fled the field. Rumors following the battle may have claimed that Lincoln himself was among the fugitive politicians. William C. Davis, *Battle at Bull Run* (Garden City, N.Y.: Doubleday & Company, 1977), 239–40.

42. The Spences may have ordered a carriage from R. H. Prince's factory in Washington, Arkansas, which had been established in 1857 or 1858 and had a reputation for quality work. If so, they probably never received it since its

owners and staff joined the army at the beginning of hostilities. H. B. McKenzie, "Confederate Manufactures in Southwest Arkansas," in *Publications of the Arkansas Historical Association,* vol. 2 (Little Rock, Ark.: Democrat Printing and Lithography Co., 1908), vol. 2: 208–9.

43. The Tiger Rifles, or Louisiana Tigers, was the First Special Battalion of Louisiana troops led by Maj. Chatham R. Wheat. Company B, of Orleans Parish, led by Capt. Alex White was known as the Tiger Rifles and gave the battalion its nickname. "Ellsworth's Pet Lambs" were the Eleventh New York Infantry, the "Fire Zouaves." Their commander, Col. Elmer Ellsworth, a personal friend of President Lincoln, was killed on the way to Manassas after the proprietor of the Marshal House in Alexandria, Virginia, shot him for removing a Confederate flag from atop the building. The Eleventh New York and Wheat's Tiger Rifles were clad in flashy zouave uniforms at First Manassas, which caused some confusion during the battle as one Confederate regiment hesitated to fire on the New Yorkers for fear they were the Louisiana troops. The New York and Louisiana units apparently did not confront each other on the field at First Manassas, despite Alex Spence's report to the contrary. Arthur W. Bergeron Jr., *Guide to Louisiana Confederate Military Units 1861–1865* (Baton Rouge, La.: Louisiana State University Press, 1989), 149–50; Davis, *Battle at Bull Run,* 9, 207–8.

44. Theophilus Hunter Holmes, an 1829 graduate of West Point and a Mexican War veteran, commanded the division that contained the First Arkansas Infantry. He was a major in the regular army when he resigned on April 22, 1861, to join the Confederate service, which may have been his greatest service to the United States. A personal friend of Jefferson Davis, Holmes was appointed brigadier general June 5, 1861, major general on October 7, 1861, and lieutenant general to rank from October 10, 1862. After a lackluster performance in the Seven Days Campaign in Virginia, Holmes was given command of the Trans-Mississippi Department. After Edmund Kirby Smith replaced him in that position, Holmes commanded the District of Arkansas until shortly after his July 4, 1863, attack on Helena, Arkansas, failed disastrously. He ended the war organizing the reserves in North Carolina. Though personally brave, Holmes was not capable of the high commands with which he was entrusted. Ezra J. Warner, *Generals in Gray: Lives of the Confederate Commanders* (Baton Rouge, La.: Louisiana State University Press, 1959), 141.

45. George W. McIntosh enlisted as first lieutenant of Company B on May 19, 1861. He was dropped from the rolls about a year later. Service Records, Roll 49.

46. Frederick M. Greene, twenty-nine, a merchant in civilian life, enrolled in Company B as a second lieutenant on May 19, 1861. He disappears from the company muster in early 1862. Service Records, Roll 48.

47. William E. Lindsey, thirty-two, who must have worked under Tom Spence as a deputy sheriff in Clark County, enrolled in Company B as a brevet second lieutenant on May 19, 1861. He left the First Arkansas in early 1862 but

later served in Capt. Reuben Reed's Company of Col. Robert C. Newton's Tenth Arkansas Cavalry. Service Records, Roll 49; "Muster Roll of Ruben C. Reed's Company A (10th Regiment of Arkansas Cavalry)," *Clark County Historical Journal—1998,* 132; "Rubin Reed's Company. Original Muster Roll in possession of Arkadelphia Lady," *Clark County Historical Journal* (1998): 132–33.

48. Tom Spence was elected ordnance sergeant of the Second Arkansas Mounted Rifles when the regiment was mustered into Confederate service on July 27, 1861. Service Records, Roll 21. The ordnance officer's duties included maintaining, storing, and transporting regimental gear. Webb Garrison with Cheryl Garrison, *Encyclopedia of Civil War Usage* (Nashville, Tenn.: Cumberland House, 2001), 182.

49. Rufus Hearn enrolled as second corporal on July 15, 1861, in Captain Roberts's Company, Clark County Light Artillery (also known as Wiggins's Battery Arkansas Light Artillery). He later was made sergeant when the battery reorganized and all of its 1861 officers resigned. Hearn was captured twice during the war, at Shelbyville and at Knoxville, Tennessee. Hearn's service records are somewhat confusing: one section says he died in a Federal hospital on April 21, 1864, after deserting and being captured by the Third Indiana Cavalry, while another says he was sent to a Chattanooga hospital on October 1, 1864, after his capture. The latter is certainly more accurate, given Hearn's distinguished postwar career. In 1870, he opened the Arkadelphia Male School, of which he was principal, and the next year was an assistant at the Arkadelphia Normal and Free High School. Hearn earned a law degree in 1873 and began practicing in Arkadelphia. He was elected prosecuting attorney for the Eighth Judicial District in 1878 and circuit judge for that district in 1886. Service Records, Roll 43; Laura Scott Butler, "History of Clark County," in *Publications of the Arkansas Historical Association,* vol. 2, ed. John Hugh Reynolds (Fayetteville, Ark.: Arkansas Historical Association, 1908), 569; Richter, ed., *Clark County Arkansas: Past and Present,* 237–38; *The Goodspeed Biographical and Historical Memoirs of Southern Arkansas,* 144.

50. William A. Alexander, a thirty-five-year-old clerk, enrolled in Company B on May 19, 1861, and was elected first sergeant. He reenlisted for two years on January 25, 1862, and was promoted to first lieutenant on April 1, 1862. Alexander became captain of the company on July 4, 1862. He was "seriously wounded in neck" on December 31, 1862, at the battle of Murfreesboro and died of his wounds on January 16, 1863. Service Records, Roll 46. Before the war, Alexander worked as a clerk for Joseph Cassart, age forty, a merchant who lived in Arkadelphia with his wife and six children. Cassart owned $11,000 in real and $6,000 in personal property, including five slaves, in 1860. He served in Reed's Company of Newton's Tenth Arkansas Cavalry Regiment later in the war. Arkansas 1860 Census, 22; Arkansas 1860 Slave Schedule, 7; "Muster Roll of Ruben C. Reed's Company A (10th Regiment of Arkansas Cavalry)," 132; "Rubin Reed's Company. Original Muster Roll in possession of Arkadelphia Lady," 132–33.

51. Cook probably is referring to Cordelia Marbury, forty-four, who lived in Arkadelphia with her husband, Leonidas, and their five children. Like Solomon Spence Sr., the Marburys operated an Arkadelphia hotel. Bobby Jones McLane, *Clark Count Census,* 58; Barbara Caffee, "Antebellum Arkansas, 1800–1850," *Clark County Historical Journal* (spring, 1981): 68.

52. Cook is probably referring to Ebenezer J. Borland, age forty-seven, a farmer who lived in Antoine Township in Clark County with his wife and five children. Babe Cook's brothers, George and Dempsey, also lived in Antoine Township. I was unable to identify "Pen." McLane, *Clark County Census,* 8, 22.

53. I was unable to find any reference to a soldier named Calhoun in the First Arkansas Infantry Regiment or any other Arkansas unit that may have been in the area at the time. The reference to "his old Masster" may indicate that Calhoun was a slave who accompanied a soldier in Company B.

54. Cook is referring to the battle of Wilson's Creek, Missouri, fought August 11, 1861, southwest of Springfield.

55. Alexander Battis, forty-two, an Irish-born minister, lived in Arkadelphia with his Canadian wife, Moriah, thirty-two, and their four children. Battis owned $3,000 in real estate and $295 in personal property in 1860. Arkansas 1860 Census, 28.

56. Caldwell, Texas, is located in Burleson County about fifty-five miles northeast of Austin.

57. Mary Ann Spence was married to John W. Hood of Texas. Hood raised the Burleson Guards in March 1861 from men living near Caldwell and was elected captain. Though the county commission initially allocated four dollars for each soldier in the company to buy equipment, a total absence of funds in the county treasury made it necessary for each soldier in the Burleson Guards to purchase his own equipment. The Burleson Guards became Company G, Second Texas Infantry, a regiment formed at Galveston in July 1861 under Col. John C. Moore, who later became a brigadier general. Hood would later be seriously wounded at the battle of Shiloh. Joseph E. Chance, *The Second Texas Infantry: From Vicksburg to Shiloh* (Austin, Tex.: Eakin Press, 1984), 6–7, 38; *Goodspeed Biographical and Historical Memoirs of Southern Arkansas,* 173; Hewett, comp., *The Roster of Confederate Soldiers 1861–1865,* vol. 13: 134; Sifakis, *Compendium of the Confederate Armies: Texas* (New York and Oxford: Facts on File, 1992), 108; Crute, *Units of the Confederate States Army* (Midlothian, Va.: Derwent Books, 1987), 323; O. M. Roberts, *Confederate Military History of Texas,* vol. 15 of *Confederate Military History Extended Edition,* ed. Clement A. Evans (Atlanta: Confederate Publishing Company, 1899; reprint, with new material, Wilmington, N.C.: Broadfoot Publishing Company, 1989), 553.

58. Galveston, Texas, was a deep-water port on an island in the Gulf of Mexico and as such an area of concern in the Union effort to establish a blockade on the Confederacy. By mid-1861, the five-gun screw steamer *South Carolina* was patrolling the mouth of Galveston Bay, though blockade runners continued

to use the harbor with little effort. By December, four other Union ships would be on blockade duty off Galveston. Despite the importance of the port, it was poorly defended by the Confederates. S. Sherman, commandant of Galveston, reported on March 8, 1861, that "we now have six 24-pounders, two siege and four battery guns, two howitzers, and two mortars, and about three hundred ball and shell . . . but it is important we should have some heavier guns, say 68-pounders." On June 12, Capt. W. H. Stevens, a Confederate engineer, requested the addition of "four or five 8-inch columbiads" for the island's defense. After Brig. Gen. P. O. Hebert took command of the Department of Texas, he reported on September 27, 1861, that "the port of Galveston is partially defended by a few open sand works, mounted with guns of calibers ranging from 18-pounders to 32-pounders, and of course totally inadequate to resist a bombardment with heavy guns. The few large guns now on the way, should they not arrive too late, will in some measure increase the efficiency of the harbor defenses." Those guns, the caliber of which were not specified, by October 16 were "reported on the way, strung along the road from Alexandria to Niblett's Bluff. Two or three of them are expected by the end of this or the beginning of next week. I have ordered them to be placed in battery as they arrive and, as the number is limited, distributed to the best advantage." It was not until a year later, on October 9, 1862, that the Union conducted an assault on the island, landing five hundred men who captured Galveston without firing a shot. On January 1, 1863, Confederate troops under John B. Magruder attacked Galveston in the early morning and drove the Federal defenders away, though the blockade was maintained at the mouth of the bay. Galveston would remain in Confederate possession for the remainder of the war. Jack D. Coombe, *Gunfire Around the Gulf: The Last Major Naval Campaigns of the Civil War* (New York: Bantam Books, 1999), 32–33; *OR*, Series 1, vol. 1: 610–11; *OR*, vol. 4: 92, 112, 123; Kerby, *Kirby Smith's Confederacy*, 18–19.

59.   "Ulto" is short for "ultimo," which means "the previous month." Garrison, *Encyclopedia of Civil War Usage*, 253.

60.   The original chaplain of the First Arkansas Infantry Regiment was Robert W. Trimble. Hammock, *With Honor Untarnished*, 144.

61.   While this rumored attack apparently never transpired, artillery fire was common between Federal forces and the Confederate batteries. Pvt. Samuel H. Williams of Company I, First Arkansas, wrote in a letter to the *Washington (Arkansas) Telegraph* that "not a day passes that does not witness an artillery duel between our gunners and the enemy. At times the cannonading becomes quite spirited, and the shells fall thick and fast on both sides. The Yankees, I must accord them the credit to say, shoot well. Their bombs often explode in and over our batteries. Notwithstanding, they have thus far done little damage." Capt. William A. Crawford of Company E, First Arkansas, noting that the regiment was encamped near the battery, wrote that "the men have become so accustomed to the cannonading tht they verry often do not break a conversation or get off their seats, when a heavy firing is going on. . . ." *Washington (Arkansas) Telegraph*, January

22, 1862, p. 1; Charles G. Williams, ed., "A Saline Guard: The Civil War Letters of Col. William Ayers Crawford, C.S.A., 1861–1865," *Arkansas Historical Quarterly* 31, no. 4 (winter 1972): 355.

62. Professor Thaddeus S. C. Lowe first demonstrated the use of observation balloons on June 17, 1861, ascending in Washington and communicating with President Lincoln by telegraph wire. Lowe first observed Confederate troops by balloon on June 23, 1861, at Falls Church, Virginia. Wiley Washburn of Company H, First Arkansas, also noted that "as we had much pretty weather, they would go up in balloons daily to prospect." Long, *The Civil War Day by Day*, 86–87; Nichols and Abbott, eds., "Reminiscences of Confederate Service by Wiley A. Washburn," 53.

63. James F. Fagan, a native of Clark County, Kentucky, and a Mexican War veteran, was appointed colonel of the First Arkansas Infantry on May 8, 1861. Fagan led the regiment at the April 6–7, 1862, battle of Shiloh, after which the regiment's officers sent a letter to Jefferson Davis urging his promotion to brigadier general. Fagan resigned on April 12, 1862, after Gen. Braxton Bragg refused his request for leave to address family needs. Fagan returned to Arkansas by August 1862, where he reentered the Confederate Army and was promoted to brigadier general to rank from September 12, 1862. Fagan led troops at Prairie Grove, during the Camden Expedition, and during Sterling Price's 1864 invasion of Missouri. He was promoted to major general to rank from April 25, 1864, the date of his stunning victory at Marks' Mills. He was an active politician and planter after the war, dying in Little Rock on September 1, 1893. Fagan is buried in Little Rock's Mount Holly Cemetery. Service records, Roll 47; *Washington (Arkansas) Telegraph*, August 13, 1862, p. 2; Warner, *Generals in Gray*, 85–86.

64. John H. S. Swink, a fifty-two-year-old North Carolina native, was a farmer in Antoine Township in Clark County in 1860 but apparently did not join the Confederate military. His son, Leander D. Swink, age twenty-two, enlisted as a private in Company B, First Arkansas Infantry Regiment, on May 19, 1861. He was discharged on January 27, 1862, after a long struggle with typhoid fever. The younger Swink was five feet, eleven inches tall and had a dark complexion, blue eyes, and dark hair. Dumfries, Virginia, was about ten miles north of Aquia Creek on Quantico Creek. McLane, *Clark County Census*, 87; Desmond Walls Allen, *Index to Arkansas Confederate Soldiers*, vol. 3 (Conway, Ark.: Arkansas Research, 1990), 116; Service Records, Roll 51; Calvin D. Cowles, comp., *Atlas to Accompany the Official Records of the Union and Confederate Armies* (Washington, D.C.: Government Printing Office, 1891–95) Plate 8, 1 (cited hereafter as *OR Atlas*).

65. James A. Coffman, twenty-seven, enrolled as a second corporal in Company C of the First Arkansas Infantry on May 19, 1861. The former clerk was listed as sick in Fredericksburg in the November 1861 muster sheet and "died of disease" on December 5, 1861. Service Records, Roll 47. Coffman likely worked for Robert T. Cook, forty-five, a Virginia-born merchant who lived in Arkadelphia with his wife and five children. Most of the other Cooks listed in the 1860 cen-

sus were farmers (though one was a carpenter and Isaac Cook was a clerk) who lived in either Alpine or Caddo Townships. McLane, *Clark County Census*, 19.

66.   William F. Cowen, twenty-two, a farmer in civilian life and a private in Company B, First Arkansas Infantry, died of disease in Fredericksburg on December 25, 1861. Service Records, Roll 47.

67.   John G. Walker, a Missouri native, commanded a brigade consisting of the First Arkansas, Second Tennessee, and Twelfth North Carolina. The Mexican War veteran had achieved the rank of captain in the regular army before resigning on July 31, 1861, for service in the Confederate army. Walker was promoted to brigadier general on January 9, 1862, and major general on November 8, 1862. Walker transferred to the Trans-Mississippi after the battle of Antietam to command a Texas infantry division and later replaced Richard Taylor as the head of the District of West Louisiana. When the war ended, Walker commanded a division in the District of Texas, New Mexico, and Arizona, and went to Mexico rather than sign his parole. He apparently repatriated himself, as he later served as U.S. consul general in Bogota, Colombia. Warner, *Generals in Gray*, 319–20; Hammock, *With Honor Untarnished*, 38.

68.   Thomas B. Yancey, twenty-four, a clerk in civilian life, enrolled in Company B, First Arkansas Infantry, on May 19, 1861 as third corporal. He was appointed second lieutenant on April 1, 1862, and resigned August 28, 1862 because of his health. A surgeon certified him as unfit for service because of "chronic diarrhea and general debility, the disease returning with renewed violence from every exposure in camp." Service Records, Roll 52. James P. Bourland, a twenty-one-year-old clerk, enlisted as a private in Company B, First Arkansas Infantry Regiment, on May 19, 1861. He was wounded slightly in the thigh at Shiloh and was detailed to the quartermaster's department between September 1862 and February 1863. Beginning in 1864, he served as ordnance sergeant. Service Records, Roll 46.

69.   Newton S. Love recruited a company that became Company A, Eighth Battalion, Arkansas Infantry, and was elected captain on February 26, 1862. The thirty-year-old South Carolina native was killed near Holly Springs, Mississippi, on October 15, 1862. The Eighth Battalion surrendered at Port Hudson, Louisiana, on July 8, 1863. Service Records, Roll 108; Sifakis, *Florida and Arkansas*, 84–85.

70.   Franklin Roberts organized the Clark County artillery company and enlisted as captain on July 15, 1861, in Little Rock. The reports of dissatisfaction with Roberts apparently were not universal, as Roberts was reelected captain on May 25, 1862. Roberts was transferred to the Trans-Mississippi on November 25, 1862, and placed in charge of the small arms factory at Arkadelphia. On October 22, 1863, he was again transferred, this time to Marshall, Texas, where he was in charge of an armory that manufactured small arms. Service Records, Roll 43.

71.   Union operations had indeed gone far toward cutting Arkansas and the Trans-Mississippi off from most of the rest of the Confederacy. New Orleans had

been under Federal blockade since May 26, 1861; Union troops would control the Crescent City by April 29, 1862. Cairo, Illinois, commanding the upper reaches of the Mississippi, had been under Union control since mid-1861. U. S. Grant's troops had taken two major fortifications commanding two Tennessee rivers, which would ultimately yield control of Kentucky and most of Tennessee to Federal forces. It is understandable in light of these and other developments that Alex Spence would feel isolated from his home state. Long, *The Civil War Day by Day,* 64, 79, 81, 209.

72. Forts Henry and Donelson were key Confederate fortifications guarding the Tennessee and Columbia rivers in Tennessee. Union troops under U.S. Grant captured Fort Henry on February 6, 1862, then turned their attention to Fort Donelson. Within a week, the Federal army surrounded the fort, attacking with troops on February 13 and with gunboats on February 14. The next day, the Confederate defenders attacked, actually breaching the Union lines but failing to exploit their victory to allow Fort Donelson's garrison to escape. By February 16, some twelve thousand Confederate troops surrendered, minus Nathan Bedford Forrest's cavalry, which had slipped out and escaped through the Yankee lines during the evening. The loss of Forts Henry and Donelson left Tennessee open to Union invasion, placed two major rivers under Federal control, and effectively lost Kentucky for the Confederacy. Long, *The Civil War Day by Day,* 166–72.

73. "Long home" is slang for a grave or a burial trench. Garrison, *Encyclopedia of Civil War Usage,* 149.

74. After Fort Henry fell and as U.S. forces began investing Fort Donelson, Confederate troops started withdrawing from Bowling Green in western Kentucky on February 11. A fire on February 13 burned several buildings. The last Rebel troops left Bowling Green the next day and soon were replaced by Union forces. The Confederates abandoned Columbus, Kentucky, the last bastion of what had been a defensive line stretching from the Mississippi River to the Cumberland Gap, on February 20, ceding Kentucky to the Union. Long, *The Civil War Day by Day,* 170–73.

75. The fall of Fort Donelson on February 16 caused panic throughout Confederate Tennessee and the state capital at Nashville was abandoned without a fight. Union troops occupied Nashville on February 25, 1862, and used it as a base of operations for the rest of the war. Long, *The Civil War Day by Day,* 175.

76. Union troops under Brig. Gen. Samuel Curtis entered Arkansas on February 17, 1862. That afternoon, at James Dunagin's farm on Little Sugar Creek, advance Union elements fought soldiers from Ben McCulloch's Confederate army and troops from Sterling Price's Missouri forces, the latter of which had been retreating before Curtis's army. The battle ended in a practical draw, as all of the troops engaged withdrew from the field. This battle, the first in the war fought entirely on Arkansas soil, left thirteen Federals dead and about twenty wounded, and about twenty-six Confederates dead. William L. Shea and Earl J. Hess, *Pea*

Ridge: Civil War Campaign in the West (Chapel Hill, N.C.: University of North Carolina Press, 1992), 41–43.

77. Gov. Henry M. Rector, angry about Richmond's perceived disdain for the Trans-Mississippi and perturbed by the depletion of Arkansas state troops by enrollment into Confederate service or outright release from service, in January 1862 ordered the state's militia to muster. This call was largely ignored; in Clark County, two-thirds of the militia refused to muster, "claiming that by recent law they could not be fined for nonattendance." Large-scale conscription would not occur in Arkansas until T. C. Hindman arrived to build an army after Earl Van Dorn stripped the state of troops and equipment in the spring of 1862. Dougan, *Confederate Arkansas,* 76–78, 86–88; Bobby L. Roberts, "General T. C. Hindman and the Trans-Mississippi District," *Arkansas Historical Quarterly* 32, no. 4 (winter 1973): 305.

Chapter 2: "We had a very hard Fight . . .": The Second Arkansas Mounted Rifles in the Trans-Mississippi

1. Maj. Gen. Ben McCulloch formed "the battalion of Mounted Riflemen because the companies that will comprise it are well acquainted with the country around here and will be of much use as scouts." Stephen B. Oates *Confederate Cavalry West of the River* (Austin: University of Texas Press, 1961), 14; Sifakis, *Florida and Arkansas,* 53; Wesley T. Leeper, *Rebels Valiant: Second Arkansas Mounted Rifles (Dismounted)* (Little Rock, Ark.: Pioneer Press, 1964), 12, 31; Service Records, Roll 21.

2. Leeper, *Rebels Valiant,* 13–31 passim.

3. Warner, *Generals in Gray,* 202–3.

4. Brig. Gen. N. Bart Pearce wrote after the war of the Arkansians at Wilson's Creek: "It was a new thing to most of them, this regular way of shooting by word of command, and it was, perhaps, the old-accustomed method of using rifle, musket, or shot-gun as gamesters or marksmen that won them that battle when pressed into close quarters with the enemy." N. B. Pearce, "Arkansas Troops in the Battle of Wilson's Creek" in *Battles and Leaders of the Civil War,* ed. Robert Underwood Johnson and Clarence Clough Buell, vol. 1 (New York: Century Company, 1887; reprint, New York: South Brunswick, 1956), 299.

5. Moneyhon, "1861," 14–15.

6. William Riley Brooksher, *Bloody Hill: The Civil War Battle of Wilson's Creek* (Washington and London: Brassey's, 1995), 186–87, 237–39.

7. Pearce, "Arkansas Troops in the Battle of Wilson's Creek," 301.

8. Brooksher, *Bloody Hill,* 183.

9. Lt. Col. Benjamin T. E. Embry led the Second Arkansas Mounted Rifles through most of the fighting at Wilson's Creek. Though McIntosh would not become a brigadier general until January 24, 1862, he already served that function. *OR,* 3: 111; William Garrett Piston and Richard W. Hatcher III, *Wilson's*

Creek: The Second Battle of the Civil War and the Men Who Fought It (Chapel Hill, N.C.: University of North Carolina Press, 2000), 215–17; Jonathan Callaway to J. H. Thomas, 11 August 1861; Warner, *Generals in Gray*, 203.

10.   Thomas W. Cutrer, *Ben McCulloch and the Frontier Military Tradition.* (Chapel Hill, N.C.: University of North Carolina Press, 1993), 232–33. William Tunnard of the Third Louisiana Infantry Regiment remembered McCulloch saying, "Come, my brave lads, I have a battery for you to charge and the day is ours!" William H. Tunnard, *A Southern Record: The History of the Third Regiment, Louisiana Infantry* (Fayetteville, Ark.: University of Arkansas Press, 1997), 30.

11.   *OR*, 3: 111–12; Piston and Hatcher, *Wilson's Creek*, p. 276–77.

12.   "We watched the retreating enemy through our field glasses, *and we were glad to see him go,*" Pearce reported. Pearce, "Arkansas Troops in the Battle of Wilson's Creek," 303.

13.   Brooksher, *Bloody Hill*, 236; *OR*, 3: 112.

14.   Jonathan Callaway to J. H. Thomas, October 5, 1861; Callaway to Thomas, October 11, 1861.

15.   Moneyhon, "1861," 17.

16.   While there is no record of Thomas Spence participating in this campaign, he may have been included in the troops from Company E. He was back from his recruiting mission in Arkansas by December.

17.   W. Craig Gaines, *The Confederate Cherokees: John Drew's Regiment of Mounted Rifles.* (Baton Rouge, La.: Louisiana State University Press, 1989), 49–54.

18.   *OR*, 8: 22–25, 29.

19.   William L. Shea, "1862: 'A Continual Thunder'" in *Rugged and Sublime*, 21–22; Shea and Hess, *Pea Ridge*, 20–21.

20.   Shea, "1862," 23–24.

21.   Shea, "1862," 25–27.

22.   Shea and Hess, *Pea Ridge*, 27–29.

23.   Van Dorn's insistence on a rapid march would cost him about one-fourth of his 16,500 men, who either dropped out of the march exhausted or were in no shape to fight when they arrived at the battlefield. Shea, "1862," 29–31, 37.

24.   Shea, "1862," 32; Shea and Hess, *Pea Ridge*, 110; Cutrer, *Ben McCulloch*, 304.

25.   Shea and Hess, *Pea Ridge*, 114–15.

26.   Shea, "1862," 33; Shea and Hess, *Pea Ridge*, 335. Tom Spence's comrade Jonathan Callaway missed the battle, but wrote home later that "the Boys say that Oak Hills was but a picket fight compared with it." Jonathan Callaway to "My Son," March 16, 1862.

27.   Shea, "1862," 34–37.

28.   Shea, "1862," 38.

29.   Van Dorn began moving his troops out of Van Buren on March 17, 1862, planning to gather them at Des Arc before marching across east Arkansas for a

crossing of the Mississippi River to Memphis. While advance units under Sterling Price entered Memphis on April 11, 1862, four days after the Battle of Shiloh ended, at least three Arkansas regiments were still stalled between Van Buren and Little Rock by the wretched traveling conditions as late as April 20. Harris Flanagin left DeValls Bluff on April 16, arriving in Memphis with Company E and two other companies of the Second Arkansas Mounted Rifles (Dismounted) on April 18. They left Memphis on April 23 and finally arrived in Corinth on May 3. Leeper, *Rebels Valiant*, 72; Robert G. Hartje, *Van Dorn: The Life and Times of a Confederate General* (Nashville, Tenn.: Vanderbilt University Press, 1967), 166–68; Wendy Richter, ed., "The Letters of Harris Flanagin," *Clark County Historical Journal*, (spring, 1986 [1988]): 97, 98, 101.

30. Harris Flanagin, a native of New Jersey, worked as a lawyer in Arkadelphia in 1860, where he lived with his wife and four children and was one of the town's wealthier citizens. Flanagin owned $30,000 in real and $25,000 in personal property, including seven slaves. He was forty-three years old when he was enrolled as captain of Company E, Second Arkansas Mounted Rifles, on July 27, 1861. Flanagin would be elected colonel of the regiment when it reorganized on May 8, 1862, and would hold that position until he resigned on October 20, 1862, after being elected governor of Arkansas. Arkansas 1860 Census, 19; Arkansas 1860 Slave Schedule, 7; Service Records, Roll 18.

31. Jonathan W. Callaway, twenty-seven, enrolled in the Second Arkansas Mounted Rifles as first lieutenant of Company E at Camp McRae on July 27, 1861. He was appointed regimental commissary officer with the rank of captain on March 22, 1862, and replaced as first lieutenant by J. L. Stroope. He soon attained the rank of major when he was made commissary officer for the division. Callaway served with the regiment through the Kentucky Campaign, at least, and later moved west of the Mississippi where he became assistant chief of the Bureau of Subsistence for the Trans-Mississippi Department. After the war, he was elected clerk of the Arkansas State Senate in 1876 and Pulaski County chancery court clerk in 1878, a post he held for ten years before retiring. Service Records, Roll 17; Richter, ed., "The Letters of Harris Flanagin," 102.; Wendy Richter, comp., "The Reminiscences of Samuel Callaway, *Clark County Historical Journal* (1991): 97.

32. McIntosh noted Spence's injury in his official report on the battle: "Orderly Sergeant Spencer [*sic*] was conspicuous for his gallantry. He was wounded while leading his men." *OR*, vol. 3, 111.

33. The Kansas Rangers was one of ten companies of three-month volunteers who responded to President Lincoln's initial call for state troops that collectively were designated the Second Kansas Infantry Regiment. The Kansas Rangers under Capt. Samuel P. Wood served as a mounted unit at Wilson's Creek, the regiment having captured dozens of horses in the march from Springfield. The Second Arkansas Mounted Rifles and the Kansas Rangers apparently never

confronted each other on the field at Wilson's Creek. Piston and Hatcher, *Wilson's Creek,* 62, 126.

34. James L. Witherspoon was captain of Company F, Second Arkansas Mounted Rifles. John D. McCabe replaced him as captain when the regiment reorganized in Corinth, Mississippi, in May 1862. Witherspoon assumed command of Company H, Thirty-seventh Arkansas Infantry on October 23, 1862; Gen. Theophilus Holmes then detailed him as a recruiting officer on February 4, 1863. He organized Witherspoon's Sixteenth Battalion Arkansas Cavalry on June 10, 1863, and was promoted to major. Federal forces captured Witherspoon, either on November 17, 1863, in Montgomery County or October 14, 1863, at Benton. He was exchanged in July 1864. Service Records, Rolls 21, 36, 234.

35. George Ashby, twenty-eight, enrolled in Company F of the Second Arkansas Mounted Rifles on July 27, 1861, at Camp McRae, Arkansas, and was elected second lieutenant. He was slightly wounded at Wilson's Creek. W. A. Wilson replaced him as second lieutenant when the regiment reorganized in Corinth. Service Records, Roll 17.

36. Marvell H. Moseley, a fifty-two-year-old farmer, enrolled as a private in Company F of the Second Arkansas Mounted Rifles on July 27, 1861, at Camp McRae, Arkansas. He was born in Christian County, Kentucky, was five feet, eight inches tall, and had a brown complexion, gray hair, and hazel eyes. He was "dangerously wounded" at Wilson's Creek and discharged from service on July 16, 1862, because of a gunshot wound to the thigh and chronic diarrhea. Before the war he lived with his wife and two young daughters in Clark County's Caddo Township. Service Records, Roll 20; McLane, *Clark County Census,* 64.

37. Pvt. William H. Wilson, who was born June 7, 1838, in Independence County, Arkansas, was a member of Company B, Third Arkansas Infantry Regiment (State Troops) when he was killed at Wilson's Creek. Service Records, Roll 70; information cited in Wilson-McFadden Family Bible, cited in August 8, 2001, personal correspondence of Margaret Curley of Minden, Nevada, with the author. Wilson's father was James Wilson, a Cumberland Presbyterian minister who had been ordained in Independence County, Arkansas. The elder Wilson was born in Hickman County, Tennessee, in 1809 and died in Clark County, Arkansas, in 1875. Margaret Curley posting of February 16, 1999, at http://boards.ancestry.com/; INTERNET.

38. T. D. Kingsbury apparently was visiting his brother, George, a sergeant in Company F, Second Arkansas Mounted Rifles. Service Records, Roll 19.

39. Hogeye, Arkansas, is located about seven miles southwest of Fayetteville in the Boston Mountains. Hogeye boasted a stop on the Butterfield Overland Mail Route and later in the war was the location of a Federal "post colony," where Unionist families gathered together for protection from guerrillas. Shiloh Museum, *History of Washington County* (Springdale, Ark.: Shiloh Museum, 1989), 158, 203–4.

40. Curtis sent a reconnaissance in force of about twelve hundred cavalry

and artillery under Brig. Gen. Alexander S. Asboth into Fayetteville on February 22. They occupied Fayetteville until February 26, when Curtis ordered them to return to the main Union force around Cross Hollows in Benton County. Shea and Hess, *Pea Ridge*, 53–54.

41. James E. M. Barkman, forty-two, enrolled in Company F of the Second Arkansas Mounted Rifles on July 27, 1861, at Camp McRae, Arkansas, and was elected first lieutenant. He was discharged after the regiment reorganized at Corinth, Mississippi, in May 1862. Service Records, Roll 17.

42. Following the defeat at Pea Ridge, Van Dorn's tired, hungry troops struggled south through the Boston Mountains toward Van Buren on the Arkansas River near the border with Indian Territory. The demoralized troops set up camps along Frog Bayou, east of Van Buren. Shea and Hess, *Pea Ridge*, 266–67.

43. After the Union victory at Pea Ridge, a lack of supplies and foraging opportunities in northwest Arkansas caused Curtis to pull the Army of the Southwest back into Missouri. The Yankees began their march to the Keetsville, Missouri, area on March 18. Shea and Hess, *Pea Ridge*, 277–78.

44. James C. Bridges, nineteen, enrolled in the Second Arkansas Mounted Rifles on July 27, 1861, at Camp McRae, Arkansas. He was captured at Pea Ridge and exchanged on May 17, 1862. Bridges was promoted to second sergeant on November 10, 1862. Service Records, Roll 17. L. W. Bushnell, who also is listed in the service records as Lyric Brouchellon, was twenty-two years old when he enrolled in the Second Arkansas Mounted Rifles on July 27, 1861, at Camp McRae. Captured at Pea Ridge, he died of erysipelas on April 26, 1862, at the military prison at Alton, Illinois. Service Records, Roll 17. Martin V. Cole, age twenty, enrolled as a private in Company E of the Second Arkansas Mounted Rifles on July 27, 1861, at Camp McRae. Captured at Pea Ridge, he was listed as "taken prisoner, taken the oath" on the March 1 to June 30, 1862, muster. He was again listed as present on the May and June 1863 muster. Cole deserted on January 8, 1864, taking $14.35 worth of ordnance stores with him. Service Records, Roll 18. George E. May, twenty-two, enrolled as a private in Company E of the Second Arkansas Mounted Rifles on July 27, 1861, at Camp McRae. A farmer and Georgia native, he lived before the war with his parents and seven other family members in Clark County's Caddo Township. He was listed as sick in a Little Rock hospital on the March and April 1862 muster sheet. May deserted January 8, 1864, but did not leave Confederate service. He was among the Southern soldiers killed at the battle of Poison Spring on April 18, 1864, near Camden in southwest Arkansas. Service Records, Roll 20; McLane, *Clark County Census,* 60; "Company E, 2nd Regiment Arkansas Mounted Rifles," *Clark County Historical Journal* (1998): 140. Sterling Burton, twenty-eight, enrolled as a private in the Second Arkansas Mounted Rifles on July 27, 1861, at Camp McRae. There are no records on Burton after his capture at Pea Ridge. Service Records, Roll 17. H. C. Ellis enlisted in Company E of the Second Arkansas Mounted Rifles on February 4, 1862, for a three-year stint. He was captured at Pea Ridge, but the January and

February 1863 muster roll shows him back with the company. He was hospitalized in the spring then discharged from an Atlanta hospital in May or June 1863, after which he disappears from the muster rolls. Service Records, Roll 18.

45. Henry Benjamin, twenty-eight, enrolled as a private in the Second Arkansas Mounted Rifles on July 27, 1861, at Camp McRae. He was wounded at Pea Ridge, and there is no record of him after June 30, 1862. Service Records, Roll 17. Hendrick H. Osburn, an eighteen-year-old farmer, enrolled as a private in Company E of the Second Arkansas Mounted Rifles on March 1, 1862, at Hogeye, Arkansas. He was five feet, five inches tall and had a swarthy complexion, gray eyes, and light hair. He was discharged from service on June 21, 1862, for a "spinal disability from gunshot wound received at Elk Horn." Service Records, Roll 20. He was the son of P. M. Osburn, 51, a farmer from North Carolina who lived in Southfork Township, Clark County, with his wife and their children. McLane, *Clark County Census,* 67.

Chapter 3: "Until endurance ceased to be a virtue . . .": Shiloh and Corinth

1. Hammock, *With Honor Untarnished,* 52.

2. Spence was appointed second lieutenant of Company B on April 1 and would lead his men into battle in that capacity five days later. Service Records, Roll 51.

3. Hammock, *With Honor Untarnished,* 52–53; Shelby Foote, *The Civil War: A Narrative,* vol. 1 (New York: Random House, 1958), 324.

4. Foote, *The Civil War,* 1: 324, 327. Private William Bevens wrote later, "General Johnston was cheered as he rode by our command and I remember his words as well as if they had been today: 'Shoot low boys; it takes two to carry one off the field.'" Sutherland, *Reminiscences of a Private,* 67.

5. *OR,* vol. 10, pt. 1: 489.

6. Larry J. Daniel, *Shiloh: The Battle That Changed the Civil War.* (New York: Simon & Schuster, 1997), 211–13; Hammock, *With Honor Untarnished,* 56; Wiley Sword, *Shiloh: Bloody April* (New York: Morrow, 1974; reprint, Dayton, Ohio: Press of Morningside Bookshop, 1999), 255.

7. *OR,* 10: 488.

8. *OR,* 10: 480.

9. Daniel, *Shiloh,* 215; Service Records, Roll 51.

10. Thomas R. Stone, diary, 1861–1862, Small Manuscript Collection, Box 4, No. 10, Arkansas History Commission, Little Rock, 33–34.

11. James Lee McDonough, *Shiloh—In Hell Before Night* (Knoxville, Tenn.: The University of Tennessee Press, 1977) 162.

12. Daniel, *Shiloh,* 236.

13. McDonough, *Shiloh,* 178–79.

14. Johnston received a slight leg wound, which apparently was unnoticed

until Tennessee governor Isham G. Harris, riding with the general's entourage, noticed that he was growing pale. "General, are you wounded?" Harris asked, to which Johnston replied "in a very deliberate and emphatic tone: 'Yes, and, I fear, seriously.'" An errant minnie ball had nicked an artery in Johnston's leg, a possibly minor wound if caught in time. Johnston, however, had previously ordered his personal surgeon to tend to several wounded Yankees, and the general bled to death. William Preston Johnston, "Albert Sidney Johnston at Shiloh," in vol. 1, *Battles and Leaders of the Civil War,* 565.

15. Beauregard's decision to not attempt a final assault on the Federal lines in a gamble to drive the Yankees into the Tennessee River was hotly argued after the battle and well into the postwar years by the participants, and it continues to be discussed by modern historians. Johnston, "Albert Sidney Johnston at Shiloh," 567–68, 590–91; McDonough, *Shiloh,* 180–83; Daniel, *Shiloh,* 238–61.

16. *OR,* 10: 488.

17. McDonough, *Shiloh,* 197.

18. *OR,* 10: 488–89.

19. McDonough, *Shiloh,* 206–8.

20. McDonough, *Shiloh,* 186–88, 214.

21. Thomas Spence's muster sheet for March and April 1862 lists him as "absent with leave went home with wounded brother." Service Records, Roll 21.

22. *Battles and Leaders of the Civil War,* 1: 538–39. The combined losses at Shiloh exceeded those of the American Revolution, the War of 1812, and the Mexican War, and they were dwarfed by the casualty tolls of future Civil War battles. Foote, *The Civil War,* 1: 351.

23. *Battles and Leaders of the Civil War,* 1: 529; Hammock, *With Honor Untarnished,* 60. Gibson's losses were 97 killed, 488 wounded, and 97 missing; there is no individual breakdown of killed, wounded, and missing for the First Arkansas.

24. The soldiers of the Second Arkansas may have found some comfort in continuing to receive forty cents per day for the use of their horses for some time following abandonment of their mounts. Leeper, *Rebels Valiant,* 71–72.

25. T. Michael Parrish, "Siege of Corinth, Mississippi" in *The Civil War Battlefield Guide,* ed. Frances H. Kennedy, 2d ed. (Boston: Houghton Mifflin, 1998), 52–53.

26. Leeper, *Rebels Valiant,* 81–82.

27. Hammock, *With Honor Untarnished,* 67–68. Fagan reported that "the enemy was driven hurriedly before us from one point to another until we reached a morass or swamp, which prevented farther pursuit. At this point, by order, the troops were withdrawn, and returned in good order and high spirits to camp." *OR,* vol. 10, pt. 1: 830. Private Bevens of Company G dismissed the battle at Farmington thus: "The Yankee forces advanced to Farmington, and we had a little more fighting. They captured one of our outposts, then we drove them back to their lines." Sutherland, *Reminiscences of a Private,* 77. The Second Arkansas

Mounted Rifles also took part in this operation against the Federal left at Farmington. Leeper, *Rebels Valiant*, 88.

28. Leeper, *Rebels Valiant*, 88. Halleck also faced heavy losses from disease; by the end of May, 55,000 of his 150,000 troops were ineffective, and more than half of the Union high command, including "Old Brains" himself, suffered from dysentery. Parrish, "Siege of Corinth, Mississippi," 53.

29. Parrish, "Siege of Corinth, Mississippi," 53–54; Leeper, *Rebels Valiant*, 95.

30. Hammock, *With Honor Untarnished*, 69–70. The *Washington (Arkansas) Telegraph* reported that Fagan resigned after being refused a leave of absence to assist his family in Arkansas, and John Harrell in *Confederate Military History* asserts that Fagan "became offended by General Bragg's treatment, which he deemed harsh and unreasonable." In any event, Fagan was soon back in uniform in Arkansas, and as a general he commanded troops at Prairie Grove, at Helena, during the Camden Expedition, and in Price's Missouri Raid. *Washington (Arkansas) Telegraph*, August 13, 1862, p. 2; John M. Harrell, *Confederate Military History of Arkansas* in vol. 14 of *Confederate Military History Extended Edition*, ed. Clement A. Evans (Atlanta, Ga.: Confederate Publishing Company, 1899; reprint, with new material, Wilmington, N.C.: Broadfoot Publishing Company, 1988), 324; Warner, *Generals in Gray*, 86.

31. Hammock, *With Honor Untarnished*, 70, 145; Service Records, Roll 46.

32. The Confederacy discontinued the practice of allowing wounded soldiers to recover at home after 1863 because of improper care received there and "an increasing reluctance of those on furlough to return to camp." Wiley, *The Life of Johnny Reb*, 262–63; Service Records, Rolls 21, 51.

33. Following the loss at Pea Ridge, Confederate general Earl Van Dorn began moving his troops eastward, informing his superiors that he would gather them at Jacksonport on the White River by early April. He changed the marshalling point from Jacksonport to Des Arc after receiving orders on March 25 to send his army to Memphis to join Gen. Albert Sidney Johnston's army in attacking Federal troops at Pittsburg Landing, Tennessee, Pocahontas had been a key strategic point in Confederate military thinking in 1861 and early 1862; it was erroneously believed to be a good point from which to send troops to defend the Mississippi or to operate in the west. Bordered as it was by swamps to the east and mountains to the west, Pocahontas was a bad location from which to operate in either direction. Shea and Hess, *Pea Ridge*, 286–88; Dougan, *Confederate Arkansas*, 76–77.

34. Two sons of Dr. Benjamin P. Jett of Washington, Arkansas, likely were present at Pea Ridge: Benjamin P. Jett Jr. and Edward Davenport Jett. Jett Jr. first served as the elected second lieutenant of the "Hempstead Riflemen" of the Eighth Arkansas Militia, which he joined on January 12, 1861, before Arkansas left the Union. At age twenty-three, he organized Captain Jett's Company of Arkansas Infantry at Fort Smith on December 4, 1861, which became Company H of the Seventeenth Arkansas Infantry Regiment. He was appointed major of the regi-

ment to date from April 16, 1862, and retained that position after the Eleventh and Seventeenth Arkansas were consolidated. He signed his parole at Jackson, Mississippi, on May 14, 1865. Service Records, Rolls 122, 154, 256; Bobbie Jones McLane, *Hempstead County, Arkansas, United States Census of 1850* (Hot Springs, Ark.: self-published, 1967), 40. Edward Davenport Jett, twenty-five, enrolled as second lieutenant in his brother's company of the Seventeenth Arkansas Infantry on December 15, 1861, at Bentonville. He was promoted to first lieutenant by February 1862 and was captain of Company H when captured at Port Hudson, Louisiana, on July 8, 1863. He spent the remainder of the war in Federal prison camps at Fort Columbus in New York Harbor, Johnson's Island, Ohio, and Fort Delaware, Delaware. Edward Jett was paroled on June 12, 1865. He had a light complexion, black hair, gray eyes, and was five feet, eleven inches tall. The *Washington (Arkansas) Telegraph* noted on March 26, 1862, that Edward Jett had fought at Pea Ridge. Service Records, Rolls 154, 122; Mrs. Capitola Glazner and Mrs. Gerald B. McLane, *Hempstead County, Arkansas, United States Census of 1860* (Privately printed: Hot Springs National Park, Ark., 1969), 39; *Washington (Arkansas) Telegraph,* March 26, 1862. A soldier named Jett served in the Second Arkansas Mounted Rifles with Tom Spence, but he was not a son of Washington's Dr. Jett. Finis E. Jett, nineteen, enrolled in Company K, Second Arkansas Mounted Rifles, on December 22, 1861, at Cantonment Bee. Jett was promoted to third sergeant on May 23, 1862, then to second sergeant on June 17. He was wounded in the right thigh on August 3, 1864, and placed in a hospital in Ocmulgee, Georgia. He was later among the survivors of the Second Arkansas who surrendered at Greensboro, North Carolina, in 1865. Service Records, Roll 19; Leeper, *Rebels Valiant,* 308. Dr. Benjamin P. Jett, fifty-two, a Virginia native, lived in Washington, Arkansas, with his wife. Ten children also lived in their household. Glazner and McLane, *Hempstead County Census,* 2.

35. Jacob L. Stroope, thirty-six, joined the Second Arkansas Mounted Rifles on July 27, 1861, at Camp McRae and was elected second lieutenant. He was then elected first lieutenant at the regiment's reorganization at Corinth, Mississippi, in May 1862 and later promoted to captain of Company E on April 4, 1864, to date from December 31, 1862, the date of Tom Spence's death. Service Records, Roll 21. Henry Waldrop, twenty-four, also enrolled July 27, 1861, and was elected second sergeant. Elected second lieutenant at the Corinth reorganization, he replaced Stroope as first lieutenant when the latter was promoted to captain on April 4, 1864. Service Records, Roll 21. William J. Rowe, twenty-eight, enrolled in Company E as a private on July 27, 1861, but was soon listed as a second corporal on the muster rolls. He was among the men detailed to take the company's horses home from DeVall's Bluff after the Second Arkansas Mounted Rifles were designated a dismounted regiment. He was elected third lieutenant at the Corinth reorganization. Service Records, Roll 20.

36. This letter probably was sent to Col. Harris Flanagin of the First Arkansas Infantry, who wrote in a July 29, 1862, letter home that "the only news I have

heard from home lately was by Mr. Spence's letter." Richter, ed., "The Letters of Harris Flanagin,"103.

37. After the battle of Pea Ridge, the Federal Army of the Southwest skirted along the Missouri border to guard against any incursions from Arkansas. After learning that Van Dorn had crossed the Mississippi, Maj. Gen. Henry Halleck ordered Samuel R. Curtis to head back into Arkansas. Curtis entered the state near Salem on April 29 and captured Batesville on May 2. A separate Union column under Brig. Gen. Frederick Steele came in from southeast Missouri and occupied Jacksonport on the White River. Curtis combined the Union forces with the intent of taking Little Rock, but his overextended supply lines caused him to abandon the plan. Little Rock residents panicked at the prospect of the Federal invasion, and Gov. Henry M. Rector fled to Hot Springs with the state archives. Curtis's army ended up at Helena on July 12 after rampaging through eastern Arkansas seizing supplies, freeing slaves, and destroying both public and private property. Helena would remain an important Union troop and supply depot throughout the rest of the war. Shea, "1862," 41–44.

38. Maj. Gen. Thomas C. Hindman, a fire-eating Helena lawyer and politician before the war, assumed command of the Trans-Mississippi District on May 31, 1862, and immediately began trying to alleviate the manpower shortage caused by Van Dorn's move east of the Mississippi River. He requested that any unemployed regiments in Texas be sent to Arkansas, ordered all white troops and a six-gun battery in Indian Territory to Little Rock, and succeeded in having Mosby M. Parsons's Missouri State Guard sent to Arkansas from Tupelo, Mississippi. Hindman also authorized Partisan Rangers to harass Union operations in the state. Roberts, "General T. C. Hindman and the Trans-Mississippi District," 302–7.

39. The Confederate Congress authorized conscription of all eligible males between ages eighteen and thirty-five on April 21, 1862. Brig. Gen. John Seldon Roane was given authority to conscript sufficient troops to defend Arkansas but nothing substantial would occur until Hindman took command. Roberts, "General T. C. Hindman," 298–99. Hindman later claimed that "in Arkansas there were raised and organized under my orders thirteen regiments and one battalion of infantry, two regiments and one battalion of cavalry, and four batteries— all war troops—besides upward of 5,000 irregulars of the independent companies." Hindman does not mention a Colonel Bruce in a lengthy list of officers who he credits with assisting him in raising troops, nor could I find any record of a colonel of that name from Arkansas. It is possible that Spence is referring to Col. W. H. Brooks, who is mentioned in the report. *OR*, 12: 43, 45.

40. James Gunter was a Baptist preacher born in Chatham County, North Carolina, on September 2, 1824. He lived in Caddo Township in 1850 and was ordained in 1851. Miles Ledford Langley was pastor of Pleasant Hill Baptist Church in Clark County from 1850 to 1855. Initially a conservative, he became

opposed to slavery and served as a delegate to the 1864 Arkansas constitutional convention. While serving as a delegate to the 1868 convention, Langley argued strongly against a constitutional ban of interracial marriages and in favor of women's suffrage. While I could find no record of the two preachers being arrested in 1862, Langley alluded to his tribulations during the war at the 1868 convention. In one speech at the convention, Langley said that "six years ago, if a man said he was in favor of universal freedom, he was thrown into a cell as noisome as the Black Hole of Calcutta,—as close, and apparently as hopeless as the Bastile [*sic*]. I was called non compos mentis [mentally incompetent] at that time, because I said all men ought to be free. . . ." Before another speech, Langley claimed that he had been shot in the lung and had difficulty speaking. Langley and Gunter probably had expressed antislavery views and were arrested and sent to Little Rock in the tense days when Curtis threatened the capital. *Arkansas Baptist,* January 23, 1895, p. 8; Bobby Jones McLane, *Clark County, Arkansas, 1850 United States Census* (Hot Springs, Ark.: Arkansas Ancestors, 1985), 18; Russell Grigson, "Miles Ledford Langley: In Defense of Truth," TMS, Special Collections, Riley-Hickingbotham Library, Ouachita Baptist University, Arkadelphia, Arkansas, 2, 4–5,12–16.

41. Cook is probably referring to Robert Adams of Company B, a nineteen-year-old student before he joined the army, rising to the rank of first sergeant. Two other soldiers named Adams are listed in the First Arkansas's service records, but both were dead by the time this letter was written. Charles A. Adams, twenty-five, a farmer in civilian life, died of disease in Fredericksburg in November 1861 and William M. Adams, a twenty-year-old clerk in Company C, was killed in action at Shiloh. Robert Adams would not survive the war either: he was listed as sick and hospitalized on August 14, 1863 and again on October 1, 1863; finally he was listed as having died on June 30, 1864. Service Records, Roll 46.

42. George Washington Cook enlisted March 1, 1862, at Washington, Arkansas, as first sergeant in Company F, Twentieth Arkansas Infantry Regiment. He was elected second lieutenant of the regiment on May 13, 1862, but died on June 1, 1862, at the home of Campbell Bull in Yazoo County, Mississippi. He apparently was well known throughout the region, as the *Washington (Arkansas) Telegraph* ran a notice on July 2, 1862, reading: "Late arrivals from across the Mississippi give us melancholy assurance of the death of our young friend an[d] fellow-citizen, George W. Cook. He had many friends in this and adjoining counties, by whom he was much esteemed, and to whom his death will be cause of unfeigned sorrow." The *Telegraph* also ran a lengthier obituary on Cook two weeks later. Before the war Cook and his wife farmed in Clark County's Antoine Township. Service Records, Roll 170; *Washington (Arkansas) Telegraph,* July 2, 1862 and July 27, 1862; McLane, *Clark County Census,* 22.

43. Demps Cook, twenty-seven, enrolled May 22, 1862, at Washington, Arkansas, as second corporal in Company D, First (Monroe's) Arkansas Cavalry

Regiment. The unit's muster rolls list him present through January and February 1864. Dempsey Cook, too, lived in Antoine Township with his wife and child. Service Records, Roll 4; McLane, *Clark County Census*, 22.

44. By the time this letter was written, Samuel Curtis's Federal army had safely occupied Helena since July 12. Hindman's only direct attempt to confront Curtis had occurred on July 7, when a force of Texas and Arkansas horsemen under Brig. Gen. Albert Rust hit Federal troops at Hill's Plantation on the Cache River north of Cotton Plant, Arkansas. The outgunned Confederates suffered as many as 136 fatalities, at least that number wounded, and lost 66 horses killed in the battle. Curtis's force lost only 6 killed and 57 wounded in driving the Confederates from the field. Shea and Hess, *Pea Ridge*, 302–4.

45. Tom and Liza Ewing did not name their baby after George Washington Cook, instead naming the child, who was born around 1863, William B. Ewing. Dempsey and Madora Cook apparently did name a child after the deceased brother, however, as she wrote Liza Ewing in May 1864: "Charlie and George talks a heep a bout willie and wants to see him so bad." Bobby Jones McLane, *Clark County Arkansas 1870 United States Census* (Hot Springs, Ark.: Arkansas Ancestors, 1989), 199; Madora Cook to "Dear Liza," Ewing-Weber-Dews Collection, Special Collections, Riley-Hickingbotham Library, Ouachita Baptist University, Arkadelphia, Arkansas.

46. William S. Gorham, age eighteen, enlisted as a private in Company B, First Arkansas Infantry, on May 19, 1861. He was severely wounded in the shoulder at Murfreesboro on December 31, 1862, and disappears from the muster rolls in June with the notation that he was furloughed, went to Arkansas, and is probably in service there. Gorham did return to service, enlisting March 25, 1863, in Company D, First (Monroe's) Arkansas Cavalry for three years or the war. Service Records, Rolls 4, 47.

47. Gen. George B. McClellan's Army of the Potomac had threatened Richmond for much of the spring of 1862. On June 25, the Seven Days Campaign began, in which Confederate forces under new commander Robert E. Lee engaged Federal troops at Oak Grove, Mechanicsville, Gaines Mill, Savage's Station, Frayser's Farm, and, on July 1, Malvern Hill. The week of hard fighting drove McClellan back to the James River and cost the Confederates some twenty-thousand casualties, while Union forces suffered nearly sixteen-thousand casualties. Long, *The Civil War Day by Day*, 230–35.

48. Yancey is mistaken in thinking that Maj. Gen. John Bankhead Magruder, then serving in Virginia, was being sent to command Trans-Mississippi forces. "Prince John" would, however, take command of the District of Texas, New Mexico, and Arizona on October 10, 1862, where he would lead the successful effort to recapture Galveston Island. After the war, Magruder joined several other Confederate generals west of the Mississippi in offering their services to Emperor Maximillian in Mexico instead of seeking parole from U.S. authorities. Warner, *Generals in Gray*, 207–8; Robert L. Kerby, *Kirby Smith's Confederacy: The Trans-*

Mississippi South, 1863–1865 (New York: Columbia University Press, 1972; Tuscaloosa, Ala.: University of Alabama Press, 1991), 18–19.

49. Maj. Gen. William Joseph Hardee was no stranger to Arkansas troops, having held command of the state before moving east of the Mississippi shortly before the battle of Shiloh. The author of *Rifle and Light Infantry Tactics*—the standard textbook on the subject—Hardee would rise to the rank of lieutenant general and serve through most of the battles of the Army of Tennessee, earning recognition as one of the Confederacy's ablest corps commanders. Warner, *Generals in Gray,* 124–25.

50. William A. Crawford, thirty-six, a farmer, enlisted as captain of Company E, First Arkansas Infantry, on May 19, 1861, at Lynchburg, Virginia. He was severely injured in the leg at 9 A.M. at Shiloh on April 6, 1862. Crawford was appointed lieutenant colonel of the regiment on May 18, 1862, and commanded it in the fighting at Farmington, Mississippi, on May 9, 1962. Crawford resigned on July 21, 1862, and continued to fight under Gen. James F. Fagan in the Trans-Mississippi. Service Records, Roll 47; Hammock, *With Honor Untarnished,* 68. There were two Monroes in the First Arkansas: James C. Monroe, the regiment's first lieutenant colonel who later commanded Monroe's Arkansas Cavalry in the Trans-Mississippi, and Edward F. Monroe, twenty-five, a private in Company F who was killed December 31, 1862, at Murfreesboro. There is no indication in the service records that either served as captain of Company B, and William A. Alexander ultimately replaced Charles Stark as company commander. Service Records, Roll 50; Hammock, *With Honor Untarnished,* 70. Nathaniel Edwards, twenty-eight, a lawyer in civilian life, enlisted as second sergeant of Company H, First Arkansas Infantry, on May 19, 1861. He transferred to the Commissary Department on June 2, 1861, but was appointed second lieutenant of Company H on July 25, 1862. He served as company commander later in the war. Service Records, Roll 47. The only man named Kirk in the First Arkansas's service records is Pvt. John W. Kirk, twenty-four, a former clerk who enlisted in Company B on May 19, 1861, but transferred to Company A four days later. Though his records do not show that he ever officially rose above the rank of private, one card in his service records contains the typewritten notation: "Subject: 2nd Lt., 1st Ark Regt Army of Miss, June 16/62." As Yancey indicates, Kirk may have been appointed but later replaced. Service Records, Roll 49. The man who was appointed first lieutenant of Company K was Abram J. Fowler, twenty-nine, a blacksmith in civilian life who enrolled in Confederate service as a second sergeant on May 21, 1861. Fowler was promoted to first sergeant by January 1962 and appointed first lieutenant to date from April 1, 1862. Though he tendered his resignation on May 9, 1863, Fowler apparently remained in service and died on October 31, 1863. Service Records, Roll 47.

51. Guntown, Mississippi, is about thirty-five miles south of Corinth and twelve miles north of Tupelo on the Mobile and Ohio Railroad. Cowles, comp., *OR Atlas,* Plate 154, D-14.

52. There is no record of a soldier named Dickerson in the First Arkansas Infantry Regiment. Private Elisha Brown of Company B was discharged on July 1, 1862. The only other record pertaining to him notes that he lost his weapon at Shiloh, "no excuse given." Service Records, Roll 46. John S. T. Hemphill was not discharged as Yancey indicates. The twenty-five-year-old farmer was severely wounded in the left chest and captured during the battle of Murfreesboro on December 31, 1862. He was taken to the military prison at Louisville, Kentucky, then transferred to City Point, Virginia, where he was exchanged on March 27, 1863. He was promoted to second corporal after Murfreesboro, but the damage to his lung kept him in hospitals and disabled camps for the duration of the war. Service Records, Roll 48.

53. Yancey is probably referring to Frederic M. Greene, the former second lieutenant of Company B, and George W. McIntosh, the company's former first lieutenant, both of whom had resigned. Service Records, Rolls 48, 49.

54. John D. McCabe, twenty-three, enrolled in Company F of the Second Arkansas Mounted Rifles on July 27, 1861, at Camp McRae and was elected first sergeant. He was promoted to captain of Company F on July 18, 1862, and was wounded "slight in head" at Murfreesboro. McCabe was sent back to Arkansas on recruiting detail in February 1863 and apparently never returned to the regiment. Company muster rolls have no record of his serving as third lieutenant. Service Records, Roll 20. Joel Dickinson, twenty-three, also enrolled in Company F on July 27, 1861, and was elected second corporal. He was promoted to second lieutenant on July 19, 1862. Dickinson's brother, Shadrick, was among the men detailed to return the regiment's horses home after the Second Arkansas was dismounted and he was pressed into service with the Thirty-seventh Arkansas Infantry under the orders of T. C. Hindman. Shadrick Dickinson was captured in the July 4, 1863, battle of Helena, Arkansas, leading Joel Dickinson to request a fifty-day furlough in December 1863 to protect their families, who were located between the Union and Confederate armies in Arkansas and "liable to be plundered and insulted by the thieves and ruffians of each." Dickinson apparently never returned to the regiment and was dropped from the muster rolls by August 1864. Service records, Roll 18.

55. Spence probably crossed the Mississippi River at Gaines Landing, which was located about forty miles southeast of Monticello and twelve miles north of Lake Village in southeast Arkansas. Richard M. Venable, *Topographical Map of the District of Arkansas, Complied from Surveys and Military Reconnaissances by Order of Lieut' Col. H. T. Douglas, Chief Engineer, Dept.* (Washington, D.C.: War Department, 1865).

56. Though his service records list his occupation as "clerk," Alex may be referring to George Carter, who enlisted in the First Arkansas Infantry Regiment but transferred to the Clark County Light Artillery on May 26, 1862. He was listed as a doctor in several articles in Arkadelphia's *Southern Standard* newspaper in the early twentieth century. Carter served as a private and a corporal in the

artillery battery. He was captured at Shelbyville, Tennessee, on June 27, 1863, and held at Federal prison camps at Camp Chase, Ohio, and Fort Delaware, Delaware, before being exchanged on March 7, 1865. Service Records, Roll 42; *Clark County Historical Journal* (1998): 134, 139.

57.   Stephen Saunders Ewing, Tom Ewing's father, was indeed still alive at his home in Aberdeen, Monroe County, Mississippi, at this time. He died after the war, and his will was read in 1871. Betty Couch Wiltshire, comp., *Mississippi Index of Wills, 1800–1900* (Bowie, Md.: Heritage Books, 1989), 62.

Chapter 4: "Two faces we shall never meet up with again . . .": Kentucky and Murfreesboro

1.   James M. McPherson, *Battle Cry of Freedom: The Civil War Era* (New York: Oxford University Press, 1988), 515–16. Bragg brought fifteen thousand extra rifles along on his invasion to arm the anticipated influx of Kentucky recruits.

2.   In addition to the captured troops, Union losses at Richmond included 206 killed and 844 wounded. Confederate casualties totaled 600; the Second Arkansas lost 2 killed and fatally wounded, 3 wounded, and 2 captured in the battle. McPherson, *Battle Cry of Freedom,* 517; James Lee McDonough, *War in Kentucky: From Shiloh to Perryville* (Knoxville, Tenn.: University of Tennessee Press, 1994), 129–46 *passim;* Leeper, *Rebels Valiant,* 107–11.

3.   The First Arkansas was present at the surrender, having arrived on September 17. Thomas Lawrence Connelly, *Army of the Heartland: The Army of Tennessee, 1861–1862* (Baton Rouge, La.: Louisiana State University Press, 1967), 228–30; Sutherland, *Reminiscences of a Private,* 91.

4.   McPherson, *Battle Cry of Freedom,* 519; Joseph Wheeler, "Bragg's Invasion of Kentucky," in vol. 3, *Battles and Leaders of the Civil War,* ed. Robert Underwood Johnson and Clarence Clough Buell (New York: Century Company, 1887; Secaucus, N.J.: Castle, undated), 15.

5.   Paul Hawke, "Perryville, Kentucky," in *The Civil War Battlefield Guide,* 125–27; McPherson, *Battle Cry of Freedom,* 519–20. Private William Bevens of Company G, First Arkansas Infantry, reported the regiment's involvement at the Battle of Perryville: "When called into action we crossed a bridge in the center of town, formed a line and advanced to the top of the hill. Our battery was planted and had begun its work when we received orders to recross the bridge and occupy our former lines. We had to retreat under battery fire, and after we had got our battery over the bridge we marched along the pike. The enemy opened on us with grape and canister and did deadly work. We double-quicked into line and their sharpshooters gave us a terrible assault from behind the houses. But when our line was formed, our sharpshooters deployed and our battery opened fire, they had to retreat. So the battle went on, but finally we had to give up the struggle and evacuate the town." Sutherland, *Reminiscences of a Private,* 99. Casualties were

high at Perryville. Of the 22,000 Union troops involved, Buell lost 845 killed, 2,851 wounded, and 515 missing or captured, a total of 4,211. About 16,000 of Bragg's men were engaged, and some 20 percent became casualties, with 510 killed, 2,635 wounded, and 251 missing, a total of 3,396 soldiers. There is no individual breakdown of casualties from the First Arkansas Infantry. *Battles and Leaders of the Civil War,* 3: 30, Hawke, "Perryville, Kentucky," 127.

6. Dougan, *Confederate Arkansas,* 95; Leeper, *Rebels Valiant,* 114.

7. Lucius Polk, a nephew of Leonidas Polk, and the Irish-born Cleburne both were from Helena, Arkansas. Polk had served with Cleburne since 1861, rising from the ranks to assume command of Cleburne's brigade. Warner, *Generals in Gray,* 243–44. Cleburne learned his craft as a soldier in a British regiment prior to his emigration to the United States and was renowned as a stubborn, savage fighter. Warner, *Generals in Gray,* 53–54. The Army of Tennessee resulted from a consolidation of Bragg's Army of Mississippi and Kirby Smith's Army of Kentucky. Peter Cozzens, *No Better Place to Die: The Battle of Stones River.* (Urbana, Ill.: University of Illinois Press, 1990), 31.

8. The cavalry under Maj. Gen. Joseph Wheeler rode completely around the Union army, capturing and destroying four Federal wagon trains and capturing one thousand Yankee soldiers. James Lee McDonough, "Cold Days in Hell: The Battle of Stone's River," *Civil War Times Illustrated* 25, no. 4 (June 1986): 20.

9. Grady McWhiney, "Stones River, Tennessee," in *The Civil War Battlefield Guide,* 151.

10. Cozzens, *No Better Place to Die,* 73.

11. Cozzens, *No Better Place to Die,* 83–96; *OR,* vol. 20, pt. 1, 845, 950. After the battle, Lycurgas Sallee of Company C, First Arkansas Infantry Regiment, went to a field hospital to check on his brother, George, also of Company C, who had been wounded. After being told his brother was beyond aid, Sallee remained with him until he died. While Sallee was there, "an ambulance came to the door to take the body of Capt. Spence of Co. B 1st Ark. [actually Company E, Second Arkansas Mounted Rifles] to Col. Butlers apple orchard for interment but was informed that it was by the Masons and could not allow me to go." Lycurgas Sallee to Comrade J. A. Reeves, February 26, 1910, Sallee Collection, Small Manuscript Collection, Box 15, No. 8, Roll 9, Arkansas History Commission, Little Rock.

12. William Mathews, bearing the colors of Company G of the First Arkansas, saw his first action at Murfreesboro. While chasing the retreating Federals, Mathews said, "Boys, this is fun." A comrade replied, "Stripes, don't be so quick, this is not over yet; you may get a ninety-day furlough yet." Twenty minutes later, the color bearer's arm was "shot to pieces." Sutherland, *Reminiscences of a Private,* 113–15.

13. Lt. Col. Don McGregor of the First Arkansas was mortally wounded in this assault. Captain William A. Alexander of Company B also was among the fatalities at Murfreesboro; Alex Spence would succeed him as captain on

January 20, 1863. *OR,* 20: 854; Hammock, *With Honor Untarnished,* 80; Service Records, Roll 51.

14. *OR,* 20: 852–54.

15. McDonough, *Cold Days in Hell,* 42–44. David Urquhart, "Bragg's Advance and Retreat," in *Battles and Leaders of the Civil War,* 3: 607.

16. *Battles and Leaders of the Civil War,* 3: 611–12.

17. *OR,* 20: 680–81; *Washington (Arkansas) Telegraph,* February 25, 1863, p. 2. Lycurgus Sallee of Company C, First Arkansas Infantry, wrote after the war that the regiment "entered a deep draw parallel to Nashville Pike, when the 15th Ky. Federal Reg't. suddenly appeared over a sharp ridge in front of our regiment, the 1st Arkansas. They were at short range and a volley from our regiment literally cut them down killing their Major. Soon after our Major Don McGregor was shot in the thigh dying soon. While in this draw and pressing forward in a dense cedar brake and under an awful fire of artillery all shots passing over our lines save two, one killing Backus of Co. C. and one killing Babe Cook of Co. B." Lycurgas Sallee to Comrade J. A. Reeves, February 26, 1910.

18. The newspaper from which this clipping came is unidentified, but the reference to "Henry Waldrop of this place" and the list of Clark County casualties indicate it was located in Arkadelphia. Two newspapers were published in Arkadelphia in 1863, *The War Times,* a Baptist newspaper that Rev. N. P. Moore published, and the *Arkadelphia Intelligencer,* which John Messenger published for about ten months. Richter, ed., *Clark County: Past and Present,* 35.

19. Erastus G. Chrice enlisted as a private in Company B, First Arkansas Infantry, on May 19, 1861, at Lynchburg, Virginia. The twenty-two-year-old farmer died January 3, 1863, from wounds suffered December 31, 1862, at the battle of Murfreesboro. Service Records, Rolls 46, 47.

20. James Tarver, twenty-one, enrolled as a private in Company E, Second Arkansas Mounted Rifles, on July 27, 1861, at Camp McRae, Arkansas. He was wounded severely in the hip at Murfreesboro and died from that wound on January 17, 1863. Isaac Jeff Thompson, nineteen, enrolled as a private in Company E on October 15, 1861. Though wounded severely in the head at Murfreesboro, he was back with the unit by March 1863. Simeon Dunn, twenty-four, enrolled as a private in Company E on July 27, 1861. He also suffered a severe head wound at Murfreesboro but returned to the unit and was wounded again on July 26, 1864, during the Atlanta Campaign. John W. Andrews, an eighteen-year-old farmer, enrolled in Company B, First Arkansas Infantry, on May 19, 1861. He was severely wounded in the face at Murfreesboro and sent to a hospital at Rome, Georgia. His wound rendered him unfit for service, and he was discharged from service on March 3, 1863. Andrews, a native of Maury County, Tennessee, was five feet, eleven inches tall and had a fair complexion, hazel eyes, and brown hair. William H. Tweedle, twenty-two, enrolled as a private in Company E, Second Arkansas Mounted Rifles, on July 27, 1861. He was wounded in the thigh at

Murfreesboro and promoted to first corporal, the promotion to date from November 10, 1862. Tweedle deserted on January 8, 1864. William B. W. Brown, twenty-on, enrolled as a private in Company E on July 27, 1861. He was wounded severely in the arm at Murfreesboro, then captured at Corinth on January 24, 1863. Brown was exchanged at City Point, Virginia, on April 1, 1863, but died from diarrhea on April 22, 1863. Service Records, Rolls 17, 18, 21, 46.

21. Tom Spence apparently was much loved by his friends and comrades. Writing years after the war, a Clark Countian noted that "the mere mention of this name will stir feelings of emotion in the breast of not a few, as it does in the breast of the writer. As schoolmate, companion and boyhood friend, as fellow-soldier and messmate, in all these relations, he was admirable, superb. . . . The survivors of Company 'E' will keep green the memory of Tom Spence, until they too in turn shall receive the last order to stack arms." N. S. and H. B. Arnold Jr., "Old Clark County," *Clark County Historical Journal*, (1986 [1988]): 54. The *Southern Standard*, Arkadelphia's preeminent postwar newspaper, published Spence's lengthy eulogy ten years after his 1865 reburial in Arkadelphia; it is included in this volume as Appendix 3. "Eulogy on Capt. T. F. Spence," *Arkadelphia, (Arkansas) Southern Standard*, June 19, 1875, p. 1.

22. Robert E. Hearn, who was born in Wilson County, Tennessee, on December 7, 1838, enlisted as a private in Company B, Fourth Tennessee Cavalry Regiment, at Camp Cheatham in Tennessee on November 28, 1861. He was promoted to second lieutenant on July 15, 1863. R. E. Hearn would die of wounds received near Dalton, Georgia, on May 9, 1864, during the Atlanta Campaign. Hearn Family Group Record—Ancestral File [database on-line] accessed August 6, 2001, available at http://www.familysearch.org/Eng/Search/af/family_group_record.asp?familyid=1198205 (hereafter cited as Hearn Family Group Record—Ancestral File); Compiled Service Records of Confederate Soldiers Who Served in Organizations from the State of Tennessee, National Archives Microcopy No. 268, Roll 18.

23. Susan A. Hearn, born around 1847 in Wilson County, Tennessee, was the daughter of William F. Hearn, an older brother of the writer of this letter, Robert E. Hearn. Her younger brother was Rufus D. Hearn, the Arkansas artillerist mentioned in many of the Spence family letters. Hearn Family Group Record—Ancestral File.

24. There were two Harlans in the Fourth Tennessee Cavalry Regiment, neither listed in the service records as "Jack," though it may have been a nickname. George W. Harlan, a farmer from Wilson County, served with Robert E. Hearn in Company B, having enrolled at Hartsville, Tennessee, on November 7, 1861. He was discharged from service on December 6, 1862. George Harlan was five feet, eleven inches tall and had a fair complexion, blue eyes, and dark hair. The other Harlan was Edward F. Harlan, who enrolled in Company H at Camp Cheatham, Hartsville, Tennessee, on November 28, 1861. Service Records, Microcopy No. 268, Roll 17.

25. Lebanon, Kentucky, is about sixty miles southeast of Louisville. The armies did not fight there during the 1862 Kentucky Campaign. Cowles, comp., *OR Atlas,* Plate 118, 1.

26. Orin Dillon Hearn, an older brother of R. E. Hearn, was born December 11, 1827, in Wilson County, Tennessee. He enrolled as a private in Company H, Seventh Tennessee Infantry Regiment, on July 9, 1861, at Camp Trousdale, Tennessee. He was discharged on July 8, 1862, after hiring a substitute to serve in his place. Hearn Family Group Record—Ancestral File; Service Records, Microcopy 268, Roll 145.

27. Granderson Turner Hearn, an older brother of R. E. Hearn, was born March 11, 1830, in Wilson County, Tennessee. He, too, served in Company B of the Fourth Tennessee Cavalry Regiment, having enrolled as a private on October 11, 1862, at Lebanon, Kentucky. He served through the war, surrendering May 9, 1865, at Washington, Georgia, and taking the oath of allegiance to the United States on June 15, 1865. Granderson Hearn was five feet, eleven inches tall and had a fair complexion, light hair, and blue eyes. Hearn Family Record Group—Ancestral File; Service Records, Microcopy No. 268, Roll 17.

28. R. E. Hearn's mother was Elizabeth Turner Hearn, born May 17, 1788, and married to Ebeneezer Hearn on November 28, 1816. His sister, Susan Turner Hearn, was born February 25, 1835, in Wilson County, Tennessee. "Little Orin" is Orin H. Belcher, the son of Susan Turner Hearn and her husband, Sutton E. Belcher. Orin Belcher was born January 20, 1861. Hearn Family Record Group—Ancestral File.

29. "Brother Whit" is Whitson Page Hearn, born April 11, 1820, in Wilson County, Tennessee. "Sister" is likely Louisa F. Hearn, born January 29, 1824, in Wilson County, and the only Tennessee member of the family not mentioned earlier in the letter. Hearn Family Record Group—Ancestral File.

30. Charles Carter enlisted as second lieutenant of Company H of the Second Arkansas Mounted Rifles on August 4, 1861, at Crane Creek, Missouri. He was elected first lieutenant on September 23, 1861, and then promoted to captain when the company reorganized on May 8, 1862. Carter was killed at Richmond, Kentucky, on August 30, 1862. Service Records, Roll 17.

31. Hessekiah L. Cash, nineteen, enrolled as a private in the Second Arkansas Mounted Rifles on October 15, 1861, at Camp Holloway. He was five feet, eight inches tall and had a fair complexion, light hair, and gray eyes. Cash was paroled at Raleigh, North Carolina, on June 22, 1865. Service Records, Roll 17. Daniel T. McCallum, twenty-two, enlisted as third sergeant of the Second Arkansas Mounted Rifles on July 27, 1861, at Camp McRae. He was elected brevet second lieutenant on December 21, 1862. McCallum was wounded in the right hip in 1864 and requested leave of absence on April 27, 1865. He signed his parole on May 16, 1865. Service Records, Roll 20.

32. The fortifications at Cumberland Gap were strengthened by both Union and Confederate troops to defend the strategically important gateway between

east Tennessee and eastern Kentucky. At the beginning of the Kentucky campaign, Kirby Smith flanked the Federal defenders out of the works at Cumberland Gap by crossing into Kentucky at Big Creek Gap to the west, avoiding a lengthy siege. Leeper, *Rebels Valiant*, 103; McDonough, *War in Kentucky*, 80–81; George W. Morgan, "Cumberland Gap," in *Battles and Leaders of the Civil War*, 3: 62–69 *passim*.

33.   Jonathan Calloway wrote home on October 27, 1862: "I saw the first Arkansas regt. a few days since they all look dingy—they have no advantage in looks over 'the Western rabble' Uniforms have done and played out They have seen hard times as well as ourselves—Lt. Alex Spence's wound has rendered him unable to do service." Jonathan Calloway to J. H. Thomas, October 27, 1862. Alex Spence did tender his resignation on November 17, 1862, but apparently was persuaded to remain in service. Service Records, Roll 51.

34.   Tom Spence probably is referring to William J. Edwards of Company B, Second Arkansas Mounted Rifles, who was the regiment's adjutant at the time, though not a captain. Edwards, twenty-three, was mustered into service on July 15, 1861, at a camp near Bentonville, where he was elected second lieutenant. He is listed in muster rolls as acting adjutant by that fall, was then promoted to first lieutenant and made inspector general on June 30, 1862, and finally was promoted to adjutant on September 23, 1862. Service Records, Roll 18.

35.   B. Painter, a thirty-two-year-old Virginia native, was a gunsmith in Arkadelphia in 1860. He owned $3,000 in real and $425 in personal property, and it is possible that he owned some of the real estate in partnership with Tom Spence. *Arkansas 1860 Census*, 15.

36.   The retreat from Kentucky was a harsh one for most of the Confederate soldiers involved, who had to travel through a sparsely populated region that already had been picked over by both armies. One officer reported that he had to place armed guards to protect the fodder for the army's horses and mules, but that hungry soldiers still would search for kernels of shelled corn from areas where the stock had been fed, then "wash it and parch it. I did it several times myself." McDonough, *War in Kentucky*, 311.

37.   Readyville, Tennessee, was located about twelve miles east of Murfreesboro. Cowles, comp., *OR Atlas*, Plate 30, 2.

38.   Major Hiram S. Bradford served as acting adjutant general for John Porter McCown's division and was a close personal friend of Tennessee governor Isham Harris. Joseph H. Crute, *Confederate Staff Officers, 1861–1865* (Powhatan, Va.: Derwent Books, 1982), 136–37; Connelly, *Army of the Heartland*, 41.

39.   Tom Spence was elected Clark County sheriff in 1860 but abandoned the office when he enlisted in the Second Arkansas Mounted Rifles. His brother-in-law, Joshua Elder, was elected Clark County sheriff in 1862. An article in the 1986 *Clark County Historical Journal* surmises that Elder also finished out Spence's unexpired term before being elected himself. Nicholas Dyer, who also was Arkadelphia's postmaster, was serving the last of his six terms as Clark County

judge in 1862. N. S. and H. B. Arnold Jr., "Old Clark County," *Clark County Historical Journal*, (1986 [1988]): 46–47; Richter, ed., *Clark County Arkansas Past and Present*, 71, 531.

40. Only a typewritten transcription of this initial leave request is known to exist; there is not an original copy in the Spence Family Collection at the Old State House Museum.

41. Tom Spence is referring to four members of the Confederate Congress as character witnesses. Augustus Hill Garland (1832–1899) of Arkansas served as a member of the 1861 Provisional Confederate Congress, then as a representative in the regular Congress. He ran for a seat in the Confederate Senate in 1863 but was defeated, though he was reelected to the House. Garland became a senator in 1864, being appointed to complete the unexpired term of Sen. Charles B. Mitchel. Garland later served as governor of Arkansas, as a U.S. senator, and as attorney general in Pres. Grover Cleveland's first cabinet. Charles Burton Mitchel (1815–1864) of Arkansas was serving in the United States Senate in 1861, but went South in early May and was expelled from that body. He was elected to the Confederate Senate and served there through both Confederate congresses, focusing his efforts on often-futile attempts to aid Arkansas and the Trans-Mississippi Department. He died at Little Rock on September 20, 1864, between sessions of Congress. William Paris Chilton (1810–1871) of Alabama was a former state legislator and chief justice of the state Supreme Court and served as a representative in the Provisional Confederate Congress and both regular congresses. Jabez Lamar Monroe Curry (1825–1903) was serving in the U.S. House of Representatives when the Civil War broke out, leaving that post to serve in the Provisional Confederate Congress. After serving in the House in the first Confederate Congress, Curry lost a Senate bid and served on the staffs of generals Joseph E. Johnston and Joseph Wheeler with the rank of lieutenant colonel of cavalry. After the war he served as a college president and as an ambassador to Spain in the administrations of Grover Cleveland and Theodore Roosevelt. Curry spent much of his effort in the years following the Civil War promoting and achieving advances in public education for both white and black students in the states of the old Confederacy. Ezra J. Warner and W. Buck Yearns, *Biographical Register of the Confederate Congress* (Baton Rouge, La.: Louisiana State University Press, 1975), 47–48, 67–70, 95–96, 176–77.

42. Lebanon, Tennessee, was about twenty-five miles northwest of Readyville and twenty-six miles northeast of Murfreesboro. Cowles, comp., *OR Atlas*, Plate 118, 1.

43. Tom Spence's harsh criticism of James A. Williamson, who succeeded Harris Flanagin as commander of the Second Arkansas Mounted Rifles (Dismounted) after the latter was elected governor of Arkansas, does not seem warranted by his record, which indicates he was a respected member of the regiment. Williamson enrolled in the Second Arkansas as first lieutenant of Company H on August 4, 1861, at Crane Creek, Missouri, and was elected captain of the

company on September 25 of that year. The regiment elected him lieutenant colonel when it reorganized at Corinth on May 8, 1862. He was not appointed full colonel until November 5, 1863, a promotion confirmed on February 16, 1864. Williamson was wounded at Resaca, Georgia, on May 18, 1864, and his leg was amputated at an Atlanta hospital. Williamson apparently did not share Tom's enmity, as he later seemed genuinely saddened by the young captain's death at Murfreesboro. Service Records, Roll 21; *OR*, vol. 20, pt.1: 950.

44.   It would actually be another three months before Alex would have an opportunity to face Federal soldiers again. Rosecrans would not begin the march south from Murfreesboro, Tennessee, until June 23, 1863, beginning the Tullahoma Campaign. Long, *The Civil War Day by Day*, 370.

45.   Alex is referring to the skirmish at McGrew's Mill, fought February 15, 1863. In that fight, Lt. Col. William A. Crawford, former captain of Company E of the First Arkansas Infantry Regiment, led some 250 volunteers against a band of 83 men under Capt. Andy Brown, an Arkadelphia Unionist. Brown's force, described as "jayhawkers" and "a party of deserters and disloyal citizens" had been stealing wagons, horses, and mules in the Ouachita Mountains northwest of Arkadelphia. The Confederates attacked Brown on the Walnut Fork of the Ouachita River in what was then Montgomery County, killing eleven, wounding about twenty-four, and capturing about twenty while suffering one dead and four wounded. Brown and twenty-seven survivors of his band made their way to Fayetteville by March 9, 1863, where some joined the First Arkansas Infantry (Union). The looted wagons, horses, and mules were returned to their original owners on proof of ownership. Frank Arey, "The Skirmish at McGrew's Mill," *Clark County Historical Journal*, (2000): 63–65.

46.   Sterling Price crossed the Mississippi on March 18, 1863, and on April 1 took command of an infantry division. If Price changed Arkansas's prospects, it certainly isn't in the manner that Alex Spence had hoped. Price would lead his division in a disastrous attack at Helena on July 4, 1863, abandon Little Rock and all of northern Arkansas that September, and lead his army to destruction in a lengthy raid into Missouri in late 1864. Albert Castel, *General Sterling Price and the Civil War in the West* (Baton Rouge, La.: Louisiana State University Press, 1968), 139.

47.   The First Arkansas Infantry would not consolidate until July 1864, when it merged with the Fifteenth Arkansas Infantry Regiment. Joseph H. Crute Jr., *Units of the Confederate States Army* (Midlothian, Va.: Derwent Books, 1987), 42. John W. Colquitt, twenty-two, a school teacher, enlisted as second lieutenant of Company I, First Arkansas Infantry, on May 19, 1861. A graduate of the Georgia military institute at Marietta, Colquitt was promoted to major when the First Arkansas reorganized. He was seriously wounded at Shiloh and was captured by Union troops on the way home on furlough after the battle but escaped after two weeks. The native of Columbus, Georgia, was promoted to colonel of the First Arkansas on July 21, 1862. Colquitt was wounded July 22, 1864, in the battle of

Atlanta, resulting in the loss of his right leg. He served the rest of the war in post duty at West Point, Mississippi. After the war, he lived in Monticello and Little Rock. He was elected Drew County judge in 1866 but was removed from office eighteen months later during the turmoil of Reconstruction. He would serve as Pulaski County tax assessor and in 1899 and 1901 was elected state land commissioner. He later was involved in the real estate business. Service records, Roll 47; Harrell, *Confederate Military History of Arkansas*, 459–60; *Confederate Veteran* 13 (May 1905): 240i.

48. I was unable to find any information about this soldier.

49. J. Walker Stansell was a thirty-seven-year-old farmer and native of South Carolina who lived with his wife and six children in Arkadelphia in 1860. He enlisted on July 23, 1861, in Patrick Cleburne's Yell County Rifles, which later became part of the First (Cleburne's) Arkansas Infantry, a unit later designated the Fifteenth Arkansas Infantry. The Fifteenth Arkansas was consolidated first with the Thirteenth Arkansas Infantry in December 1862, then with the Second Arkansas Infantry in September 1863, and finally with the Twenty-fourth Arkansas Infantry in December of that year. In July 1864 the regiment consolidated with the First Arkansas Infantry Regiment, of which Alex Spence was a member. Stansell was appointed assistant regimental commissary on November 15, 1861, which resulted in his promotion to captain if his experience mirrors that of Jonathan Callaway of the Second Arkansas Mounted Rifles. He was on detached duty, gathering stragglers in Mississippi, from November 1862 to April 1863. After his return, he served with the corps commissary department. McLane, *Clark County Census,* 83; Service Records, Roll 142; Crute, *Units of the Confederate Army,* 51; Richter, ed., "The Letters of Harris Flanagin," 102.

Chapter 5: "We gained a great Victory at Chickamauga . . .": Tullahoma to Ringgold Gap

1. Foote, *The Civil War,* 2: 663.

2. Foote, *The Civil War,* 2: 666–68.

3. William M. Lamers, *The Edge of Glory: A Biography of General William S. Rosecrans, U.S.A.* (New York: Harcourt, Brace & World, 1961), 273–89; *OR,* vol. 23, pt. 1: 587; McPherson, *Battle Cry of Freedom,* 669. No reports of killed and wounded exist for the Confederate army in the Tullahoma Campaign, but the total probably is small. Michael R. Bradley, *Tullahoma: The 1863 Campaign for Control of Middle Tennessee* (Shippensburg, Pa.: Burd Street Press, 2000), 92.

4. Lt. Gen. Daniel Harvey Hill took command of Hardee's Corps, which included Cleburne's division, on July 24, 1863, after Hardee was transferred to Alabama. Hammock, *With Honor Untarnished,* 87.

5. Hammock, *With Honor Untarnished,* 86; McPherson, *Battle Cry of Freedom,* 670.

6. McPherson, *Battle Cry of Freedom,* 671–74.

7. Thomas Lawrence Connelly, *Autumn of Glory: The Army of Tennessee, 1862–1865* (Baton Rouge, La.: Louisiana State University Press, 1971), 201–6.

8. *OR*, vol. 30, pt. 2: 179.

9. Craig L. Symonds, *Stonewall of the West: Patrick Cleburne and The Civil War* (Lawrence, Kans: The University Press of Kansas, 1997), 146.

10. This hole was caused when a staff officer failed to see a Yankee division concealed in a stand of woods and Rosecrans ordered another division to fill the gap. Longstreet's men exploited the resulting opening, pouring fire into both flanks. McPherson, *Battle Cry of Freedom*, 672.

11. Cleburne praised Polk's brigade for this final charge in his official report: "I have already incidentally called attention to the gallant conduct of Brigadier-General Polk, but it is due to him and to the country, which wishes to appreciate its faithful servants, to say that to the intrepidity and stern determination of himself and men, I was principally indebted for the success of the charge on Sunday evening which drove the enemy from his breastworks and gave us the battle." *OR*, 30: 156.

12. William Glenn Robertson, "Chickamauga, Georgia," in *The Civil War Battlefield Guide*, 230–31; McPherson, *Battle Cry of Freedom*, 672–74; Symonds, *Stonewall of the West*, 150–51; *OR*, 30: 179. Wiley Washburn of Company H, First Arkansas, was among those who felt Bragg lost a chance to destroy Rosecrans's army by not vigorously pursuing the fugitive Yankee army, writing that "all knew we should have kept on[,] could have captured their army few no[w] doubt. It was a complete rout. . . . If we had gone that night and opened fire from Missionary ridge on Chattanooga Rosecranz would have been ours, but Ah! it was a Shiloh." Nichols and Abbott, ed., "Reminiscences of Confederate Service," 59.

13. *Battles and Leaders of the Civil War*, 3: 673–76; *OR*, 30: 179.

14. Lamers, *The Edge of Glory*, 374–76, 391–92; Charles P. Roland, "Chattanooga-Ringgold Campaign: November 1863," in *The Civil War Battlefield Guide*, 241–42. Abraham Lincoln was unhappy with Rosecrans's desultory performance in the wake of Chickamauga, saying the general seemed "confused and stunned like a duck hit on the head." Roland, "Chattanooga-Ringgold Campaign," 245.

15. Peter Cozzens, *The Shipwreck of Their Hopes: The Battles for Chattanooga.* (Urbana and Chicago, Ill.: University of Illinois Press, 1994), 23–29, 103–5; Roland, "Chattanooga-Ringgold Campaign," 244. Longstreet was unsuccessful in driving Ambrose Burnsides's Yankees from their strong fortifications and went into winter quarters in east Tennessee in late December after losing some sixteen hundred casualties in fighting around Knoxville. The survivors would rejoin the Army of Northern Virginia in April. Roland, "Chattanooga-Ringgold Campaign," 248–49; Jeffry D. Wert, *General James Longstreet: The Confederacy's Most Controversial Soldier, a Biography.* (New York: Simon & Schuster, 1993), 371.

16. Roland, "Chattanooga-Ringgold Campaign," 245; Hammock, *With Honor Untarnished*, 101.

17. Roland, "Chattanooga-Ringgold Campaign," 245; *OR*, vol. 31, pt. 2: 749–53.

18. *OR*, 31: 755, 760. Wiley Washburn of Company H, First Arkansas Infantry, wrote of the battle: "Just the cavalry which was on the crest, came back & the yanks rushed up and swarmed. We moved forward & fired on them just a few shots and in a minute we [were] up to they were coming up and as it was steep they did not get a firm footing. Our loss was light and theirs was heavy." Nichols and Abbott, eds., "Reminiscences of Confederate Service," 61.

19. *OR*, 31: 756, 761. The captured colors were the regimental colors of the Seventy-sixth Ohio Regiment. The regiment lost eight color bearers and two officers in defending their national colors from the attacking Arkansians. The fight for the flag was fierce. Maj. Willard Warner of the Seventy-sixth Ohio wrote in his after-action report: "Captain French was killed planting the colors. Lieutenant Metzgar was wounded, and Captain Blackburn struck, and 4 of the color guard and Sergeant Preston, of Company C, were wounded; and Private Joseph W. Jennings, Company C, killed while carrying the colors." Regimental color bearer Silas Priest was hit just as the Ohioans were ordered to withdraw and the flag fell into a gully; several men were shot trying to retrieve it. On September 20, 1916, a party of First Arkansas veterans went to a convention of Seventy-sixth Ohio veterans and returned the flag that had been captured at Ringgold Gap. Sgt. William C. Montgomery, whose right arm was shot off by a shell while carrying the flag, received it on behalf of the Ohioans. Cozzens, *The Shipwreck of Their Hopes*, 380–81; *OR*, 31: 612; *Confederate Veteran* 25 (February 1917): 131, 136.

20. *OR*, 31: 760–61; Roland, "Chattanooga-Ringgold Campaign," 246–48; William Bevens of Company G remembered, "Captain Shoup and John Baird rolled rocks down the hill and when a Yankee dodged the other boys shot him. We picked off dozens." Sutherland, *Reminiscences of a Private*, 147.

21. *Battles and Leaders of the Civil War*, 3: 729–30. Grant contended that the Confederate losses were higher, and that sixty-one hundred Rebel prisoners were sent north "and there must have been hundreds, if not thousands, who deserted." Ulysses S. Grant, "Chattanooga," in *Battles and Leaders of the Civil War*, 3: 711.

22. On March 25, 1863, Brig. Gen. Nathan Bedford Forrest surrounded Brentwood, Tennessee, and its 529-man Union garrison surrendered without a shot being fired. Forrest then led the bulk of his men a little closer to Franklin, Tennessee, where they captured 230 additional Yankees who were defending a railroad bridge, and also destroyed the bridge. Brian Steel Wills, *A Battle from the Start: The Life of Nathan Bedford Forrest* (New York: HarperCollins, 1992), 106.

23. Rawlings Young, twenty-five, a doctor, enlisted as a private in Company G, First Arkansas Infantry, on May 19, 1861. He was appointed brigade surgeon on July 2, 1862, after Surgeon R. A. Burton was detached to serve as medical

director in Arkansas. Young survived the war to surrender at Greensboro, North Carolina, in May 1865. Service Records, Roll 52; Hammock, *With Honor Untarnished*, 70.

24. Dempsey Cook was still alive, being reported present on the muster rolls for Company D of Monroe's First Arkansas Cavalry through February 1864. He survived the war and died in 1891. Service Records, Roll 14; Bob Ewing, genealogical information transmitted through e-mail correspondence with the author, August 7, 2001.

25. The first major religious revival to occur in the Confederate armies took place in spring 1863, which may have led to the order to make Sunday a day of rest for the Army of Tennessee. Bragg himself professed Christian faith during such a revival. Wiley, *The Life of Johnny Reb*, 180–82.

26. Sallie and Alfred Hearn had two daughters during the early 1860s. Elizabeth Eba Hearn was born August 10, 1857, and Fannie Hearn was born June 13, 1860 and died September 6, 1862. Alex Spence's other sister in Arkadelphia, Martha Spence Elder, also had two daughters: Fannie, who was born on November 18, 1858 and died March 16, 1860, and Lizzie Alexandra, born June 4, 1861. Alex Spence apparently is referring his two surviving nieces in this letter. Hearn Family Group—Ancestral File; Wilson-McFadden Family Bible, cited in August 8, 2001, e-mail message from Margaret Curley to the author; information from Fannie Elder and Fannie Hearn tombstones, Rose Hill Cemetery, Arkadelphia, Arkansas.

27. Spence is referring to 2nd Lt. Henry Waldrop and Capt. John D. McCabe of Company F, Second Arkansas Mounted Rifles (Dismounted), who were in Arkansas on recruiting duty at this time, and Capt. Samuel O. Cloud of the Fourth Battalion, Arkansas Infantry. Cloud, age thirty, a Kentucky native, was a farmer in Antoine Township in Clark County when he enlisted as a private in Company C of the Fourth Battalion at Little Rock on October 12, 1861. He was elected first lieutenant of the company on May 8, 1862, and later made captain. He was relieved when the company was consolidated on February 28, 1863, then sent on recruiting duty in Arkansas. The Fourth Battalion was part of Evander McNair's brigade during this period. Service Records, Rolls 20, 21, 76; McLane, *Clark County Census*, 18; Sifakis, *Florida and Arkansas*, 75–76.

28. All of the references in this section of the letter are to various members of the extended Spence family. "Pete" is Dudley Spence, Alex Spence's brother; Miss Sarah Ann is Dudley Spence's wife; Mr. Hearn is Alfred Hearn, Sallie Spence Hearn's husband; Mr. Elder is Joshua Elder, whose wife, Martha Spence Elder, died during the war; Liza and Mr. Ewing are Mary E. Cook Spence Ewing, widow of Solomon Spence Jr. and Thomas Ewing.

29. Spence, as he wrote in his letter of March 22, 1863, is probably again referring to the February 15, 1863, skirmish at McGrew's Mill, which involved many residents of Arkadelphia and Clark County fighting on both sides.

30. The Sequatchie River cuts through the Cumberland Plateau south and

east of Tullahoma, Tennessee, and just north of the Alabama state line. *Battles and Leaders of the Civil War*, 3: 636.

31. I could find no reference to a Tom Dodson in the Fourth Tennessee Cavalry Regiment.

32. Jannedens H. Wiggins enlisted at Little Rock in July 1861 as a private in the Clark County Light Artillery Battery. By early 1862 he was promoted to first sergeant and was commissioned a second lieutenant on February 25, 1862. Wiggins was elected senior first lieutenant on April 18, 1862, then reelected to that position on May 10. He took command of the battery after the original captain, Franklin Roberts, transferred to the Trans-Mississippi in November 1862. Wiggins was captured at Shelbyville, Tennessee, with thirty of his men on June 27, 1863. He was sent to the Federal prison camp at Johnson's Island, Ohio, on July 6, 1863, and was paroled May 16, 1865, at Talladega, Alabama. Service Records, Rolls 42, 43.

33. J. H. Wiggins's Battery, in which Rufus Hearn served, was part of Maj. Gen. Joseph Wheeler's Cavalry Corps during the retrograde Tullahoma Campaign. On June 27, at Shelbyville, Tennessee, two guns of Wiggins's Battery were placed in a small earthwork at the junction of the Shelbyville Pike and a line of Confederate rifle pits about three miles north of town when Maj. Gen. Gordon Granger's Union cavalry division struck them. Granger, hearing that Leonidas Polk's corps was retreating across the Duck River, charged the line and drove its defenders back to within three-fourths of a mile from town. A stronger force here was supported by three of Wiggins's guns "planted in the town in such position as to command all of the approaches thereto from the north." At 6 P.M., Granger ordered a cavalry charge that swept the defenders away and captured the "three superior brass guns, one of which was rifled, . . . and the captain commanding the battery." An additional gun of the battery got away, but Granger reported that its wheels broke through the Duck River bridge and it was abandoned. Another account claims that the gun was left after one of its team of horses was shot, blocking the bridge. Polk was informed of the disaster at Shelbyville in a terse note from his chief of staff, W. W. Mackall, which read: "Push on your trains at once with the greatest dispatch. Martin's cavalry has been utterly defeated before Shelbyville." Granger ultimately "captured between 400 and 500 prisoners . . . and [J. H.] Wiggins' battery and all of its officers and men." Granger also claimed that 200 to 225 Confederates were killed, wounded, or drowned in Duck River during the frenzied retreat, a number that is likely excessive. *OR*, vol. 23, pt. 1: 534–37, 620; Bradley, *Tullahoma*, 76–80; Butler, "History of Clark County," *Publications of the Arkansas Historical Association*, ed. John Hugh Reynolds, vol. 2. (Little Rock, Ark.: Democrat Printing and Lithographing, 1908), 555.

34. Anson S. Brackett enrolled in Company B, Fourth Tennessee Cavalry Regiment, on January 3, 1862, at Camp Cheatham, Tennessee. The twenty-five-year-old's service record lists him as killed on June 2, 1863, near Columbia, Tennessee. Service Records, Microcopy 268, Roll 16. The closest name to Seddeth

in the Fourth Tennessee records is W. Suddeth, and the only record of him notes that he was wounded in the hip at Thompson's Station on March 5, 1863. Service Records, Microcopy 268, Roll 18.

35. There were two soldiers named Hankins on duty with the Fourth Tennessee in July 1863, Alfred and Robert, both of whom served in Company G. A third man, Henry Hankins, had been captured on January 12, 1863. Service Records, Microcopy 268, Roll 17.

36. William M. Sea, thirty, enrolled as a private in Company H, Fourth Tennessee Cavalry, on January 1, 1862, at Camp Cheatham, Tennessee. He was captured January 24, 1863, near Nashville and sent to the prison camp at Camp Chase, Ohio. Sea was exchanged on March 28, 1863. He was six feet, one inch tall and had hazel eyes, dark hair, and a fair complexion. Service Records, Microcopy 268, Roll 18. I could find no information on James Bryan or Adolph Sweat.

37. The siege of Vicksburg, Mississippi, ended on July 4, 1863, with the surrender of about twenty-nine thousand Confederate soldiers. The seven thousand or so Rebels at Port Hudson, Louisiana, surrendered four days later, removing the last Confederate garrison from the banks of the Mississippi River. Though guerrilla attacks would continue to threaten Union shipping on the river for the rest of the war, Federal forces maintained effective control of the Mississippi. Long, *The Civil War Day by Day,* 378–79, 381.

38. Federal troops would not cross the Tennessee until August 29 and 30, 1863, beginning the Chickamauga Campaign. Daniel H. Hill, "Chickamauga—The Great Battle of the West," in *Battles and Leaders,* 3: 640.

39. Charles S. Stark, the first captain of Company B, First Arkansas Infantry Regiment, resigned his commission and left Confederate service in Arkansas in July 1862, moving to Georgia. He died at Athens, Georgia, on October 4, 1899. Bobby Roberts and Carl Moneyhon, *Portraits of Conflict: A Photographic History of Arkansas in the Civil War* (Fayetteville, Ark.: University of Arkansas Press, 1987), 226.

40. Alex Spence is probably referring to Confederate congressman William Paris Chilton of Alabama, who Tom Spence had cited as a character reference in his December 23, 1863, request for leave. Warner and Yearns, *Biographical Register of the Confederate Congress,* 47–48.

41. Frederick Greene was a former second lieutenant in Company B, First Arkansas Infantry Regiment. Service Records, Roll 48.

42. Alabama natives Alexander and John Henry Erskine both served as doctors in the Army of Tennessee. During the winter at Tullahoma, Alexander R. Erskine served as medical inspector of Cleburne's division and as a brigade surgeon in Leonidas Polk's corps. John Henry Erskine served as senior surgeon on Cleburne's staff, chief surgeon of Cleburne's division, medical inspector and chief surgeon of Hardee's corps and, toward the end of the war, acting medical director of the Army of Tennessee. James D. Porter, *Confederate Military History of*

Tennessee in *Confederate Military History,* vol. 10, ed.Clement A. Evans (Atlanta: Confederate Publishing Company, 1899; reprint, with new material, Wilmington, N.C.: Broadfoot Publishing Company, 1987), 464–66; H. H. Cunningham, *Doctors in Gray: The Confederate Medical Service,* 2d edition (Baton Rouge, La.: Louisiana State University Press, 1960), 269.

43. Alcohol—including contraband liquors known by such names as "bust-head," "pop-skull," "old red eye," "spill skull" and "rifle knock-knee"—was a serious cause of disciplinary problems in the Confederate army, but soldiers would go to ingenious lengths to smuggle liquor into their camps. Braxton Bragg recognized this problem early on, forbidding the sale of alcohol in December 1861 within five miles of the Rebel camps at Pensacola, Florida. Confederate troops also would bet on virtually anything, from card games to races pitting the soldier's lice against each other. When battle drew near, however, it was a common sight to see decks of cards and dice scattered around as soldiers divested themselves of symbols of vice before going into combat. Wiley, *The Life of Johnny Reb,* 36–43.

44. No action at Arkadelphia until about two weeks after this letter was written, though there was skirmishing at Tulip, about twenty-four miles east of Arkadelphia. Federal cavalry under Col. Powell Clayton hit approximately two hundred Confederate troops under Col. Archibald Dobbins at Tulip at about 4 A.M. on October 11, 1863, driving them from their camps. This column "captured all of [Dobbins's] camp and garrison equipage and transportation, and took a number of prisoners and horses. This affair caused great consternation in Arkadelphia," Maj. Gen. Frederick Steele reported on October 24. The Yankees left Tulip the next day, with part of the column going to Benton and part to Pine Bluff. *OR,* vol. 12, pt. 2: 674, 1042–43; Venable, *Topographical Map of the District of Arkansas.*

45. Two divisions of Gen. James Longstreet's Corps of the Army of Northern Virginia reinforced the Army of Tennessee, some in time for the battle of Chickamauga. William Tecumseh Sherman, who assumed command of the Army of the Tennessee from U. S. Grant, brought four divisions from Vicksburg to Chattanooga. The Eleventh and Twelfth Corps of the Army of the Potomac under Gen. Joseph Hooker also were sent from Virginia to assist the beleaguered Army of the Cumberland. Connelly, *Autumn of Glory,* 151–52; McPherson, *Battle Cry of Freedom,* 675.

46. Wilson McCauley enrolled as a private in Company B, First Arkansas Infantry, on April 5, 1862, at Corinth, Mississippi, and was killed September 20, 1863, at Chickamauga. Service Records, Roll 49.

47. Moses M. Sanders, a twenty-three-year-old physician, enlisted as a private in Company B, First Arkansas Infantry, on May 19, 1861. He was elected brevet second lieutenant on December 10, 1862, then formally promoted from third lieutenant to second lieutenant on January 20, 1863. His service records say

he resigned on February 19, 1864, but he must have stayed with the unit, as Alex Spence will note Sanders in another casualty list accompanying his letter of August 10, 1864. Service Records, Roll 51.

48. Edward G. McBride, age eighteen, a farmer, enlisted as a private in Company B, First Arkansas Infantry, on May 19, 1861. By fall of 1862 he was promoted to fifth sergeant, and he was promoted to second sergeant on August 1, 1863. The Mississippi native died September 30, 1863, of wounds received at Chickamauga. Service Records, Roll 49.

49. Edwin T. Allen, a twenty-four-year-old painter, enlisted as a private in Company B, First Arkansas Infantry, on May 19, 1861. He was wounded September 20, 1863, at Chickamauga and sent to a hospital in Newman, Georgia. The last entry in his service record indicates he returned to the company, receiving a clothing allotment on March 12, 1864. Service Records, Roll 46.

50. David C. Neill, a twenty-two-year-old laborer, enlisted as a private in Company B, First Arkansas Infantry, on May 19, 1861. Neill was reported missing in action at Shiloh. He was promoted to fourth corporal in the summer of 1863 and wounded at Chickamauga on September 20, 1863. He was listed absent wounded on the muster rolls until granted a furlough on April 30, 1864. Service Records, Roll 50.

51. Simon L. Sanders, a twenty-one-year-old artist, enlisted as a private in Company B, First Arkansas Infantry, on May 19, 1861. He was seriously wounded in the arm at Shiloh, and promoted to first corporal in the fall of 1862. The resident of Rockport, Arkansas, also received a slight arm wound on December 31, 1862, at the battle of Murfreesboro, and a severe leg wound September 20, 1863, at Chickamauga. His obituary in *Confederate Veteran* reported that his arm was shattered by grapeshot at Murfreesboro, but he refused to hand the regimental flag to another soldier and instead continued to carry it through the action. His disability resulted in his being placed on detached duty in early 1864. Sanders surrendered at Citronelle, Alabama, on May 5, 1865, and was paroled at Meridian, Mississippi, eleven days later. Born at Alcorn, Mississippi, in 1839, Sanders died at Corinth on October 31, 1908. Service Records, roll 51; *Confederate Veteran* 18, no. 3 (March 1910): 128.

52. Isaiah D. Ellis, sixteen, enlisted as a private in Company B, First Arkansas Infantry, on March 9, 1862, at Arkadelphia. He was wounded at Chickamauga on September 20, 1863, and placed on detached duty on March 15, 1864, to serve as a nurse at Asylum Hospital in Atlanta. Ellis was five feet, eight inches tall and had light hair, a fair complexion, and hazel eyes. He signed his parole on May 22, 1865, at Montgomery, Alabama. It is likely that Alex Spence met his future fiancée, Amanda Willson of Madison, Georgia, through Ellis, as he is mentioned in Willson's November 30, 1866, letter to Sallie Hearn, Alex Spence's sister. Service Records, Roll 47.

53. Joshua McDaniel, thirty-two, a farmer, enlisted as a private in Company B, First Arkansas Infantry, on March 12, 1862, at Arkadelphia. He was injured

February 25, 1864, in a fall from a railroad car in Atlanta. McDaniel was killed at the battle of Atlanta on July 22, 1864. Service Records, Roll 49.

54. James L. Newton, twenty-five, a farmer, enlisted as a private in Company B, First Arkansas Infantry, on May 19, 1861. He was killed at the battle of Ringgold Gap on November 27, 1863. Service Records, Roll 50.

55. Thomas Bryan Norris, seventeen, a student, enlisted as a private in Company B, First Arkansas Infantry, on March 9, 1862, at Arkadelphia. Norris was wounded at the battle of Perryville on October 8, 1862, and captured two days later at Harrodsburg, Kentucky, returning to the company in early 1863. He was wounded at Chickamauga on September 20, 1863, and sent to a hospital in Marietta, Georgia. His final service records list him as absent wounded. Service Records, Roll 50.

56. Charles Trickett, twenty-one, a painter, enlisted as a private in Company B, First Arkansas Infantry, on May 19, 1861. He was captured on April 8, 1862, after the battle of Shiloh, and sent to Camp Douglas, Illinois, then to Vicksburg, Mississippi, where he was exchanged on September 3, 1862. Trickett was wounded at Chickamauga, but returned to the company by late 1863. He would be placed on the Roll of Honor, the Confederate equivalent of the Medal of Honor, on August 10, 1864. Trickett survived the war and was paroled at Greensboro, North Carolina, in May 1865. Service Records, Roll 52; Garrison, *Encyclopedia of Civil War Usage*, 215.

57. James L. Hicks, thirty-nine, a shoemaker, enlisted as a private in Company B, First Arkansas Infantry, on May 19, 1861. He was captured during the Kentucky Campaign and spent several months in Chattanooga, Tennessee, before being paroled on January 11, 1863. Hicks, a native of Haywood County, North Carolina, was six feet tall, had a sandy complexion, and had dark hair and hazel eyes. Service Records, Roll 48.

58. Alexander W. Hughes, a twenty-six-year-old mechanic, enlisted as a private in Company B, First Arkansas Infantry, on May 19, 1861. Wounded at Chickamauga, he died of disease while in camp near Tunnel Hill, Georgia, on December 21, 1863. Service Records, Roll 48.

59. Jairus G. Robertson, nineteen, a farmer, enlisted as a private in Company B, First Arkansas Infantry, on May 19, 1861. He was promoted to third corporal in September 1862, appointed first sergeant December 31, 1862, and promoted to second lieutenant by June 1863. Robertson was wounded at Ringgold Gap on November 27, 1863, and died in the hospital at Marietta, Georgia, on December 1, 1863. Service Records, Roll 51.

60. Officers were relatively well paid in the Confederate army. Colonels made $195 per month, lieutenant colonels $170, majors $150, captains, as Spence noted, $130, first lieutenants $90, and second lieutenants $80. Enlisted men and non-commissioned officers fared far worse, with sergeant majors receiving $21 per month, first sergeants $20, sergeants $17, corporals $13, and musicians $12. The lowly privates had to scrape by on $11 per month, when they were paid at all.

John L. Ferguson, ed., *Arkansas and the Civil War* (Little Rock, Ark.: Pioneer Press, 1962), 316–17.

61.   C. Mitchel was a forty-year-old physician and Tennessee native who lived in Arkadelphia with his wife and daughter in 1860. McLane, *Clark County Census*, 62.

62.   Following Brig. Gen. John Sappington Marmaduke's October 25, 1863, attack on the Federal post at Pine Bluff, Arkansas, Maj. Gen. Frederick Steele sent "all my available cavalry" along with two brigades of infantry and two six-gun artillery batteries under Brig. Gen. Samuel A. Rice in pursuit of the Confederate raiders. "My troops have orders to break up the post of Arkadelphia, if anything remains there," Steele noted. Lt. Col. H. C. Caldwell of the Third Iowa Cavalry reported capturing "2 lieutenants, some $1,370 in Confederate money, belonging to the Confederate Government, being proceeds of sale of Government salt; 3 six-mule teams, belonging to the Confederate Government; a large mail, and 8 or 10 Confederate soldiers" at Arkadelphia. On October 31, 1863, Steele reported that the Union troops had "captured some prisoners and 8 wagons" but the manufacturing facilities in Arkadelphia had already been transferred to Marshall, Texas. Confederate reports state that a Union force "4,000 strong, with three four-gun batteries" was still present at Arkadelphia on November 2. Tom Ewing reported a November 5 raid by 300 Yankees that caused considerable damage, writing: "About 300 came into town about 12 oclk at night . . . They went to every house & got something to eat—took all the jewlry and watches they could find— Treated the citizens very well with one or two exceptions . . . Peter Greene's Drug store was torn open & all his goods scattered thro the streets—He estimates his damage at $5000 . . . did not stay in town more than two hours." Another Union column of about 1,500 cavalry was sent toward Arkadelphia between December 8 and 10 in pursuit of Brig. Gen. William L. Cabell's brigade. *OR,* vol. 22, pt. 2: 681–85, 1091; Thomas Ewing to "Dear Liza," November 8, 1863, Ewing-Weber-Dews Collection, Special Collections, Riley-Hickingbotham Library, Ouachita Baptist University, Arkadelphia, Arkansas; *OR,* vol. 22, pt. 1: 729.

63.   Spence probably is referring to the home of A. L. B. Green, thirty, who was a merchant in Arkadelphia. The Virginia native lived in Arkadelphia with his wife, Roenia, twenty-one. McLane, *Clark County Census,* 34.

64.   By 1863, there was considerable dissent to Confederate authority in much of southwest Arkansas, with "union leagues" forming in many counties and armed bands of Unionists and deserters living in the hills and in the country. For an in-depth discussion, see Carl H. Moneyhon, "Disloyalty and Class Consciousness in Southwestern Arkansas" in *Civil War Arkansas: Beyond Battles and Leaders,* eds. Ann J. Bailey and Daniel E. Sutherland (Fayetteville, Ark.: University of Arkansas Press, 2000), 117–32.

65.   Edward W. Gantt, a lawyer at Washington, Arkansas, was a secessionist elected three times as district prosecutor and elected to the U.S. Congress in 1861, though he never took his seat. He was appointed colonel of the Twelfth Arkansas

Volunteer Infantry Regiment on July 28, 1861. Gen. P. G. T. Beauregard appointed him as an acting brigadier general in early 1862. The Twelfth Arkansas was evacuated from Fort Thompson, part of the Island No. 10 defenses on the Mississippi River, on March 14, 1862, and surrendered near Tiptonville, Tennessee, on April 7, 1862. A letter in his service records indicates that he tendered his resignation on March 31, 1862. He was released for exchange on July 31, 1862. In 1863, Gantt switched loyalties and became a leading proponent of returning Arkansas to the Union, actually traveling to Washington to meet with President Lincoln, who issued him a pardon. He served as supervisor of the Freedmen's Bureau in southwest Arkansas from 1865 to 1866 and also served during Reconstruction as a state prosecutor in Little Rock. Charles T. Jordan, thirty-four, was an Arkadelphia lawyer who was elected attorney general in Unionist elections held in mid-March 1864. He also served on the 1864 constitution committee. Service Records, Roll 125; Bruce S. Allardice, *More Generals in Gray* (Baton Rouge, La.: Louisiana State University Press, 1995), 95–96; Ruth Caroline Cowen, "Reorganization of Federal Arkansas, 1862–1865" in *Arkansas in the Civil War*, 256, 263, 265, 267–68, 270; McLane, *Clark County Census*, 48.

66. Solomon Spence Sr. apparently had quit the hotel business but moved back into the hotel building because of the Union raids on Arkadelphia. Tom Ewing noted that "the old man has moved back to his Hotel, was afraid the Yankees would burn it if it was left empty." Thomas Ewing to "Dear Liza," November 8, 1863.

67. Jesse D. Jenkins enrolled as a private in Company K, Sixth Arkansas Infantry Regiment, at Camden on September 14, 1861. He was later wounded in the hand in the fighting at Murfreesboro on December 31, 1862. He was detailed to carry mail to Arkansas in February 1864. Service Records, Roll 87.

68. After brief service in the First Arkansas Infantry Regiment, Tom Ewing served for a time as a clerk in the Confederate quartermaster's department in Arkadelphia. By late 1863, he was in Marshall, Texas, apparently still serving in the commissary department, as he wrote home that he planned to set up a bed in the quartermaster's office. Tom Ewing brought his slaves to Texas with him, telling his wife that "the negroes are doing very well. All improving. I will not start them to The Brazos [River] yet awhile, but will hire them all out to pick Cotton until Christmas." His brother, William B. Ewing, was a twenty-five-year-old farmer living with farmer M. P. House in Clark County's Caddo Township in 1860. He apparently did not serve in the Confederate army. He was in Columbus, Arkansas, in November 1863. *The Goodspeed Biographical and Historical Memoirs of Southern Arkansas*, 139; Thomas Ewing to "My Dear Liza," December 2, 1863; McLane, *Clark County Census*, 44; Thomas Ewing to "Dear Liza," November 8, 1863.

69. General Order No. 54 from Kirby Smith demanded that "all officers in the Department of Trans-Mississippi whose commands are east of the Mississippi river, unless on duty under orders of from Department or District Headquarters,

join their respective commands forthwith." The order also instructed department and district commanders to "relieve all Officers belonging to commands east of the Mississippi, whose services can possibly be dispensed with, and order them to rejoin their proper commands without delay." *Washington (Arkansas) Telegraph,* 9 December 1863, p. 1.

Chapter 6: "There has been some hard fighting . . .": The Atlanta Campaign

1. William Bevens noted, "We had good foraging ground and could get chickens, eggs, butter, so we could live high." Sutherland, *Reminiscences of a Private,* 151. Wiley Washburn also found the accommodations acceptable, writing, "We had a very good time as long as we stayed there till after Xmas." Nichols and Abbot, eds., "Reminiscences of Confederate Service," 61.

2. Company B of the First Arkansas was so reduced by attrition that it had only been able to muster twenty-five men for the combat at Ringgold Gap. Hammock, *With Honor Untarnished,* 111.

3. *With Honor Untarnished,* 111; Symonds, *Stonewall of the West,* 196, 199–200; Daniel E. Sutherland, "No Better Officer in the Confederacy: The Wartime Career of Daniel C. Govan," *Arkansas Historical Quarterly,* 54, no. 3 (autumn, 1995): 292–93. Many historians have attributed Cleburne's failure to advance beyond division command to his unorthodox proposal to transform blacks into Southern fighting men. A balanced assessment of this argument is provided by Paul R. Fessler in "The Case of the Missing Promotion: Historians and the Military Career of Major General Patrick Ronayne Cleburne, C.S.A.," *Arkansas Historical Quarterly,* 52, no. 2 (summer 1994): 211–31.

4. Sherman's forces in this campaign included the entire armies of the Cumberland, Ohio, and Tennessee. Johnston would later be bolstered by reinforcements from Leonidas Polk's Army of Mississippi, who would bring his aggregate strength to sixty-three thousand men. William T. Sherman, "The Grand Strategy of the Last Year of the War," in *Battles and Leaders of the Civil War,* 4: 252; Hammock, *With Honor Untarnished,* 112; Symonds, *Stonewall of the West,* 202.

5. In a related action, Union cavalry under Maj. Gen. Alexander McCook hit elements of Joseph Wheeler's Confederate cavalry at Varnell's Station north of Dalton on May 7. Two days later, Col. George C. Dibrell's Confederate brigade, fighting dismounted, withstood a charge from McCook's horsemen and drove the Yankees from the field. This probably was the action in which Robert E. Hearn of the Fourth Tennessee Cavalry Regiment, Sallie Spence Hearn's brother-in-law, was killed, as the Fourth was in Dibrell's brigade during the Atlanta Campaign and Hearn died near Dalton, Georgia, on May 9. John E. Fisher, *They Rode with Forest and Wheeler: A Chronicle of Five Tennessee Brothers' Service in the Confederate Western Cavalry* (Jefferson, N.C.: McFarland and Co., 1995), 74;

Thomas A. Wigginton, et al., *Tennesseans in the Civil War: A Military History of Confederate and Union Units with Available Rosters of Personnel*, vol. 1 (Nashville, Tenn.: Civil War Centennial Commission, 1964), 63; Service Records, Microcopy 268, Roll 17.

6. *OR*, vol. 38, pt 3: 721; Leeper, *Rebels Valiant*, 227–28; Lucius Polk's brigade, including the First Arkansas, did not take part in this action. Sutherland, *Reminiscences of a Private*, 158. McPherson, meanwhile, failed to exploit his advantage at Resaca, allowing Johnston to reenforce the two brigades there before moving his entire army to the area May 12–13. Sherman censured McPherson for the lost chance: "Well, Mac, you missed the opportunity of your life." McPherson, *Battle Cry of Freedom*, 745. Cleburne also acknowledged the close shave at Resaca: "[I]f McPherson had hotly pressed his advantage, Sherman supporting him strongly with the bulk of his army, it is impossible to say what the enemy might not have achieved—more than probable a complete victory." *OR*, 38: 721.

7. *OR*, 38: 722.

8. *OR*, 38: 722.

9. McPherson, *Battle Cry of Freedom*, 743–48; *OR*, 720–26. Cleburne estimated Union casualties at Pickett's Mill at 3,000 killed, wounded and missing, while Federal reports put their losses at 1,600. Cleburne's casualties totaled only 85 killed and 363 wounded. Symonds, *Stonewall of the West*, 214.

10. Knowing Cleburne's reputation for not approving leave requests, the badly wounded Polk told his friend, "Well, I think I will be able to get a furlough now." Symonds, *Stonewall of the West*, 216.

11. John W. Tritsch of the Ninetieth Ohio Infantry had fond memories of this period, writing in 1907 that "on the Kennesaw Mountain line we were within a stone's throw of [the First Arkansas's] works from the 20th of June to the 2d of July, and during part of that time we entered into a truce not to fire at each other unless we came out of our works in line of battle. . . . This gave us an opportunity to meet between the lines and do a little trading in the way of coffee, tobacco, knives, newspapers, etc. and we would play cards with them for several hours." *Confederate Veteran* 15 (December 1907): 539.

12. William Bevens of Company G, First Arkansas Infantry, remembered the Federal attack: "The assault in seven deep lines was vigorous and persistent on Cheatham's and Cleburne's Divisions of Hardee's Corps, the Confederates being covered by strong rifle pits which could not be carried by front attack, coolly and rapidly pouring a murderous fire into the massed Federals, causing losses entirely out of proportion to those inflicted upon the Confederates." Sutherland, *Reminiscences of a Private*, 175.

13. This incident obviously made a deep impression on the soldiers of the First Arkansas, and it is the action of the regiment that is most recalled in the pages of *Confederate Veteran*, being the subject of at least five articles over an eighteen-year period. *Confederate Veteran* 12 (May 1903): 226–27; 15 (December

1907): 539; 19 (May 1911): 206; 25 (April 1917): 168; 30 (January 1922): 48–49; Sutherland, *Reminiscences of a Private*, 174.

14. McPherson, *Battle Cry of Freedom*, 748–49; James Lee McDonough and James Pickett Jones, *War So Terrible: Sherman and Atlanta*. (New York: W.W. Norton & Company, 1987), 175; Symonds, *Stonewall of the West*, 216, 218–19; Hammock, *With Honor Untarnished*, 115; Sutherland, *Reminiscences of a Private*, 176, Symonds, *Stonewall of the West*, 218–19; Albert Castel, *Decision in the West: The Atlanta Campaign of 1864*. (Lawrence, KS: The University Press of Kansas, 1992), 281. The works in front of the First Arkansas were described thus: "In front of their breastworks the Confederates had cut down trees and saplings, and had also driven rails in the ground, making it necessary for the Federals to edge their way through and as soon as they came in sight were shot down." *Confederate Veteran* 19 (May 1911): 206–7.

15. Joseph E. Johnston, "Opposing Sherman's Advance to Atlanta" in *Battles and Leaders of the Civil War*, 4: 273–74; McPherson, *Battle Cry of Freedom*, 752–53; Castel, *Decision in the West*, 352–65. Two high-ranking officers had decidedly different views on the new Confederate commander. Robert E. Lee found Hood to be a rash general: "All lion, none of the fox." William T. Sherman considered that in appointing Hood "the Confederate Government rendered us most valuable service. . . . I confess I was pleased at this change. . . . I was willing to meet the enemy in the open country, but not behind well-constructed parapets." McPherson, *Battle Cry of Freedom*, 753; Sherman, "The Grand Strategy of the Last Year of the War," in *Battles and Leaders of the Civil War*, 4: 253.

16. Castel, *Decision in the West*, 280–81; Sherman, "The Grand Strategy of the Last Year of the War," *Battles and Leaders of the Civil War*, 4: 253; Hammock, *With Honor Untarnished*, 116–18; Symonds, *Stonewall of the West*, 226–30. Among the Union dead was Maj. Gen. James M. McPherson, commander of the Army of the Tennessee, shot dead after blundering into Confederate lines and refusing to surrender. The general was a great favorite of Sherman, who considered him the man most likely to bring the Civil War to a successful conclusion should anything happen to Grant or Sherman. Hood also held the Yankee, a West Point classmate, in high esteem, writing later, "No soldier fell in the enemy's ranks who caused me equal regret." McDonough and Jones, *War So Terrible*, 229–30, 239. Private Bevens of Company G succinctly assessed the results of the fighting on July 22: "This was Hood's second defeat. In two battles, he had lost ten thousand men—more than we had lost the whole campaign, in seventy-four days' battles and skirmishes. It would not take long with such tactics to wipe out the rebel army." Sutherland, *Reminiscences of a Private*, 191.

17. McPherson, *Battle Cry of Freedom*, 755; Sherman, "The Grand Strategy of the Last Year of the War," in *Battles and Leaders of the Civil War*, 4: 254; Symonds, *Stonewall of the West*, 236–39; McDonough and Jones, *War So Terrible*, 303; *OR*, vol. 38, pt. 3: 727.

18. Symonds, *Stonewall of the West*, 240–41; McDonough and Jones, *War So*

Terrible, 303–5. Total casualties for Cleburne's division on the second day at Jonesboro were 55 killed, 197 wounded, and 659 missing, the bulk from Govan's command. *OR*, 38: 729; Cate, *Two Soldiers*, 127. William Bevens of Company G assessed the First Arkansas's tactics at Jonesboro: "We fought all day against seven corps of Yankees. We were surrounded and fought front and rear. Fought as General Cleburne always fought." Sutherland, *Reminiscences of a Private*, 191.

19.   Kennedy, ed., *The Civil War Battlefield Guide*, 343; Hammock, *With Honor Untarnished*, 119.

20.   Spence must be referring to Thomas S. Carter, twenty-five, a farmer who enrolled as a private in Company B, First Arkansas Infantry, on May 19, 1861. Carter was listed as present on the December 1863 to February 1864 muster sheets, then again on the June to August 1864 muster sheets, indicating he could have been on leave to Arkansas during March. The only other Carter in Company B, Pvt. George B. Carter, transferred to Robertson's Battery of Light Artillery on June 18, 1862, where he would have served with Rufus Hearn. Service Records, Roll 46.

21.   The three-year enlistments of many of Cleburne's troops expired during this period, and Cleburne personally urged his Trans-Mississippi soldiers to place Southern independence above their desire to return to their families. Almost everyone in his division reenlisted for the duration. Howell and Elizabeth Purdue, *Pat Cleburne, Confederate General* (Tuscaloosa, Ala.: Portals Press, 1973; 2d ed. revised, 1977), 171; Symonds, *Stonewall of the West*, 196.

22.   Hardee's Corps, including Cleburne's division, was ordered on February 17 to relieve Leonidas Polk's Army of the Mississippi in Alabama, which was retreating before an advance of Sherman's Union army from Vicksburg. Sherman's soldiers marched as far as Meridian, Mississippi, leaving widespread destruction as they went, but they began retreating westward even before Nathan Bedford Forrest crushed a supporting column of Federal cavalry at Okalona, Mississippi, on February 21. Cleburne's troops were back in Atlanta by February 24 and 25. While Cleburne's men were heading to Polk's aid, Union soldiers of George Thomas's Army of the Cumberland demonstrated against Confederate positions around Dalton, Georgia, between February 22 and 25. The camps of the First Arkansas at Tunnel Hill probably were destroyed during this demonstration. Purdue, *Pat Cleburne*, 172–73; Symonds, *Stonewall of the West*, 196–97; Long, *The Civil War Day by Day*, 466–69.

23.   In September 1863, Union forces had gained control of the line of the Arkansas River and everything north of there after Maj. Gen. Frederick Steele led a relatively bloodless campaign resulting in the capture of Little Rock and removal of Confederate government to Washington, Arkansas. Federal forces also reoccupied Fort Smith on Arkansas's western border in early September 1863. Confederate resistance to these efforts was weak. Thomas A. DeBlack, "1863: 'We Must Stand or Fall Alone'" in *Rugged and Sublime: The Civil War in Arkansas*, 85–96.

24. Alfred G. Hearn joined Captain Reuben Reed's company of cavalry sometime in late 1863 or early 1864. The unit became Company A of Robert C. Newton's Tenth Arkansas Cavalry Regiment, an outfit that does not show up in the combined service records of Confederate troops. Dudley "Pete" Spence also served in Reed's company until forced to resign "on account of ill health," and Hearn would rise to the rank of first sergeant. "Rubin Reed's Company: Original Muster Roll in Possession of Arkadelphia Lady," *Clark County Historical Journal* (1998): 132–33; "Tenth Arkansas Regiment of Cavalry," *Clark County Historical Journal* (1998): 138; *Goodspeed Biographical and Historical Memoirs of Southern Arkansas*, 173.

25. The Confederate Congress passed a Funding Act on February 17, 1864, which intended to reduce the amount of Confederate currency "by compelling holders of Treasury notes to fund them in 4% 20-year bonds or exchange them for new notes at the rate of $3 old for $2 of the new issue." The new notes were to be payable two years after peace was established. Richard Cecil Todd, *Confederate Finance* (Athens, Ga.: University of Georgia Press, 1954), 74–75.

26. The First Arkansas Infantry was consolidated with the Fifteenth Arkansas Infantry in 1864. Patrick Cleburne formed the Fifteenth Arkansas in May 1861; it initially was designated the First Arkansas Infantry but was later made the Fifteenth, with James Fagan's regiment retaining the name of the First Arkansas Infantry. By the time these two units were consolidated, the Fifteenth Arkansas had already been consolidated three times: with the Thirteenth Arkansas Infantry at Murfreesboro, with the Second Arkansas Infantry in September 1863, and with the Twenty-fourth Arkansas Infantry in December 1863. Crute, *Units of the Confederate States Army*, 51.

27. Between May 23 and June 6, 1864, Johnston's army lost about 3,000 casualties while inflicting about 4,500 casualties. By the end of June, Federal casualties would still outstrip those of the Southern army, at a rate of approximately 12,000 Union to 9,000 Confederate. That ratio would shift alarmingly in July, after John Bell Hood took command of the Army of Tennessee. That month would see some 15,000 Confederate casualties while Sherman's army suffered only about 8,000. Castel, *Decision in the West*, 261; Richard M. McMurry, *Atlanta 1864: Last Chance for the Confederacy* (Lincoln, Nebr.: University of Nebraska Press, 2000), 111; McDonough and Jones, *War So Terrible*, 263.

28. Gen. U. S. Grant threw repeated assaults against Robert E. Lee's entrenched Army of Northern Virginia between June 1 and 3, 1864. The attacks failed miserably, with Grant losing as many as 12,000 soldiers, including some 7,000 in less than an hour in a June 3 attack at Cold Harbor, Virginia. Lee lost around 1,500 men during this attack. The two armies then settled into strong fortifications. Long, *The Civil War Day by Day*, 512–15.

29. In March and April 1864, Union armies under Nathaniel Banks in Louisiana and Frederick Steele in Arkansas set out from New Orleans and Little Rock to meet at Shreveport and occupy the cotton-rich Red River region.

Confederate troops defeated Banks at Mansfield, Louisiana, on April 8, and at Pleasant Hill on April 9, blunting his westward drive. Union defeats at Poison Spring, Arkansas, on April 18 and at Marks' Mills on April 25 led Steele to retreat toward Little Rock, barely escaping across the swollen Saline River after fighting a desperate rear-guard action at Jenkins' Ferry on April 30. The failure of the Union Red River Campaign certainly would have been encouraging to Cleburne's Trans-Mississippi soldiers, who were mostly hearing of Confederate defeats in their home states. For a succinct account of the Red River Campaign, see Kerby, *Kirby Smith's Confederacy*, 283–322.

30. T. F. Moreland was a thirty-year-old grocer from South Carolina who lived in Arkadelphia with his five-year-old daughter in 1860. He enlisted as a private in Roberts' Clark County Light Artillery Battery at Little Rock on July 15, 1861, where he served with Rufus Hearn. He was appointed quartermaster and commissary sergeant for the battery on February 25, 1862, and was paroled at Talladega, Alabama, on May 16, 1865. McLane, *Clark County Census*, 63; Service Records, Roll 43.

31. The Confederate Funding Act of February 17, 1864, reduced the amount of currency in circulation without a concomitant drop in prices, increasing the difficulties of both soldiers and civilians in acquiring needed commodities. John Christopher Schwab, *The Confederate States of America 1861–1865: A Financial and Industrial History of the South During the Civil War* (New York: Burt Franklin, 1968; reprinted version of 1901 original edition) 66–67; Todd, *Confederate Finance*, 75.

32. Wiggins's Arkansas Battery was attached to Maj. Gen. William T. Martin's Cavalry Corps when it was dispatched to east Tennessee with Lt. Gen. James Longstreet's command to attack Ambrose Burnside's Yankees at Knoxville. By late November, hungry Confederates were besieging hungry Federals, who were safe within the elaborate works around Knoxville. On November 29, 1863, Longstreet attacked the Union bastion at Fort Sanders and was repulsed with heavy casualties. Learning that a relief column under William Tecumseh Sherman was headed for Knoxville, Longstreet lifted his siege and headed toward Virginia on December 4 and 5. Longstreet turned on pursuing Federal cavalry on December 14 at Bean's Station, and Wiggins's battery saw action there as Martin endeavored unsuccessfully to get his cavalry behind the Union troopers. Though it is unclear exactly when it happened, Wiggins's battery lost ten men taken prisoner during the campaign in east Tennessee. Equally unclear is when and where Rufus Hearn was wounded, though his service records indicate he was admitted February 1, 1864, to the U.S. General Hospital in Knoxville with a gunshot wound to the right thigh, the "ball pass[ing] from inner to outer side obliquely downward." Goodspeed's entry on Hearn states that he was "wounded at Pigeon River, Tennessee, by a pistol shot, in Longstreet's campaign against Knoxville." A postwar account, inaccurately saying that the incident occurred at Shelbyville, states that Hearn was shot by a guard after being captured. Wiggington, et al., *Tennesseeans in the Civil*

War, 157; Foote, *The Civil War,* 862–65; Wert, *General James Longstreet,* 354–56; *OR,* vol. 31, pt. 1: 545; Service Records, Rolls 43, 46; *Goodspeed Biographical and Historical Memoirs of Southern Arkansas,* 144; Laura Scott Butler, "History of Clark County," 2: 559.

33. Lt. Col. Benjamin F. Sawyer served in the Twenty-fourth Alabama Infantry Regiment. Janet B. Hewett, ed., *The Roster of Confederate Soldiers 1861–1865,* vol. 8 (Wilmington, N.C.: Broadfoot Publishing Co., 1996), 461.

34. William B. Spence served in Company K of the Twenty-ninth Alabama Infantry Regiment. Hewett, *Roster of Confederate Soldiers,* 14: 364.

35. Madison is located in Morgan County, Georgia, about fifty miles east of Atlanta. It was the site of a Confederate prison and was described by a prisoner of war in 1862 as "a village of a thousand inhabitants, a cultural community and the seat of a popular young ladies seminary." C. C. Andrews, "My Experiences in Rebel Prisons," *Papers Read Before the Minnesota Commandery of the Military Order of the Loyal Legion of the United States, 1892–1897.* (St. Paul, Minn.: H. L. Collins, 1898; reprint, Wilmington, N.C.: Broadfoot Publishing Company, 1992), 29.

36. "Subbers" is likely a reference to "substitutes," or men who were paid to serve on behalf of someone else. The Confederate War Department allowed substitutions as early as the fall of 1861, only at the rate of one per company per month. By late 1863, potential substitutes were bidding their availability through newspapers. "Under the best of conditions men thus inducted into service were not good soldier material," Bell Irwin Wiley noted, and "most of them were mainly concerned with getting as much money and rendering as little service as possible." Garrison, *Encyclopedia of Civil War Usage,* 242; Wiley, *The Life of Johnny Reb,* 125–26.

37. Spence likely is referring to the Camden Expedition of the Red River Campaign, which saw heavy fighting in the region around Arkadelphia.

38. There are only two soldiers named Randolph listed in *Arkansas' Damned Yankees: An Index to Union Soldiers in Arkansas Regiments,* both of whom were about the same age as Alex Spence. Madison A. Randolph enrolled in Company B of the Second Arkansas Union Cavalry at Helena on August 18, 1862. The twenty-three-year-old farmer, an Alabama native, was six feet, one inch tall and had a fair complexion, gray eyes, and auburn hair. He was reported sick in the hospital at Memphis on January 2, 1865, and was mustered out of service on May 22, 1865. John T. Randolph, twenty-four, enrolled in Company H of the First Arkansas Union Infantry on October 2, 1863, at Fort Smith. A farmer, he was five feet, six inches tall and had a fair complexion, blue eyes, and light hair. I could find no record of either Randolph living in Clark County. Desmond Walls Allen, *Arkansas' Damned Yankees: An Index to Union Soldiers in Arkansas Regiments.* (Conway, Ark.: Arkansas Research, 1987), 134; Service Records, Microcopy 399, Rolls 22, 49; Allen, *Second Arkansas Union Cavalry* (Conway, Ark.: Arkansas Research, 1987); 27; Allen, *First Arkansas Union Infantry* (Conway, Ark.: Arkansas Research, 1987); 58.

39. Humphrey Peeke was the surgeon with the Clark County artillery unit with which Rufus Hearn served. After he resigned, Dr. T. J. Scott became the battery's surgeon. I have been able to find no record of Peeke serving with Union forces. Butler, *History of Clark County*, 569.

40. I could find no reference to George Ashby serving in any other unit after the Second Arkansas Mounted Rifles; the final records in that unit's muster roll list him as absent sick after being wounded slightly at Wilson's Creek. William E. Lindsey (formerly of the First Arkansas Infantry Regiment), Alfred G. Hearn (who rose to the rank of first sergeant) and Dudley "Pete" Spence all served in Capt. Reuben C. Reed's Company A of Robert C. Newton's Tenth Arkansas Cavalry Regiment, a unit raised relatively late in the war which saw service during Steele's 1864 Camden Expedition. The Tenth is not included in the National Archives Compiled Service Records. Service Records, Roll 17; "Rubin Reed's Company. Original Muster Roll in Possession of Arkadelphia Lady," *Clark County Historical Journal* (1998): 132–33; "Tenth Arkansas Regiment of Cavalry," *Clark County Historical Journal* (1998): 138–39; Muster Roll of Rubin Reed, Company A, (10th Arkansas Confederate Cavalry)," 1884, Small Manuscript Collection, Box 85, No. 11, Arkansas History Commission.

41. Those Georgians who had not already fled their homes stood a good chance of being evicted by Sherman's army once they fell behind Union lines. Sherman adopted a policy of banishment to keep a hostile populace from operating behind his lines while burdening Confederate resources by making the Southerners care for a large refugee population. Sherman would later evict the entire population of Atlanta. Mary Elizabeth Massey, *Refugee Life in the Confederacy* (Baton Rouge, La.: Louisiana State University Press, 1964), 211–12.

42. This letter and its accompanying casualty list exist only in transcript form; no original of either is contained in the Spence Family Collection at the Old State House Museum.

43. Smith Johnston enlisted as a private in Company B, First Arkansas Infantry, on March 16, 1862, at Arkadelphia. The June 30 to August 31, 1864, muster sheet lists him as "discharged by reason of being under age by ord[er] Gen'l Hood." A postwar article states that Johnston was fourteen. Service Record, Roll 48; Butler, "History of Clark County" in *Publications of the Arkansas Historical Association,* vol. 1 (Little Rock, Ark.: Democrat Printing and Lithographing, 1906), 384. Thomas Bryan Norris was seventeen when he enlisted and had suffered a severe ankle injury during the battle of Chickamauga, as Spence noted in his letter of October 14, 1863. Service Records, Roll 50.

44. "The elephant" was Civil War slang for combat. Garrison, *Encyclopedia of Civil War Usage.*

45. Spence likely had heard of continued Confederate successes in Arkansas in the months following the failure of the Camden Expedition. On June 6, 1864, six hundred Confederate horsemen under Colton Greene inflicted at least one hundred thirty one casualties on elements of nine Union regiments at Ditch

Bayou near Lake Village. Guerillas were active that summer around much of the state, including Fayetteville, Helena, and along the White River. Long stretches of the railroad track between Little Rock and DeValls Bluff were torn up. Confederate Indian troops were active around Fort Smith, stinging the Sixth Kansas Cavalry at Massard Prairie and threatening Fort Smith itself. Fighting broke out in late July near Brownsville and Pine Bluff. Similar skirmishing and raiding bedeviled Union troops in Louisiana, Texas, and Missouri in the summer of 1864. Daniel E. Sutherland, "1864: A Strange, Wild Time" in *Rugged and Sublime*, 128–34; Don R. Simons, *In Their Words: A Chronology of the Civil War in Chicot County, Arkansas, and Adjacent Waters of the Mississippi River* (Sulphur, La.: Wise Publications, 1999), 141; Long, *The Civil War Day by Day*, 542, 546–49.

46. William J. Witcher, twenty-three, a farmer, enrolled as a private in Company B, First Arkansas Infantry Regiment, on May 19, 1861. He had previously been wounded on December 31, 1862, at the battle of Murfreesboro. Service Records, Roll 52.

47. Robert L. Davis, twenty-three, a farmer, enrolled as a private in Company B, First Arkansas Infantry Regiment, on May 19, 1861. He deserted from the unit when it was camped near Chattanooga on October 6, 1863, but returned to suffer fatal wounds in the Atlanta Campaign. Service Records, Roll 47.

48. Benjamin T. Blacknall enrolled in Company B, First Arkansas Infantry Regiment, on August 15, 1861, at Little Rock. He was promoted to third sergeant from fourth sergeant on August 1, 1863. Blacknall was injured in a fall from a railroad car on February 25, 1864, and left at Newman, Georgia. He was fatally wounded July 21, 1864, in the fighting around Atlanta. Service Records, Roll 46.

49. McDaniel enlisted at Arkadelphia on March 12, 1862. Like Blacknall, he also had fallen from a railroad car on February 25, 1864, but returned to service and was killed in action. Service Records, Roll 49.

50. Pitner was listed on the Honor Roll, the Confederate equivalent of the congressional Medal of Honor, on August 10, 1864. Service Records, Roll 50.

51. Sanders's service records indicate that he resigned on February 19, 1864, but his presence in this letter shows that he remained with Company B. Service Records, Roll 51.

52. Sinclair D. Smith, a twenty-four-year-old farmer, enrolled in Company B, First Arkansas Infantry Regiment, on May 19, 1861. He was promoted to fourth sergeant on August 1, 1863, then to first sergeant on July 22, 1864—the day he was wounded at the Battle of Atlanta. Smith survived the war and was paroled at Greensboro, North Carolina, in May 1865. Service Records, Roll 51.

53. Trickett, too, was listed on the Roll of Honor on August 10, 1864. He survived the war and was paroled at Greensboro, North Carolina, in May 1865. Service Records, Roll 52.

54. William A. Graves enlisted as a private in Company B, First Arkansas Infantry Regiment, on November 20, 1862, as a substitute for James L. Townsend. He deserted in late 1864 and took the Oath of Allegiance at Nashville, Tennessee.

A native of Logan County, Kentucky, Graves was five feet, six inches tall and had brown hair, hazel eyes, and a dark complexion. Service Records, Roll 48.

55. William V. Hughes, a farmer, enrolled as a private in Company B, First Arkansas Infantry Regiment, on May 19, 1861. There are no further records on Hughes following his wounding in the Atlanta Campaign. Service Records, Roll 48.

56. Walter A. Norris, eighteen, a student, enrolled as a private in Company B, First Arkansas Infantry Regiment, on May 19, 1861. He was promoted to fourth sergeant in the fall of 1862 but was reduced to the ranks at his own request in August 1863. He survived the war and was paroled at Greensboro, North Carolina, in May 1865. Service Records, Roll 50.

57. Joseph Pierce, twenty-five, a farmer, enrolled as a private in Company B, First Arkansas Infantry Regiment, on May 19, 1861. He also suffered a slight hip wound on April 6, 1862, at the battle of Shiloh. He survived the war and was paroled at Greensboro, North Carolina, in May 1865. Service Records, Roll 50.

58. Zacharia S. Pierce enrolled as a private in Company B, First Arkansas Infantry Regiment, on August 15, 1861, at Little Rock. Service Records, Roll 50.

59. Marion Pierce, an eighteen-year-old farmer, enrolled as a private in Company B, First Arkansas Infantry Regiment, on May 19, 1861. Service Records, Roll 50.

60. Franklin H. Stafford, a twenty-two-year-old plasterer, enrolled as a private in Company B, First Arkansas Infantry Regiment, on May 19, 1861. He was promoted to fourth corporal in the spring of 1862. Stafford was wounded slightly in the neck on April 6, 1862, at the battle of Shiloh, then received a severe chest wound on December 31, 1862, at the battle of Murfreesboro. Stafford was sent sick to the hospital at Griffin, Georgia, on September 6, 1863, and served as a nurse there until November of that year, when he returned to duty in Company B. Service Records, Roll 51.

61. Spence is probably referring to a circular issued by Hood's chief of staff, F. A. Shoup, on August 13, 1864. It said: "General Hood desires that you impress upon your officers and men the absolute necessity of holding the lines they occupy, to the very last. He feels perfectly confident that, with the obstructions in their front, and the artillery to break his masses, the enemy cannot carry our works, however many lines he may advance against them, and however determined may be his assaults, so long as the men occupy the trenches, and use their rifles. Let every man remember that he is individually responsible for his few feet of line, and that the destiny of Atlanta hangs upon the issue." *OR*, 38: 962.

62. In early August, Sherman began shelling Atlanta with four 4.5-inch rifled siege guns that he had brought up from Chattanooga. These weapons augmented the regular Federal artillery by throwing thirty-pound shells into the city at a daytime rate of one every five minutes and every fifteen minutes at night. Richard M. McMurry, *Atlanta 1864*, 164.

63. John Tyler Morgan, born in Athens, Tennessee, in 1824, was a lawyer and

a member of the Alabama secession convention. He enlisted as a private in an infantry company in 1861, at age thirty-seven, rising to major and lieutenant colonel of the Fifth Alabama Infantry. Morgan resigned in 1862 to recruit and become colonel of the Fifty-first Alabama Partisan Rangers. He was appointed brigadier general in the Army of Northern Virginia to rank from November 16, 1863, and ended his field service harassing Sherman during the March to the Sea. When the war ended, Morgan was seeking to recruit African American troops in Mississippi. After the war, he served Alabama in the U.S. Senate, where he focused much of his effort on seeking a canal route through Central America as a bene-fit to Southern trade. He died on June 11, 1907. Warner, *Generals in Gray,* 221–22.

64.   Spence probably is referring to Capt. John M. Mickle of Company I, Eighteenth Alabama Infantry, who was the only Captain Mickle in an Alabama regiment listed in Hewett's *Roster of Confederate Soldiers 1861–1865,* 11: 96.

65.   Sarah Ann Armbrester, the wife of Dudley Spence, was the daughter of Michael and Sarah Simmons Armbrester. I was unable to ascertain the date of Mrs. Armbrester's death. *Goodspeed Biographical and Historical Memoirs of Southern Arkansas,* 173.

66.   "Subbies" apparently is another reference to substitutes.

67.   Charles S. Stark, the first captain of Company B, moved to Georgia after serving in the First Arkansas and died at Athens on October 4, 1899. Apparently, his mother already lived in Georgia. Roberts and Moneyhon, *Portraits of Conflict,* 226.

68.   Thomas Alexander Hearn, son of Sallie and Alfred Hearn, was born February 10, 1863. Hearn Family Record Group—Ancestral File.

69.   "Instant," often abbreviated as "inst.," designates a day of the current month. Garrison, *Encyclopedia of Civil War Usage,* 120.

70.   Samuel G. Peeples, age twenty-three, a farmer, enlisted as a private in Company B, First Arkansas Infantry, on May 19, 1861. Service Records, Roll 50.

71.   James A. Baxley enlisted as a private in Company B, First Arkansas Infantry, on August 15, 1861, at Little Rock. He was again captured near Nashville, Tennessee, on December 16, 1864, and sent to a military prison at Louisville, Kentucky. He was later transferred to the prisoner-of-war facility at Camp Douglas, Illinois, from which he was released in June 1865. Service Records, Roll 46. Robert M. McDonald enlisted as a private in Company B, First Arkansas Infantry, on May 19, 1861. He became a corporal before suffering a serious thigh wound at the battle of Shiloh. Following his capture at Jonesboro, McDonald was transferred to Camp Douglas on October 29, 1864. Records say that while there McDonald "claims to have been loyal. Enlisted through false representations. Deserted to avail himself of the Amnesty Proclamation." He enrolled April 15, 1865, as a private in Company H, Fifth U.S. Volunteer Infantry, from which he deserted on November 4, 1865. Service Records, Roll 49.

72.   George K. Armbrester, sister of Dudley Spence's wife, Sarah Ann, was born around 1846 in Talladega, Alabama. He served as a sergeant in Company F,

Thirtieth Alabama Infantry Regiment. George K. Armbrester Individual Record in FamilySearch International Genealogical Index v4.02, [online database], available from http://www.familysearch.org/Eng/Search/individual_record.asp?recid =91891747&ldsnn=12, downloaded September 7, 2001; Hewett, *The Roster of Confederate Soldiers 1861–1865*, 1: 206.

73. William E. Bevens of Company G, First Arkansas Infantry, wrote in his memoirs that Companies B and G were consolidated after the battle of Franklin "and the two together scarcely made a full company." However, as Bevens wrote his memoirs some fifty years after the war, Alex Spence, in this letter and in his letter of November 11 to his parents, is probably correct in stating that the companies were consolidated, then made separate again, a few weeks before Franklin. Sutherland, *Reminiscences of a Private*, 213.

74. The other captain is Samuel Shoup, a Jackson County saddler who enlisted as second corporal in Company G, First Arkansas Infantry Regiment, on May 19, 1861, at the age of twenty-five. He was appointed captain of Company G on April 1, 1862, and was seriously wounded on July 21, 1864. Service Records, Roll 51.

75. James W. Ellis enlisted as a private in Company E, Fourth Arkansas Infantry Regiment, on February 11, 1862 at Washington, Arkansas. He was wounded at Murfreesboro on December 31, 1862, a wound that rendered him unfit for field service. In March 1863 he was detailed to the ordnance department and in the summer of 1864 was detailed for courier duty. Service Records, Roll 72.

Chapter 7: "Now I shall have something to live for . . .": Franklin

1. William Bevens of Company G recalled the fate of one of the captured soldiers: "One of the negroes protested against the work as he was a sergeant. When he had paid the penalty for disobeying orders the rest tore up the road readily and rapidly." At least six of the black soldiers were executed, and their white officers verbally abused. Sutherland, *Reminiscences of a Private*, 199–201.

2. Hammock, *With Honor Untarnished*, 125–27; Kennedy, ed., *The Civil War Battlefield Guide*, 391–92; Symonds, *Stonewall of the West*, 247.

3. McPherson, *Battle Cry of Freedom*, 808–11.

4. Amanda Willson was the daughter of Leroy M. Willson, sixty-one, a farmer and shoe dealer in Madison, Georgia. Willson, his wife Tabitha, fifty-one, his son Pleasant, a twenty-one-year-old medical student, and daughters Amanda, eighteen, and Martha, sixteen, were apparently well to do, with Leroy Willson claiming $6,500 in real property and $22,500 in personal property in the 1860 census. Amanda Willson graduated from the Georgia Female College in Madison in 1858. U.S. Census Bureau, Population Schedule [Free] of the Eighth Census of the United States, 1860, Georgia, National Archives Microcopy No. 653, Roll 131; *Georgia Female College Circular, 1861* (Madison, Ga.: C.B. Barrow & Co., 1861), 7.

5. Sherman decided on September 4, 1864, to order all civilians to be removed from Atlanta, though he expected the order to "raise a howl against my

barbarity and cruelty." Between September 12 and 21, 709 adults, 867 children, and 79 servants, along with many of their belongings, were sent to Rough and Ready, Georgia, where they were delivered for transport by Confederate authorities. Castel, *Decision in the West*, 548–49.

6. Newman, Georgia, was about thirty miles southwest of Atlanta. Cowles, comp., *OR Atlas*, Plate 125-A.

7. Sand Mountain, located about sixty miles due east of Decatur and thirty-five miles southeast of Chattanooga, is an eminence between Raccoon and Riley's Creeks on Raccoon Mountain. Cowles, comp., *OR Atlas*, Plate 149.

8. Northern Alabama had never embraced secession, sending delegates to the secession convention who voted against leaving the Union. Thirty-three of the north Alabama delegates refused to sign the ordinance of secession. By 1862 a "Peace Society" was active in the region, and toward the end of the war it was a haven for deserters and opponents to Confederate rule. Alabama supplied 2,578 soldiers to the Union army in the course of the war. Carl N. Degler, *The Other South: Southern Dissenters in the Nineteenth Century.* (New York: Harper and Row, 1974), 170–71, 175.

9. Hood placed a pontoon bridge across the Tennessee at Florence, Alabama. Stephen D. Lee's corps established a bridgehead on October 29 through 30, 1864, to protect the bridge-building pioneers and by November 1 the bridge was in place and trestled at both ends. It would, however, be November 13 before Cheatham's men would cross the river. Wiley Sword, *Embrace an Angry Wind: The Confederacy's Last Hurrah: Spring Hill, Franklin and Nashville* (New York: HarperCollins), 66–69.

10. Columbia, Tennessee, is located on the Duck River about seventy miles north of Decatur. Cowles, comp., *OR Atlas*, Plate 24, 3.

11. Amanda Willson apparently enclosed this letter with another she wrote to Sallie Hearn two years after Alex Spence's death at the battle of Franklin.

12. Sterling Price led a somewhat ragtag army of around twelve thousand soldiers across the Missouri line on September 19, 1864, having managed to sneak much of Arkansas's Confederate troops across the Arkansas River without opposition from Union forces. Eight days later, he suffered 750 casualties in attacking the Federal garrison at Pilot Knob, Missouri. The Confederates wandered toward Jefferson City, but declined to attack it on October 8, abandoning a plan to install Gov. Thomas Reynolds and a Confederate government in the state capital. Price continued westward at a leisurely pace, allowing Union commanders to assemble the area's troops and militias to oppose the Confederate column. On October 23, the Federal forces hit Price at Westport, Missouri, defeating the Confederates soundly and sending them on a desperate flight toward Kansas. On October 25, at Mine Creek, Kansas, Union cavalry struck and smashed the retreating Rebels, capturing two generals. The Confederate raiders then began a hungry, depressing journey south that ended with 3,500 survivors crossing back into Arkansas at Laynesport on December 2. One Confederate summed up the atti-

tude of the surviving Rebel troops: "Men are greatly demoralized, and we present a pitiable, forlorn aspect. God damn Old Price." Kerby, *Kirby Smith's Confederacy*, 341–58; McPherson, *Battle Cry of Freedom*, 787.

13. Sherman would not leave the battered remains of Atlanta and begin his "March to the Sea" until November 16, 1864. Long, *The Civil War Day by Day*, 597.

14. Noted Arkansas jurist Uriah M. Rose, on a trip to Richmond in his capacity as the official historiographer of the state's Confederate government, met Barksdale. He described the courier thus: "I had for a companion during my journey across the Mississippi River a most worthy and agreeable person, whose name was Barksdale; a resident of the State of Mississippi, a private enlisted in the Southern Army, then detailed to carry letters back and forth across the Mississippi River for officers and soldiers in the field. He was a very excellent and a very sensible person, and had a perfect knowledge of every foot of the way. Every one was glad to see him coming, as they expected to receive letters by him from their friends and relatives who were in daily peril of their lives, or from loved ones at home. Every one on the road knew him, and, so kind and obliging was he in disposition, that every one seemed to be his friend. He was probably thirty-five years old, was not highly educated, but had a sound judgment about men and things, joined with simple and agreeable manners." Uriah M. Rose, *An Episode During the Civil War*, Old State House Museum, Little Rock, Arkansas.

15. Mooresville, Alabama, lies across the Tennessee River from Decatur. Cowles, comp., *OR Atlas*, Plate 24, 3.

16. Nancy Hawkins, who would have been about seventeen years old when this letter was written, lived in Clark County's Greeneville Township with her parents and six siblings. McLane, *Clark County Census*, 39.

17. James M. Candler, twenty-four, enrolled as a private in Company F, Second Arkansas Mounted Rifles, on July 27, 1861. Service Records, Roll 117.

18. On October 29, 1864, Nathan Bedford Forrest's cavalry and artillery, blockading the Tennessee River at Fort Heiman, Tennessee, captured and burned the steamer *Mazeppa*, which was carrying a load of food, blankets, and clothing. The next day they captured the Union gunboat *Undine* and the steamers *Venus* and *J. W. Cheeseman*, though they burned the latter boat. Forrest then placed a crew aboard the *Undine* and *Venus* and headed south toward the Union stronghold at Johnsonville, Tennessee, as the remainder of his artillery slogged through the mud on the banks of the Tennessee. On November 2, a pair of Union gunboats attacked and captured the *Venus* and two of Forrest's cannon that were left aboard her, as well as some of the supplies seized earlier from the *Mazeppa*. The Confederate cavalryman set his land artillery up opposite Johnsonville and on November 4 engaged in battle with a fleet of Federal gunboats sent up from Paducah, Kentucky; the Confederates abandoned and burned the *Undine* during this action. Despite the loss of Forrest's naval flotilla, three Union gunboats were abandoned and burned and Forrest managed to shell the crowded docks at

Johnsonville, where twenty-eight steamboats and transports and mounds of supplies were lined up. Forrest reported capturing 150 Yankee soldiers and destroying "4 gunboats, 14 transports, 20 barges, 26 pieces of artillery, and $6,700,000 worth of property" during this busy week. Wills, *A Battle from the Start*, 263–72.

19. William Freeman, a North Carolina native and a farmer, lived in Greeneville Township with his wife and eight children. McLane, *Clark County Census, 1860*, 30.

20. James N. Candler Sr., forty-seven in 1860, was a river boat pilot and North Carolina native who lived with his wife and two daughters in Arkadelphia. McLane, *Clark County Census, 1860*, 15.

21. Symonds, *Stonewall of the West*, 248–53; McPherson, *Battle Cry of Freedom*, 811–12; Sword, *Embrace an Angry Wind*, 128–29.

22. Symonds, *Stonewall of the West*, 255. William Bevens of the First Arkansas described the Union fortifications at Franklin: "In front of their works was an open field with not a tree or ravine for a mile and a half. Just before the breastworks was an open ditch six feet wide and three feet deep. At the end of the ditch next to the breastworks, were placed poles sharpened spear-shape. Their main works were six feet at the base. The cannon-breast portion was cut down so that the guns, resting on oak logs, were on a level with our bodies." Sutherland, *Reminiscences of a Private*, 207–9.

23. Govan wrote after the battle, "Our advancing column was magnificently grand, my men advanced with fixed bayonetts and arms trailed and was ordered to storm the entrenchments without firing a shot." Daniel C. Govan to wife, December 14, 1864, Daniel Chevilette Govan #1000, Southern Historical Collection, the Library of the University of North Carolina at Chapel Hill. The attack against the Union lines at Franklin involved half again as many men as Pickett's charge at Gettysburg and covered twice the distance. Symonds, *Stonewall of the West*, 258.

24. William J. Hardee, Cleburne's old corps commander, later wrote of Cleburne and his men: "Where this division defended, no odds broke its lines; where it attacked, no numbers resisted its onslaught, save only once; and there is the grave of Cleburne." Foote, *The Civil War*, 3: 671.

25. Wiley Washburn of Company H, First Arkansas, was wounded here. "I raised my gun to get my man and was shot in rig[h]t elbow my hat shot off, my gun stock broken with 100 holes through my blanket. So I laid down in the ditch. They began to cross fire on us and were doing us lots and lots of harm." Nichols and Abbott, eds., "Reminiscences of Confederate Service," 82.

26. Lt. Col. Laurence H. Rousseau of the Twelfth Kentucky of Reilly's brigade reported after the battle: "The enemy had possession of the outside of the works, their officers calling on them to hold the works, 'that they had them, if they knew it.' Their colors were planted on our works, and a number of their men had gained the top and fired down into our ranks; even bayonets and clubbed muskets were used." *OR*, vol. 45, pt. 1: 416.

27. Lt. Col. Edwin L. Hayes of the 100th Ohio reported that his regiment returned to the portion of the line it had abandoned. "From this time until we were ordered to leave the works, at 10:30 P.M., six distinct charges were made upon my right, and repulsed each time." *OR,* vol. 45, pt. 1: 419. Col. Oscar W. Sterl of the 104th Ohio reported of this fighting: "[T]hey kept up a constant and destructive stream of fire, cutting down by hundreds the rebels who had accumulated and massed in the ditches and immediately in front." *OR,* vol. 45, pt. 1: 421.

28. Symonds, *Stonewall of the West,* 258–59; Sword, *Embrace an Angry Wind,* 195–96, 269.

29. Sword, *Embrace an Angry Wind,* 269–70; Sutherland, "No Better Officer in the Confederacy," 297; James Lee McDonough and Thomas L. Connelly, *Five Tragic Hours: The Battle of Franklin.* (Knoxville: The University of Tennessee Press, 1983), 136. Govan to wife, December 14, 1864; Samuel T. Foster, *One of Cleburne's Command: The Civil War Reminiscences and Diary of Capt. Samuel T. Foster, Granbury's Texas Brigade, CSA.,* Norman D. Brown, ed. (Austin, Tex.: University of Texas Press, 1980), 150–51. The other Rebel generals killed at Franklin were States Rights Gist, John Adams, Otho Strahl and John C. Carter, who died of his wounds on December 10, 1864. Foote, *The Civil War,* 3: 670–71; Warner, *Generals in* Gray, 2, 45, 106–7, 296.

30. "An Interesting Letter from an Old Soldier," *Arkadelphia Southern Standard,* May 13, 1892, in First Arkansas CSA/History John W. Colquitt Subject File, Arkansas History Commission.

Epilogue: "Many painful reminiscences are connected . . ."

1. The First and Fifteenth Arkansas was consolidated with the Second, Fifth, Thirteenth and Twenty-fourth Arkansas and the Third Confederate Infantry. The Fifteenth and Twenty-fourth Arkansas and Third Confederate would be released from the field consolidation in the early part of 1865. Sifakis, *Florida and Arkansas,* 67.

2. Total Confederate losses at Nashville were around 1,500 killed and wounded and 4,462 captured, including 3 generals. Total Union casualties were 3,061 out of 49,773 engaged. Sutherland, *Reminiscences of a Private,* 212.

3. The regiments involved in this consolidation were the First, Second, Fifth, Sixth, Seventh, Eighth, Thirteenth, Fifteenth, Nineteenth (Dawson's), and Twenty-fourth Arkansas Infantry and the Third Confederate. The mongrel unit was designated the First Infantry Regiment Consolidated. Sifakis, *Florida and Arkansas,* 67–68.

4. Sutherland, "No Better Officer in the Confederacy," 298–300; Hammock, *With Honor Untarnished,* 139–41.

5. The Second Arkansas Mounted Rifles were involved in the Vicksburg Campaign, the battle and siege of Jackson, Mississippi; the Atlanta Campaign and the battles at Dug Gap, Resaca, New Hope Church, Pine Mountain, Kennesaw

Mountain, Moore's Hill, Peach Tree Creek, Atlanta, Ezra Church, the siege of Atlanta, and the battle of Jonesboro; the battles of Lovejoy's Station, Moon's Station, Franklin, Nashville, and Sugar Creek; and the Carolinas campaign, including the battle of Bentonville. Sifakis, *Florida and Arkansas,* 53–55; Leeper, *Rebels Valiant,* 286.

6. Mrs. Pharr is likely E. Peeples, the daughter of Benjamin Peeples of Arkadelphia. Tom Ewing noted her impending nuptials in a letter home in 1863, writing that "*Capt. Polleys* left here a few days since for Arkadelphia to be married—Pharr went with him, in order to try his hand. The misses Peebles [*sic*] are at home, & not at Tyler as was reported." Lt. E. M. Pharr, C.S.A., married E. Peeples at her father's Arkadelphia home on December 5, 1863. Thomas Ewing to "My Dear Liza," December 2, 1863; Wright and McCaffee, *Clark County, Arkansas: A Genealogical Source Book,* 166.

7. Amanda Willson likely is referring to Isaiah Ellis of the First Arkansas Infantry, who recovered in Madison from the wound he suffered in the fighting at Chickamauga on September 20, 1863.

8. A little more than a year after this letter was written, on January 27, 1868, Amanda Willson married John P. Austin of Connecticut. The couple would have two sons, Leroy and Samuel. Amanda Willson died at the home of her brother, Dr. Pleasant Willson, in Morgan County, Georgia, on January 20, 1903. Amanda Willson File, Old State House Museum, Little Rock, Arkansas.

9. An annotation on an early typewritten transcription of Alex Spence's letter of November 11, 1864, presumably written by a descendant, reads as follows: "Killed in charge, minnie ball going through chest. Battle of Franklin, November 30, 1864. Body buried by friends beneath apple tree. Body recovered later by friend who did burying. Ring still on skeleton finger given him by parents before went into service. Remains carried back to family burial grounds." If this account is accurate, it bears an eerie similarity to the events following Tom Spence's burial after the battle of Murfreesboro as recounted in Lycurgus Sallee's letter of February 26, 1910, which says Tom, too, was buried in an orchard by friends. Lycurgas Sallee to Comrade J. A. Reeves, February 26, 1910, Arkansas History Commission.

Appendix 1: The Poison Spring Letter

1. Ludwell H. Johnson, "Military Strategy, Politics, and Economics: The Red River Campaign," in *The Civil War Battlefield Guide,* 265; Edwin C. Bearss, *Steele's Retreat from Camden and the Battle of Jenkins' Ferry* (Little Rock, Ark.: Pioneer Press, 1967; facsimile reprint, Little Rock, Ark.: Democrat Printing and Lithography Co., 1995), ii; Sutherland, "1864: A Strange, Wild Time," 112–14.

2. Gregory J. W. Urwin, "'We Cannot Treat Negroes . . . as Prisoners of War': Racial Atrocities and Reprisals in Civil War Arkansas," in Anne J. Bailey and Daniel E. Sutherland, eds., *Civil War Arkansas: Beyond Battles and Leaders,* 214–15; Bearss, *Steele's Retreat,* 16–34.

3. Urwin, "'We Cannot Treat Negroes . . . as Prisoners of War,'" 216–17; Bearss, *Steele's Retreat*, 32, 35. Urwin's article provides extensive and disturbing examples of Southern accounts of the aftermath of Poison Spring.

4. Price's Confederates and Steele's Federals skirmished between April 9 and 12 on Prairie D'Ane, near present day Camden. A Union column under Gen. John M. Thayer had joined Steele's forces on April 9, swelling his complement of troops to about 13,754 men. Steele diverted his force to Camden, occupying the town on April 15. Sutherland, "1864: A Strange, Wild Time," in *Rugged and Sublime*, 112–14; Grace Benton Nelson, "Federal Invasion of Clark County," *Clark County Historical Journal* (winter 1975): 2.

5. Based on the context of this letter, Henry and John likely were slaves of Alfred G. Hearn. He owned two male slaves, ages thirty-three and seventeen in 1860, who were of an age to have joined the army if they had escaped to Union lines. Arkansas 1860 Slave Schedule, 6.

6. "Old man Edwards" likely was Jordan Edwards, age sixty in 1860, a farmer and Virginia native who lived in Caddo Township with his wife and three children. Edwards owned $24,000 in real property and $1,875 in personal property in 1860, including seven slaves. One of his male slaves was fourteen years old in 1860, and may have been "Old man Edwards' boy" mentioned in this letter. It is difficult to determine the identities of the three former slaves mentioned in the letter, but the *Report of the Adjutant General of the State of Kansas* includes the names of 104 soldiers of the First Kansas Colored Infantry who were killed in action or mortally wounded at Poison Spring. Among them were Cpl. Jacob Edwards of Company A, Pvt. Silas NewBerry of Company C, and Sergeant Alfred N. Berry of Company I; it is possible that these men could be among those mentioned in the letter. Arkansas 1860 Census, 30; Arkansas 1860 Slave Schedule, 16; *Report of the Adjutant General of the State of Kansas*, vol. 1 (Leavenworth, Kans.: Bulletin Cooperative Printing Company, 1867), 574–99.

7. This was the same George May who formerly served in Company F of the Second Arkansas Mounted Rifles, as his service records show he deserted from that unit on January 8, 1864. May, a Georgia native, was a farmer in Clark County before the war. Service Records, Roll 20; McLane, *Clark County Census*, 60; "Company E, 2nd Regiment Arkansas Mounted Rifles," *Clark County Historical Journal* (1998): 40.

8. Edward L. Hitchcock, who was forty in 1860, was a Tennessee native who worked as a tinner and lived in Arkadelphia with his wife and seven children. Hitchcock was fourth corporal in Captain Rubin Reed's Company. McLane, *Clark County Census*, 42; *Clark County Historical Journal* (1998): 132–33.

9. The *Clark County Historical Journal* published a number of rolls and rosters of Clark County units that had been published in the *Arkadelphia Southern Standard* in the early twentieth century. These included the original roster of Reed's company, which showed Dudley Spence and A. G. Hearn as privates and the company being part of Robert C. Newton's Tenth Arkansas Mounted

Volunteers. An October 31, 1864, muster lists A. G. Hearn as first sergeant of Reed's Company A of Newton's Tenth Cavalry. They probably were attached to Col. W. H. Trader's Arkansas Cavalry Battalion at Poison Spring—a member of that unit mentions a "Mr. Hearne" in a letter to his wife written after the battle. "Muster Roll of Rubin Reed's Company A (10th Regiment of Arkansas Cavalry)," *Clark County Historical Journal* (1998): 132; "Tenth Arkansas Regminent of Cavalry," *Clark County Historical Journal* (1998): 138; "Senator James K. Jones," *Clark County Historical Journal* (winter, 1979–80): 181; James J. Hudson, ed., "From Paraclifta to Marks' Mill: The Civil War Correspondence of Lieutenant Robert C. Gilliam," *Arkansas Historical Quarterly* 17, no. 3 (autumn, 1958): 275, 299. Goodspeed's entry on Dudley Spence specifically mentions that he was at Poison Spring. *Goodspeed Biographical and Historical Memoirs of Southern Arkansas,* 173.

10. Tempy Spence was likely a former slave of Solomon Spence Sr., who hired her on December 25, 1865, at a rate of seven dollars per month and two suits of clothing. Some ex-slaves continued working for their erstwhile masters, though for pay, in the years immediately after being freed. John Hearn and Tempy Spence may well have known each other for many years if they were owned by close family members and exercised their freedom to marry after the war. Historians debate the frequency with which freed slaves took the names of their former masters, with some, such as Herbert Gutman, author of *The Black Family In Slavery and Freedom, 1750–1925,* maintaining that it rarely happened and others contending that many took the surnames of their master or of a respected previous owner at the time of emancipation. Register of Contracts and Labor and Register of Marriages, 1865 to 1867, both in Field Office Records, Arkansas, Bureau of Refugees, Freedmen and Abandoned Lands, Record Group 105, National Archives; Carl H. Moneyhon, *The Impact of the Civil War and Reconstruction on Arkansas: Persistence in the Midst of Ruin.* (Baton Rouge, La.: Louisiana State University Press, 1994), 207–8.

Appendix 2: Thomas Spence's Eulogy

1. Courtesy of Special Collections, Riley-Hickinbotham Library, Ouachita Baptist University, Arkadelphia, Arkansas.

2. This explanatory paragraph appeared June 19, 1875 on page 4, *Arkadelphia Southern Standard.*

3. The eulogy ran 19 June 1875 on page 1, *Arkadelphia Southern Standard.*

Appendix 4: The Places They Fought

1. More information on these and other Civil War sites is available in *The Civil War Trust's Official Guide to the Civil War Discovery Trail,* ed. Susan Braselton, (New York: Macmillan Travel, 1998), 3d ed.

Bibliography

Allardice, Bruce S. *More Generals in Gray.* Baton Rouge, La.: Louisiana State University Press, 1995.

Allen, Desmond Walls. *Index to Arkansas Confederate Soldiers.* 3 vols. Conway, Ark.: Arkansas Research, 1990.

———. *Arkansas' Damned Yankees: An Index to Union Soldiers in Arkansas Regiments.* Conway, Ark.: Arkansas Research, 1987.

———. *First Arkansas Union Infantry.* Conway, Ark.: Arkansas Research, 1987.

———. *Second Arkansas Union Cavalry.* Conway, Ark.: Arkansas Research, 1987.

Andrews, C. C. "My Experiences in Rebel Prisons." In *Papers Read Before the Minnesota Commandery of the Military Order of the Loyal Legion of the United States, 1892–1897.* St. Paul, Minn.: H. L. Collins, 1898. Reprint, Wilmington, N.C.: Broadfoot Publishing Company, 1992.

Arey, Frank. "The Skirmish at McGrew's Mill," *Clark County Historical Journal,* 2000.

Arkansas Baptist

Arnold, N. S. and H. B. Arnold Jr. "Old Clark County," *Clark County Historical Journal,* 1986 [1988].

Bailey, Anne J. and Daniel E. Sutherland, eds. *Civil War Arkansas: Beyond Battles and Leaders.* Fayetteville, Ark.: University of Arkansas Press, 2000.

Bearss, Edwin C. *Steele's Retreat from Camden and the Battle of Jenkins' Ferry.* Little Rock, Ark.: Pioneer Press, 1967. Facsimile reprint, Democrat Printing and Lithography Co., 1995.

Bergeron, Arthur W., Jr. *Guide to Louisiana Confederate Military Units 1861–1865.* Baton Rouge, La.: Louisiana State University Press, 1989.

Bradley, Michael R. *Tullahoma: The 1863 Campaign for Control of Middle Tennessee.* Shippensburg, Pa.: Burd Street Press, 2000.

Braselton, Susan, ed. *The Civil War Trust's Official Guide to the Civil War Discovery Trail.* 3d ed. New York: Macmillan Travel, 1998.

Brooksher, William Riley. *Bloody Hill: The Civil War Battle of Wilson's Creek.* Washington, D.C.: Brassey's, 1995.

Butler, Laura Scott. "History of Clark County." *Publications of the*

Arkansas Historical Association. Edited by John Hugh Reynolds. Vol.1. Little Rock, Ark.: Democrat Printing and Lithographing, 1906.

———. "History of Clark County." *Publications of the Arkansas Historical Association.* Edited by John Hugh Reynolds. Vol. 2. Little Rock, Ark.: Democrat Printing and Lithographing, 1908.

Caffee, Barbara. "Antebellum Arkansas, 1800–1850." *Clark County Historical Journal* (spring, 1981).

Callaway, Jonathan W. *Civil War Letters and Papers of Jonathan W. Callaway, C.S.A.* Arkansas History Commission, Little Rock.

Castel, Albert. *Decision in the West: The Atlanta Campaign of 1864.* Lawrence, Kans: The University Press of Kansas, 1992.

———. *General Sterling Price and the Civil War in the West.* Baton Rouge, La.: Louisiana State University Press, 1968.

Cate, Wirt Armistead, ed. *Two Soldiers: The Campaign Diaries of Thomas J. Key, C.S.A. and Robert J. Campbell, U.S.A.* Chapel Hill, N.C.: The University of North Carolina Press, 1938.

Cathey, Clyde W. "Slavery in Arkansas, Part 4: Fugitives." *Arkansas Historical Quarterly* 3, no. 2 (summer 1944): 150–63.

Chance, Joseph E. *The Second Texas Infantry: From Vicksburg to Shiloh.* Austin, Tex.: Eakin Press, 1984.

Christ, Mark K., ed. *Rugged and Sublime: The Civil War in Arkansas.* Fayetteville, Ark.: University of Arkansas Press, 1994.

"Company E, 2nd Regiment Arkansas Mounted Rifles," *Clark County Historical Journal* (1998).

Confederate Veteran

Connelly, Thomas Lawrence. *Army of the Heartland: The Army of Tennessee, 1861–1862.* Baton Rouge, La.: Louisiana State University Press, 1967.

———. *Autumn of Glory: The Army of Tennessee, 1862–1865.* Baton Rouge, La.: Louisiana State University Press, 1971.

Coombe, Jack D. *Gunfire Around the Gulf: The Last Major Naval Campaigns of the Civil War.* New York: Bantam Books, 1999.

Cowles, Calvin D., comp. *Atlas to Accompany the Official Records of the Union and Confederate Armies.* Washington, D.C.: Government Printing Office, 1891–95.

Cozzens, Peter. *No Better Place to Die: The Battle of Stones River.* Urbana, Ill.: University of Illinois Press, 1990.

———. *The Shipwreck of Their Hopes: The Battles for Chattanooga.* Urbana, Ill.: University of Illinois Press, 1994.

Crute, Joseph H., Jr. *Confederate Staff Officers 1861–1865*. Powhatan, Va.: Derwent Books.

———. *Units of the Confederate States Army*. Midlothian, Va.: Derwent Books, 1987.

Cunningham, H. H. *Doctors in Gray: The Confederate Medical Service*. 2d ed. Baton Rouge, La.: Louisiana State University Press, 1960.

Cutrer, Thomas W. *Ben McCulloch and the Frontier Military Tradition*. Chapel Hill, N.C.: University of North Carolina Press, 1993.

Daniel, Larry J. *Shiloh: The Battle That Changed the Civil War*. New York: Simon & Schuster, 1997.

Davis, William C. *Battle at Bull Run*. Garden City, N.Y.: Doubleday & Company, 1977.

Degler, Carl N. *The Other South: Southern Dissenters in the Nineteenth Century*. New York: Harper & Row, 1974.

Dougan, Michael B. *Confederate Arkansas: The People and Politics of a Frontier State in Wartime*. 2d ed. Tuscaloosa, Ala.: University of Alabama Press, 1995.

———, Tom W. Dillard, and Timothy G. Nutt, comp. *Arkansas History: An Annotated Bibliography*. Westport, Conn.: Greenwood Press, 1995.

Eisenhower, John S. D. *So Far from God: The U.S. War with Mexico, 1846–1848*. New York: Random House, 1989.

Evans, Clement A., ed. *Confederate Military History*. Vol. 10. *Confederate Military History of Tennessee*. Written by James D. Porter. Atlanta: Confederate Publishing Company, 1899. Reprint, with new material, Wilmington, N.C.: Broadfoot Publishing Company, 1987.

———. *Confederate Military History*. Vol. 14, *Confederate Military History of Arkansas*. Written by John M. Harrell. Atlanta: Confederate Publishing Company, 1899. Reprint, with new material, Wilmington, N.C.: Broadfoot Publishing Company, 1988.

———. *Confederate Military History*. Vol. 15. *Confederate Military History of Texas* by O. M. Roberts. Atlanta: Confederate Publishing Company, 1899. Reprint, with new material, Wilmington, N.C.: Broadfoot Publishing Company, 1989.

Ewing-Weber-Dews Collection, Special Collections, Riley-Hickingbotham Library, Ouachita Baptist University, Arkadelphia, Ark.

Ferguson, John L., ed. *Arkansas and the Civil War.* Little Rock: Pioneer Press, 1962.

Fessler, Paul R. "The Case of the Missing Promotion: Historians and the Military Career of Major General Patrick Ronayne Cleburne, C.S.A." *Arkansas Historical Quarterly,* 52, no. 2 (summer 1994).

First Arkansas CSA/History John W. Colquitt Subject File, Arkansas History Commission.

Fisher, John E. *They Rode with Forest and Wheeler: A Chronicle of Five Tennessee Brothers' Service in the Confederate Western Cavalry.* Jefferson, N.C.: McFarland and Co., 1995.

Foote, Shelby. *The Civil War: A Narrative.* 3 vols. New York: Random House, 1958–74.

Foster, Samuel T. *One of Cleburne's Command: The Civil War Reminiscences and Diary of Capt. Samuel T. Foster, Granbury's Texas Brigade, CSA.* Edited by Norman D. Brown. Austin, Tex.: University of Texas Press, 1980.

Gaines, W. Craig. *The Confederate Cherokees: John Drew's Regiment of Mounted Rifles.* Baton Rouge, La.: Louisiana State University Press, 1989.

Garrison, Webb, with Cheryl Garrison. *Encyclopedia of Civil War Usage.* Nashville, Tenn.: Cumberland House, 2001.

Georgia Female College Circular, 1861. Madison, Ga.: C. B. Barrow and Co., 1861.

Glazner, Mrs. Capitola, and Mrs. Gerald B. McLane. *Hempstead County, Arkansas, United States Census of 1860.* Privately printed: Hot Springs National Park, Ark., 1969.

The Goodspeed Biographical and Historical Memoirs of Southern Arkansas. Chicago and St. Louis: The Goodspeed Publishing Co., 1890.

Govan, Daniel C. Letter to wife, December 14, 1864. Daniel Chevilette Govan #1000, Southern Historical Collection, the Library of the University of North Carolina, Chapel Hill.

Grigson, Russell. "Miles Ledford Langley: In Defense of Truth." Special Collections, Riley-Hickingbotham Library, Ouachita Baptist University, Arkadelphia, Ark.

Hall, John Gladden. *Henderson State College: The Methodist Years 1890–1929.* Kingsport, Tenn.: Kingsport Press, 1974.

Hammock, John C. *With Honor Untarnished: The Story of the First Arkansas Infantry Regiment, Confederate States Army.* Little Rock, Ark.: Pioneer Press, 1961.

Hartje, Robert. G. *Van Dorn: The Life and Times of a Confederate General.* Nashville, Tenn.: Vanderbilt University Press, 1967.

Hearn Family Group Record—Ancestral File [on-line database] available at http://www.familysearch.org/Eng/Search/af/family_group _record.asp?familyid=1198205.

Hewett, Janet B., ed. *The Roster of Confederate Soldiers 1861–1865.* 16 vols. Wilmington, N.C.: Broadfoot Publishing Co., 1996.

Hudson, James J., ed. "From Paraclifta to Marks' Mill: The Civil War Correspondence of Lieutenant Robert C. Gilliam." *Arkansas Historical Quarterly* 17, no. 3 (autumn, 1958).

Hughes, William W. *Archibald Yell.* Fayetteville: University of Arkansas Press, 1988.

Johnson, Robert Underwood, and Clarence Clough Buel, eds. *Battles and Leaders of the Civil War, Being for the Most Part Contributed by Union and Confederate Officers.* 4 vols. New York: The Century Co., 1888.

Kennedy, Frances H., ed. *The Civil War Battlefield Guide.* 2d ed. Boston: Houghton Mifflin Co., 1998.

Kerby, Robert L. *Kirby Smith's Confederacy: The Trans-Mississippi South, 1863–1865.* New York, Columbia University Press, 1972. Reprint, University of Alabama Press, 1991.

Lamers, William M. *The Edge of Glory: A Biography of General William S. Rosecrans, U.S.A.* New York: Harcourt, Brace and World, Inc., 1961.

Leeper, Wesley Thurman. *Rebels Valiant: Second Arkansas Mounted Rifles (Dismounted).* Little Rock, Ark.: Pioneer Press, 1964.

Long, E. B., with Barbara Long. *The Civil War Day by Day: An Almanac 1861–65.* New York: DeCapo Press, 1971.

Massey, Mary Elizabeth. *Refugee Life in the Confederacy.* Baton Rouge, La.: Louisiana State University Press, 1964.

McDonough, James Lee. "Cold Days in Hell: The Battle of Stone's River." *Civil War Times Illustrated* 25, no. 4 (June 1986).

———. *Shiloh—In Hell Before Night.* Knoxville, Tenn.: University of Tennessee Press, 1977.

———. *War in Kentucky: From Shiloh to Perryville.* Knoxville: University of Tennessee Press, 1994.

——— and Thomas L. Connelly. *Five Tragic Hours: The Battle of Franklin.* Knoxville, Tenn.: University of Tennessee Press, 1983.

——— and James Pickett Jones. *War So Terrible: Sherman and Atlanta.* New York and London: W.W. Norton and Co., 1987.

McKenzie, H. B. "Confederate Manufactures in Southwest Arkansas." *Publications of the Arkansas Historical Association*. Vol. 2. Little Rock: Democrat Printing and Lithography Co., 1908.

McLane, Bobby Jones. *Clark County, Arkansas, 1850 United States Census*. Hot Springs, Ark.: Arkansas Ancestors, 1985.

———. *Clark County, Arkansas, 1860 United States Census*. Hot Springs, Ark.: Arkansas Ancestors, 1988.

———. *Clark County Arkansas 1870 United States Census*. Hot Springs, Ark.: Arkansas Ancestors, 1989.

———. *Hempstead County, Arkansas, United States Census of 1850*. Hot Springs, Ark.: Self-published, 1967.

McMurry, Richard M. *Atlanta 1864: Last Chance for the Confederacy*. Lincoln: University of Nebraska Press, 2000.

McPherson, James M. *Battle Cry of Freedom: The Civil War Era*. New York: Oxford University Press, 1988.

Moneyhon, Carl H. *The Impact of the Civil War and Reconstruction on Arkansas: Persistence in the Midst of Ruin*. Baton Rouge, La.: Louisiana State University Press, 1994.

"Muster Roll of Rubin Reed's Company A (10th Regiment of Arkansas Cavalry)." *Clark County Historical Journal* (1998).

Muster Roll of Rubin Reed, Company A, 10th Arkansas Confederate Cavalry, 1884, Small Manuscript Collection, box 85, no. 11, Arkansas History Commission.

National Archives and Records Administration. Records of the Bureau of Refugees, Freedmen and Abandoned Lands. Record Group 105.

Nelson, Grace Benton. "Federal Invasion of Clark County." *Clark County Historical Journal* 2 (winter 1975).

Nichols, James L. and Frank Abbott, eds. "Reminiscences of Confederate Service by Wiley A. Washburn." *Arkansas Historical Quarterly* 35 (spring 1976).

Oates, Stephen B. *Confederate Cavalry West of the River*. Austin: University of Texas Press, 1961.

Piston, William Garrett, and Richard W. Hatcher III. *Wilson's Creek: The Second Battle of the Civil War and the Men Who Fought It*. Chapel Hill, N.C.: University of North Carolina Press, 2000.

Purdue, Howell and Elizabeth, *Pat Cleburne, Confederate General*. Tuscaloosa, Ala.: Portals Press, 1973, 2nd ed. Revised, 1977.

Report of the Adjutant General of the State of Kansas. Vol. 1.

Leavenworth, Kans.: Bulletin Cooperative Printing Company, 1867.

Richter, Wendy, ed. "The Letters of Harris Flanagin." *Clark County Historical Journal* (spring 1986 [1988]).

————, comp. "The Reminiscences of Samuel Callaway." *Clark County Historical Journal* (1991).

————, ed. *Clark County Arkansas: Past and Present.* Arkadelphia, Ark.: Walsworth Publishing Company, 1992.

Roberts, Bobby L. "General T. C. Hindman and the Trans-Mississippi District." *Arkansas Historical Quarterly* 32, no. 4 (winter 1973).

———— and Carl Moneyhon, *Portraits of Conflict: A Photographic History of Arkansas in the Civil War.* Fayetteville: University of Arkansas Press, 1974.

Rose, Uriah M. *An Episode During the Civil War,* typewritten manuscript, Old State House Museum collection, unpaginated.

"Rubin Reed's Company: Original Muster Roll in Possession of Arkadelphia Lady." *Clark County Historical Journal* (1998).

Sallee Collection, Small Manuscript Collection, Box 15, No. 8, Roll 9, Arkansas History Commission, Little Rock.

Schwab, John Christopher. *The Confederate States of America 1861–1865: A Financial and Industrial History of the South During the Civil War.* New York: Burt Franklin, 1968. Reprint of 1901 edition.

Scroggs, Jack B. "Arkansas in the Secession Crisis," *Arkansas Historical Quarterly* 12, no. 3 (autumn 1953).

"Senator James K. Jones." *Clark County Historical Journal* (winter, 1979–80).

Shea, William L., and Earl J. Hess. *Pea Ridge: Civil War Campaign in the West.* Chapel Hill and London: The University of North Carolina Press, 1992.

Shiloh Museum. *History of Washington County.* Springdale, Ark.: Shiloh Museum, 1989.

Sifakis, Stewart. *Compendium of the Confederate Armies: Florida and Arkansas.* New York and Oxford: Facts on File, 1992.

————. *Compendium of the Confederate Armies: Texas.* New York and Oxford: Facts on File, 1992.

————. *Compendium of the Confederate Armies: Virginia.* New York and Oxford: Facts on File, 1992.

Simons, Don R. *In Their Words: A Chronology of the Civil War in Chicot*

County, Arkansas, and Adjacent Waters of the Mississippi River.
Sulphur, La.: Wise Publications, 1999.

Southern Standard

Stone, Thomas R. Diary, 1861–1862, Small Manuscript Collection, Box
4, No. 10, Arkansas History Commission, Little Rock.

Sutherland, Daniel E., ed. *Reminiscences of a Private: William E. Bevens
of the First Arkansas Infantry, C.S.A.* Fayetteville, Ark.: University
of Arkansas Press. 1992.

_____. "No Better Officer in the Confederacy: The Wartime Career
of Daniel C. Govan." *Arkansas Historical Quarterly,* vol. 54, no. 3
(autumn 1995).

Sword, Wiley. *Embrace an Angry Wind: The Confederacy's Last Hurrah:
Spring Hill, Franklin and Nashville.* New York: HarperCollins,
1991.

_____. *Shiloh: Bloody April.* New York: Morrow, 1974. Reprint,
Dayton, Ohio: Press of Morningside Bookshop, 1999.

Symonds, Craig L. *Stonewall of the West: Patrick Cleburne and the Civil
War.* Lawrence, Kans.: The University Press of Kansas, 1997.

"Tenth Arkansas Regiment of Cavalry." *Clark County Historical Journal*
(1998).

Todd, Frederick P. *American Military Equipage, 1851–1872: State Forces.*
vol. 2. New York: Chatham Square Press, 1983.

Todd, Richard Cecil. *Confederate Finance.* Athens, Ga.: University of
Georgia Press, 1954.

Tunnard, William H. *A Southern Record: The History of the Third
Regiment, Louisiana Infantry.* Fayetteville, Ark.: University of
Arkansas Press, 1997.

U.S. Bureau of Refugees, Freedmen, and Abandoned Lands, Arkansas.
Record Group 105, vol. 58, National Archives.

U.S. Census Bureau. Population Schedule [Free] of the Seventh Census
of the United States, 1850, Arkansas. National Archives
Microcopy No. 432.

———. Population Schedule [Slave] of the Seventh Census of the
United States, 1850, Arkansas. National Archives Microcopy No.
432.

———. Population Schedule [Free] of the Eighth Census of the United
States, 1860, Arkansas. National Archives Microcopy No. 653.

———. Population Schedule [Slave] of the Eighth Census of the
United States, 1860, Arkansas. National Archives Microcopy No.
653.

_____. Population Schedule [Free] of the Eighth Census of the United States, 1860, Georgia. National Archives Microcopy No. 653

U.S. War Department. Compiled Service Records of Confederate Soldiers Who Served in Organizations from the State of Arkansas. National Archives Microcopy No. 317.

————. Compiled Service Records of Confederate Soldiers Who Served in Organizations from the State of Tennessee. National Archives Microcopy No. 268.

Venable, Richard M. *Topographical Map of the District of Arkansas, Complied from Surveys and Military Reconnaissances by Order of Lieut' Col. H. T. Douglas, Chief Engineer, Dept.* Washington, D.C.: War Department, 1865.

Wallis, David. "The Steamboat Affair at Pine Bluff." *Jefferson County Historical Quarterly* 6, no. 1 (1975).

Warner, Ezra J. *Generals in Gray: Lives of the Confederate Commanders.* Baton Rouge, La.: Louisiana State University Press, 1959.

———— and W. Buck Yearns. *Biographical Register of the Confederate Congress.* Baton Rouge: Louisiana State University Press, 1975.

War of the Rebellion: A Compilation of the Official Records of the Union and Confederate Armies. 70 vols. in 128 books and index. Washington, D.C.: Government Printing Office, 1880–1901. In *The Civil War CD-ROM.* Carmel, Ind.: Guild Press of Indiana, 1996.

Washington Telegraph

Way, Frederick Jr., comp. *Way's Packet Directory, 1848–1994: Passenger Steamboats of the Mississippi River System Since the Advent of Photography in Mid-Continent America.* Athens, Ohio: Ohio University Press, 1983.

Wegener, Janice, ed. *Historical Report of the Secretary of State, Arkansas, 1978.* Little Rock, Ark.: Secretary of State, 1978.

Wert, Jeffry D. *General James Longstreet: The Confederacy's Most Controversial Soldier, a Biography.* New York: Simon & Schuster, 1993.

Wigginton, Thomas A., et al. *Tennesseeans in the Civil War: A Military History of Confederate and Union Units with Available Rosters of Personnel.* 2 vols. Nashville, Tenn.: Civil War Centennial Commission, 1964.

Wiley, Bell I. *The Life of Johnny Reb: The Common Soldier of the Confederacy.* New York: Essential Classics of the Civil War, Book-of-the-Month Club, 1994

Williams, Charles G., ed. "A Saline Guard: The Civil War Letters of Col. William Ayers Crawford, C.S.A., 1861–1865." *Arkansas Historical Quarterly* 31, no. 4 (winter 1972).

Wills, Brian Steel. *A Battle From the Start: The Life of Nathan Bedford Forrest*. New York: HarperCollins, 1992.

Willson, Amanda, File. Old State House Museum, Little Rock, Ark.

Wilson-McFadden Family Bible. Cited in e-mail message from Margaret Curley to author, August 8, 2001.

Wiltshire, Betty Couch, comp. *Mississippi Index of Wills, 1800–1900*. Bowie, Md.: Heritage Books, 1989.

Wright, Pauline Williams, and Barbara McDow McCaffee. *Clark County, Arkansas: A Genealogical Source Book*. Baltimore, Md.: Gateway Press, 1982.

Yearns, W. Buck. *The Confederate Governors*. Athens, Ga.: University of Georgia Press, 1985.